Landmark Visitors Guide

Cornwall

& the Is|

G000167146

Rita Tre

Editor's Note

In chapter 4 mention is made of the Tregellas Tapestry, now on display at the Cornwall Centre (*Kresenn Kernow*) in Redruth. The 58 panels of the tapestry tell the story of Cornwall in pictures, each individually designed and produced using a variety of techniques such as embroidery, appliqué and collage. The inspiration for this fascinating work came from the Cornish Bard, Tregellas an Bluven – Rita Tregellis Pope, the author of this book. She researched the subject matter and under her direction it was designed and executed by a team of skilled craftspeople. Indeed she embroidered the final panel 'Plen-an-Gwary'. For some years no place had been found to display all the panels of the tapestry together but with the opening of the Cornwall Centre this has now been made possible. This work of art is a truly remarkable achievement and well worth a visit.

Acknowledgement

The editor would like to thank all those people in Cornwall, especially the staff of the Tourist Information Centres visited, for the help and kindness received during the recent revision of this book.

Published by
Landmark Publishing
Ashbourne Hall, Cokayne Ave, Ashbourne,
Derbyshire DE6 1EJ England

Isles of Scilly
(28 miles/45km south-west of Penzance)

CORNWALL
& the Isles of Scilly

Opposite page: Land's End

Landmark Visitors Guide

Cornwall
& the Isles of Scilly

Rita Tregellas Pope

Contents

Contents

Feature Boxes

Introduction

The land of King Arthur – the Cornish Riviera – the Delectable Duchy – call it what you will. Few places have as many facets as Cornwall but this is because the land west of the Tamar is not just a holiday region, it is much more. It is almost a 'nation' in its own right. Look carefully and you will find what you seek, whether it be tales of the past, pleasures of the present or even glimpses into the future.

Until the middle of the last century, few people visited Cornwall. Roads were dangerous and sea travel largely restricted to packet-ships and merchantmen. But this state of affairs ended abruptly in 1859 when Brunel's great railway bridge carried the first train over the Tamar into Cornwall. That historic event was the 'Open

Sesame' for visitors. At first they came in a thin trickle, but others soon realised the attraction of the land beyond England and the era of the holidaymaker had begun.

There are, however, those who say that they can find nothing to do in Cornwall. Perhaps they have not troubled to look. The Cornish motto of 'One and All' has numerous interpretations but the right choice for this guide is 'One Place and Something for All'. SPB Mais said that Cornwall has a 'diversity of riches', and as those are the very treasures that shaped its development, a brief look at the past will show how their mosaic influences have formed the region as it is today.

EARLY SETTLERS

With the sea on three sides and the Tamar making the fourth boundary, Cornwall has always been almost an island. So when wandering tribes from Europe arrived, they were able to enjoy a life of comparative peace – scarcely disturbed by the hordes who ravaged the rest of the mainland. That is why, with only wind and weather to affect them, so many Neolithic and Bronze Age monoliths and barrows remain.

The richness of Cornwall's mineral deposits was not exploited until about 350BC when Iron Age tribes from Europe came in search of tin. The people of this fair-haired, blue-eyed race were tall and finely built, probably the originals of the 'giants' in Cornish folklore. They brought their knowledge of tin production with them as well as their culture and a completely new social structure. Evidence of this important occupation is still to be seen in hill forts, cliff castles and the 'trevs' or settlements. The area of West Penwith, beyond Penzance, also retains low dry-stone walls and unique small fields – the latter having been cultivated contin-uously ever since Iron Age times.

The much-maligned Druids were Celtic priests who, far from being mere growers of mistletoe, lovers of apples and makers of bonfires, were, in fact, the most highly respected scholars of their day. Men travelled across Europe to learn from them, early Greek was indebted to them and even the great Cicero paid tribute to their knowledge. People who laugh at their customs have only heard about the more sensational aspects and would doubtless be surprised to know that these same Druids were among the first of the so-called pagans to proclaim the doctrine of immortality.

Visitors interested in Roman remains will find few here. Romans did not settle in Cornwall but their merchants came here for tin, so the Romano-Cornish association was mainly through trade.

ARRIVAL OF CHRISTIANITY

The next arrivals were of great importance, for they led the Cornish people away from paganism to Christianity. These

---

Cornish Language

The Tre-, Pol- and Pen- prefixes to family and place names which are so typical of Cornwall, also stem from that Iron Age period. For those tribes introduced the Indo-European Celtic language which, as Cornish, is the Brythonic branch. Although it seemed to die as the universally spoken tongue more than two centuries ago, it has now come out of hibernation. This revival, which began at the turn of the century, was inspired by dedicated men like Henry Jenner and Morton Nance. Today the language is studied and spoken by linguists such as a former Bishop of Leicester, the Right Reverend Richard Rutt. It is an examination subject for school children and has recently become the first language in a number of homes. Many bards are fluent Cornish speakers and at their annual Gorsedd, awards are given for literary compositions in the Cornish tongue. Weddings, baptisms and other church services are also conducted in the language.

were holy men and women from Wales and Ireland who established their 'cells' near water – rivers, wells or streams. Many of these, previously objects of pagan worship, then became shrines and places of pilgrimage. Today about a hundred holy wells still exist, most of them pleasant places to visit, others looked upon as serving a special purpose – turning the affections of a loved one in the right direction, for example! Cornish churches (many near wells or water) are dedicated to those 'saints' and have names not seen in other English counties, such as St Gluvias, St Probus and St Petroc.

For centuries, Cornwall was entirely Celtic, but once the Anglo-Saxons had overcome England they turned to the west for further conquests. Here they met fierce resistance from Cornish chiefs or kings. One was Arthur, a Celtic ruler born in the late fifth century AD who led the last great Celtic battle against the Anglo-Saxons. The legends that grew up after his death and the medieval romances associated with his name, have so obscured the historical figure that it is now almost impossible to discover the truth about him. By the end of the seventh century the Anglo-Saxons had conquered Devon but it was not till after AD926 that King Athelstan finally conquered the Cornish. A few Anglo-Saxons settled in Cornwall, mostly along the eastern border. Some ventured further and there is evidence of this in the scattering of non-Cornish place names found elsewhere – Wicca at Zennor is a good example.

FROM THE NORMANS TO THE VICTORIANS

The Norman Conquest, however, did bring many changes. King William's custom of rewarding his barons with large estates held good in Cornwall – even to Land's End. The *Domesday Book* must have looked impressive with its accounts of groups of manors belonging to this or that Norman overlord. But many of the so-called manors were little more than small farmsteads or 'trevs' run by perhaps two people as they had been since Celtic times. In many cases, these homesteads are still farmed today – to be found almost hidden in a maze of narrow winding lanes. Here Cornwall has scarcely altered for centuries and those who would like to walk back in time need simply take the latest OS map and explore the narrow lanes of a remote parish. These lead to the very heart of Cornwall.

The castles the Normans built for defence – Launceston, Restormel and Trematon, also served to restore the sense of security the Cornish had lost since the Saxon conflicts. By the mid-twelfth century, Cornwall was Europe's largest supplier of tin, and stannary towns grew up at places where tin was tested. Royal charters for markets and fairs also encouraged trade while the building of numerous collegiate and other churches resulted in a more settled way of life. By 1337, Cornwall was therefore a fitting land for King Edward III to bestow on his heir, the Black Prince.

Beach Guide

Golden sands, rocky coves, surf, cliffs, blue sea, bracing wind – everyone wants something different from a beach but Cornwall has all of these if you know where to look. No matter where one is on the peninsula the sea and wonderful beaches are not far away. Everyone will have their favourite and these are just a few suggestions:

Safe bathing beaches

East Looe** and **Plaidy**
Readymoney Cove*, Fowey
Porthpean*, St Austell
Gorran Haven, south of Mevagissey
Porthluney Cove, (by Caerhays Castle)
Pendower, near Veryan
Gyllingvase*; **Flushing**; **Swanpool***; **Maenporth***; all at Falmouth
Gunwalloe*, near Helston
Praa Sands*, west of Helston
Marazion*, nr Penzance
Porthcurno*, south of Land's End
Porthgwidden, St Ives
Port Joke, near Newquay
Porth*, Newquay
Treyarnon Bay, Padstow
Summerleaze Beach, Bude
Widemouth Bay (North)*
Widemouth Bay (South)

Surfing beaches

Whitesand Bay, Land's End
Godrevy*, Hayle
Perranporth, south of Newquay
Tolcarne*, Newquay
Great Western, Newquay
Fistral, Newquay
Crooklets*, Bude

Rock pools can be found at

Hannafore, West Looe
Castle*, nr Gyllingvase, Falmouth
Godrevy*, Hayle
Widemouth Bay*, Bude

Quieter beaches which may be more difficult to reach

Towan, nr St Anthony Head
Vault, nr Gorran Haven
Prussia Cove and **Kenneggy Sands**, both at Mount's Bay
Peter's Point, Hayle

* Dogs not allowed from Easter Day to 1 October.

** Dogs not allowed all year.

Many beaches have lifeguards in attendance but whether this is the case or not, care should always be taken when bathing. Always keep well away from an estuary. Sea conditions can change rapidly and a system of warning flags is used to advise bathers.

When the red flag is flying bathing is not permitted. Red-over-yellow flags at the water's edge mean bathe between these flags. Black and white flags at the water's edge indicate malibu board and surf craft areas.

Above: Lizard Point and Lizard Lighthouse

Left: Lanhydrock Gardens

Below; Top left: Polperro

Bottom left: Polkerris

Bottom right: The preserved winder or whim at East Pool Mine, Pool, near Redruth. It is now in the care of The National Trust

In the Middle Ages, however, there was less need for defensive castles so the landowners built manors with only a degree of fortification. A good example is Cotehele, overlooking the Tamar, one of Cornwall's most beautiful great houses.

At sea, as on land, Cornwall prospered. Her sailors and fishermen gained renown at home and abroad. Perhaps one of her proudest occasions was when Fowey sent 47 ships to help the king besiege Calais in 1346. This was nearly twice the number mustered by the City of London.

But sad times lay ahead. When the Reformation came, Cornwall's beautiful churches were stripped and most of her collegiate establishments closed. Men no longer travelled from Europe to study at Glasney Collegiate Church in Penryn and the place, which might have been Cornwall's university, is now remembered in a few scattered remains. The final blow came, however, when Bibles were printed in English – a language that Cornishmen did not want to understand and certainly could not read.

Prosperity returned briefly, however, in the eighteenth and nineteenth centuries when underground mining came into its own. The inventions of great Cornishmen like Richard Trevithick, Michael Loam and Goldsworthy Gurney, enabled shafts to be sunk deep into the ground and even under the sea bed so that the increasing number of engine houses transformed much of the landscape. Fortunes were made and lost almost overnight but Cornwall faced a major disaster once again when cheap surface tin was imported from Malaya. This time miners emigrated to look for work. Many settled in Canada, Australia, South Africa, Tasmania and the United States and this often meant that whole families died out and Cornwall's glory faded again.

CORNWALL TODAY

But there is much of the phoenix in this land. Its story has always been influenced by the rocks of its landscape and its coast. Granite has been the source of shelter in life and protection in death; of prosperity with tin and copper and

Cornish rebellion

In an effort to preserve their culture, their way of life and their long heritage, the people rebelled. Many lost their lives in the 1549 revolt, but in vain. From then on the language began to decline. There is a saying in Cornish – *An lavar goth, yu lavar gwyr*. It means: 'He who loses his tongue (his language) shall lose his land.' And that was so, for as the language faded so did the customs and the essence of the nation. But Cornwall's identity was never completely overwhelmed and is still to be found today – very easily recognised.

more recently, china clay. Some feel that Cornwall's granite stones are only subjects for artists and photographers but scientists with vision have already begun to realise the great potential of this vast treasure store. The first dish scanners ever used for inter-satellite communication were built on the firm foundation of granite in the Lizard Peninsula. Once they are across the Tamar motorists are soon aware of a subtle change in the atmosphere of the countryside through which they are driving. This can be noticed as they pass groups of granite farm buildings or cottages often built against the shelter of a hilly slope and it is these 'trevs' or homesteads that reflect the way of life in Cornwall since Celtic times. 'Tre', 'Pol' and 'Pen' are first syllables that appear on many signposts as the road heads west. 'Lan' and 'Men' are other indications that this land is both Celtic and ancient.

Throughout the year there is an abundance of entertainment with festivals, plays, music and dance to be seen everywhere. The venues range from the unique Minack Theatre in the west, the solemn Gorsedd ceremony in a different open-air site each year, to local arts centres, National Trust properties and halls in every village.

At any place in Cornwall – town, village or hamlet – visitors will be certain to discover outstanding talent in arts and crafts. It is not only artists who abound but others skilled in weaving, pottery, woodcarving, metal work, leather work and the creation of stained glass items. The list is endless and fascinating to the tourists whose visits form such an important part of Cornwall's economy.

The Cornish language has its living presence in place names everywhere. Perhaps this is one reason why there is such an increase in the number of people studying it. Celtic associations are to be found across the Continent, place names with a Celtic prefix appear even on maps of Slovenia. There is a selection of Cornish words in the Fact File at the end of this book.

The geography of Cornwall offers 'much in little' for visitors who come for an activity holiday. There is rock and cliff climbing at coastal resorts, while sailing, surfing, windsurfing, diving, canoeing and fishing are also to be found there. Golf, walking and riding can be enjoyed throughout Cornwall too.

Archaeology, painting, visits to the many lovely gardens and various summer workshops are only some of the holiday pastimes that visitors can enjoy. Sample the fresh seafood, locally grown produce and of course a true Cornish pasty accompanied by the local speciality ale Hick's Special Draught. The only difficulty is deciding how to spend the precious time.

And now from the general outline of Cornwall to a closer look at the region. It has been divided into eight areas all with different characteristics – avoiding main roads as far as possible. In this way, it is hoped that visitors will see Cornwall's many facets and so appreciate to the full, the variety and individuality of this ancient and beautiful land.

GARDENS

The gardens of Cornwall are justly famous and many visitors will wish to include some in their visit. Before embarking on an exploration of the county it may be helpful to note some of the finest.

As the Gulf Stream washes the Cornish coast it is not surprising that sub-tropical and some tropical species flourish in Cornwall. William and Thomas Lobb were the first plant hunters sent overseas for a commercial firm and although some of their discoveries are not well known, many of the plants they found now thrive in their native Cornwall.

Those interested in such matters should note the William Lobb section of **Fox Rosehill Gardens** in Falmouth.

These and other plant hunters of earlier centuries, good soil, landowners seeking ever more exotic gardens to set off their newly acquired mansions, the influence of the Gulf Stream and long hours of sunshine – all have played their part in making Cornwall the 'garden capital of the world'. This was the description used by Tim Smit, Project Director for the restoration of the **Lost Gardens of Heligan**, surely one of the most remarkable garden events in recent years. The 80 acres (32 hectares) of Heligan, abandoned to nature at the outbreak of the First World War, have been uncovered from the overgrowth of ivy, laurel and bramble and restored as a living museum of nineteenth-century horticulture. Magnificent as Heligan is it is only one of many lovely gardens, large and small, formal and informal that can be seen in Cornwall throughout the year.

Mild winters lead to an early spring with wonderful displays of camellias, rhododendrons, azaleas and magnolias. Many subtropical species flourish and a number of gardens have special plant collections.

Left: Trelissick Gardens

The earliest eighteenth-century landscaped garden in Cornwall can be found at **Mount Edgcumbe Country Park** near Saltash, the only Grade I listed historic garden in the south-west. It is a place of romance, magic and delight with follies, a shell seat and temples. If you like to be quiet, there is peace in the wooded areas and gardens full of flowers. Formal gardens in varying styles, a National Camellia Collection, lovely woodlands and stunning views are all to be found here.

Many of the gardens in Cornwall are on the coast and combine wonderful views with outstanding plant collections. **Caerhays Castle,** overlooking Veryan Bay was once the home of Mr J C Williams who gave his name to many species of camellia. The garden still houses many fine rhododendrons, camellias and magnolias. **Trelissick Garden** is lovely in all seasons with rare shrubs and plants, extensive parklands, woods and farmland. The superb views include vistas of the Fal Estuary and Falmouth harbour.

The area around Falmouth boasts several fine gardens. Originally planted by the Fox family, starting in the 1820s, but now cared for by the National Trust, **Glendurgan** is a valley garden running down to the Helford River. There are many rare and exotic plants and fine trees here with particularly lovely magnolias and camellias in the spring. The laurel maze dating from 1833 has recently been restored.

Another garden running down to the Helford River and originally planted by the Fox family is **Trebah.** Trebah Estate was sold in 1939 and the garden neglected and nearly lost over the next forty years. The Hibbert family bought it in 1980 and began the restoration which is being carried on today by the Trebah Garden Trust. This garden will appeal to plantsmen, artists and families, with special attractions for children. A stream running through gives home to Koi carp and exotic plants and eventually runs out on to the private beach which is open to visitors to the garden for picnics and swimming.

Penjerrick Garden, found on this peninsula too, features ponds in a woodland setting and lovely sea views. In addition to rhododendrons and camellias there are bamboos and tree ferns in this sub-tropical garden, also originally planted by the Fox family.

There are fewer gardens as the far west is approached but **Trevarno** near Helston should not be missed. This too was nearly a lost garden and has been undergoing an extensive programme of restoration. Many rare shrubs and trees are to be found here together with garden features and a fascinating Gardening Museum. The 98 acres (40 hectares) of park and garden at **Trengwainton** near Penzance were given to the National Trust in 1961 by Lieutenant Colonel Sir Edward Bolitho. It is interesting to learn that today's beauty has been created mainly over the last 40 years with help from three great Cornish gardeners – Mr J C Williams of Caerhays, Mr P D Williams of

Lanarth and Canon Boscawen of Ludgvan. The walled gardens contain many tender plants which cannot be grown in the open anywhere else in Britain, and although Trengwainton is always lovely it is perhaps only fair to say that it is at its best in the spring.

On Cornwall's north coast there are few gardens of note, an indication of the different conditions that prevail there. However there are three further properties which should not be missed on a gardening tour of Cornwall: Lanhydrock, Pencarrow and Prideaux Place. Of these only **Prideaux Place** is near the north coast. It lies on the outskirts of Padstow and offers newly restored areas of garden overlooking the Camel estuary, a formal sunken garden and a deer park.

Lanhydrock, owned by the National Trust, is situated just south of Bodmin. Dating from 1857 the formal garden includes a unique circular herbaceous garden and there is a stunning collection of magnolias, rhododendrons and camellias. With its many rare trees and shrubs this garden offers fine colours right through to autumn.

To the north-west of Bodmin lies **Pencarrow**, with its formal and woodland gardens laid out in the 1840s by Sir William Molesworth Bt. Over 650 species of rhododendrons can be seen here along with an internationally known specimen conifer collection. A huge granite rockery, formal Italian and American gardens, a lake and woodland walks will all delight the visitor.

These are some of the most well-known gardens but the following list will also reward the visitor.

Antony House and Garden (National Trust)
Torpoint
Formal garden at Antony House featuring National Collection of Hemerocallis.
☎ (01752) 812364
Open: 1.30-5.30pm Tuesday to Thursday and Bank Holiday Mondays, April to October; plus Sundays in June, July and August.

Antony Woodland Garden
Natural woods and woodland garden including National Collection of Camellia Japonica.
☎ (01752) 812364
Open: 11am-5.30pm daily except Monday and Friday (but open bank holidays), March to October.

Bosvigo
Truro
3 acres (1.2 hectares), mainly herbaceous, best in summer.
☎ (01872) 275774
Open: March to September, Thursday and Friday, 11am-6pm.

Burncoose Nurseries and Garden
Gwennap
30 acre- (12 hectare) woodland garden alongside working nursery.
☎ (01209) 860316
Open: Daily, all year.

Carwinion
Mawnan Smith, Nr Falmouth
Valley garden with reference collection of bamboos, unusual exotics and The Towan Camellia collection. Specialist nursery within the garden.

☎ (01326) 250258
Open: Daily all year, 10am-5.30pm.

Cotehele
(National Trust)
Nr Saltash
Valley garden dropping steeply to River Tamar, much of interest throughout the year.
☎ (01579) 351346
Open: 10.30am to dusk, daily all year.

Creed
Grampound
5 acres (2 hectares) including alpine and herbaceous gardens. Woodland walks.
☎ (01872) 530372
Open: Daily February to October, 10am–5.30pm.

Fox Rosehill Gardens
Melvill Road, Falmouth
2 acre- (0.8 hectare) garden, many exotic trees and shrubs. Free admission.
☎ (01872) 224376
Open: Daily, all year round, dawn to dusk.

Japanese Garden
St Mawgan Village
Water, Stroll and Zen gardens. Bonsai nursery.
☎ (01637) 860116
Open: Daily, all year, 10am-5.00pm.

Lamorran House
St Mawes
4 acres (1.6 hectares). Water gardens. Palms and sub-tropical plants. ☎ (01326) 270800
Open: April to September, Wednesday, Friday, 1st Saturday each month,10am-5pm.

Tresco Abbey Gardens
Tresco, Isles of Scilly
A delightful place where an immense number of varied plants are grown. The whole atmosphere is charming and laid out to delight all visitors – whether or not they are gardeners. In the spring, arum lilies, camellias and azaleas begin the main flowering season. By the old pump, the Pump Garden leads to the ruins of the old priory, inside which are graves dating from the Dissolution of 1539, to 1820. There is also a small stone under the archway that suggests that it was a Christian tombstone of the fifth or sixth century AD. Pebble Gardens, Neptune's Steps and terraces are other delights in the Tresco Abbey Gardens.
☎ (01720) 424105
Open: 10am-4pm daily all year. Shop shut in winter.

Trewithen
Grampound Road, Truro
Rare trees and shrubs. Plants for sale.
☎ (01726) 883647
Open: 10am-4.30pm Monday to Saturday, March to September; plus Sundays in April and May.

Cornwall Festival of Spring Gardens
Each year, from mid-March to the end of May, the Cornwall Festival of Spring Gardens takes place when many gardens not to be seen at other times, open specially for the Festival, often in aid of local charities. Details of gardens participating and their opening times may be obtained from the Cornwall Tourist Board.
☎ (01872) 322900

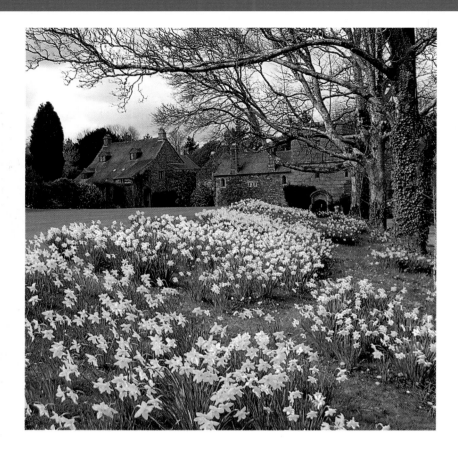

O n the Cornwall side of the River Tamar lies Saltash, and visitors generally arrive either by way of the Tamar Bridge or train via Plymouth. The name is a reminder of days when Romans, Anglo-Saxons and Normans used this 'passage' or 'esse' which was the meeting place of salt and fresh water. King John granted Saltash borough status and in 1270 the lords of nearby Trematon Castle owned the ferry. Soon the town held jurisdiction over the tidal reaches of both Tamar and Lynher, extending their claims on oysterage and anchorage till they controlled all tolls as far as the Calstock salmon weirs.

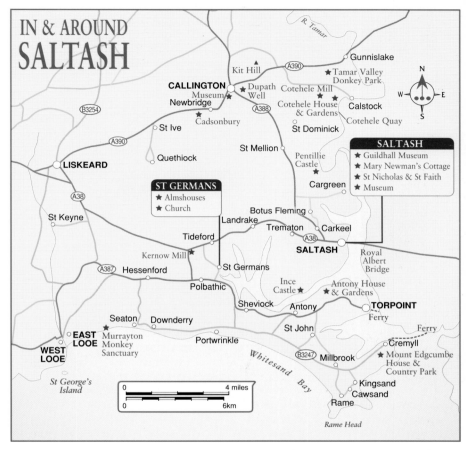

IN & AROUND
SALTASH

R. Tamar

Gunnislake

Kit Hill — A390

★ Tamar Valley
Donkey Park

CALLINGTON
Museum ★
Newbridge

★ Dupath Well — Cotehele Mill
A388

Cotehele House
& Gardens

Calstock

Cotehele Quay

B3254

★ Cadsonbury

St Ive

St Dominick

A390

St Mellion

LISKEARD

Quethiock

Pentillie Castle ★

Cargreen

SALTASH
★ Guildhall Museum
★ Mary Newman's Cottage
★ St Nicholas & St Faith
★ Museum

A38

ST GERMANS
★ Almshouses
★ Church

Botus Fleming

St Keyne

Landrake

Trematon

Carkeel

A38

SALTASH

Royal
Albert
Bridge

Tideford

Kernow Mill

A387 Hessenford

St Germans

Ince Castle ★

Antony House
★ & Gardens

Polbathic

Sheviock

Antony

TORPOINT
Ferry

Seaton

Downderry

St John

Ferry

Cremyll

EAST LOOE
Murrayton
Monkey
Sanctuary

WEST LOOE

Portwrinkle

B3247 Millbrook

★ Mount Edgcumbe
House &
Country Park

St George's
Island

Whitesand Bay

Kingsand

Cawsand

Rame

Rame Head

0 — 4 miles
0 — 6km

N
W — E
S

By 1752, traders and fishermen rebelled against the Saltash monopoly and refused to pay their tolls. The burgesses applied to parliament for confirmation of rights but were strongly opposed by James Tillie of Pentillie Castle. As he owned Halton Quay, which was a little way up river, and several trading vessels, he was considerably affected. He gained support from the governor of Plymouth and eventually won the law suit brought against him. Finally he instructed the ships' masters to pay only 1s, an act that made them free for ever 'from all encroachments of the unjust and iniquitous Saltashers.'

The town no longer sent members to parliament after 1832 and consequently declined in political importance. It kept its reputation as a great 'nursery' for sailors, however, but even more celebrated were its fisherwomen who frequently beat all comers in the four-oared gig races at various regattas.

Brunel's Triumph

On 6 May 1859, the Prince Consort opened Isambard Brunel's masterpiece, **the Royal Albert Bridge**, which had taken two years to build. That was the day when the Great Western Railway carried the first holiday makers into Cornwall. Still an impressive sight today, the handsome structure was the first to be built in a unique combination of suspension and conventional style. It was the great engineer's last work but he was too ill to attend the ceremony. However, although he was a dying man, Brunel had an open truck made especially for him and by the end of that same month travelled in quiet triumph over the Tamar to Cornwall.

This new influx of visitors gave the town of **Saltash** a brief revival but when the Admiralty bought the oyster rights in 1901, its long maritime history came to an end. Today it is a friendly shopping centre with a scattering of historic buildings to remind people of its past and although the bypass in its tunnel gives it the appearance of standing alone, it is proud to know that it is still very much a part of Cornwall.

On the corner of Fore Street and Station Road is the present fine **Guildhall**. Over the centuries it has been market hall and town hall, now resplendent inside and out – worthy of its name. The latter building was added at the end of the eighteenth century and since 1890 has been called the Guildhall. The upstairs assembly hall is used for every kind of meeting from politics to popular markets as well as the mayor-choosing ceremony. The mayoral insignia has a special local interest in that it incorporates three silver oars with maceheads. Almost opposite is the Heritage Museum.

Closely associated with the Guildhall is the **church of St Nicholas and St Faith**. A chapel of ease until 1881, it dates from about 1225, (although the tower is earlier) while the clock – probably 1720 – is a rarity in a Cornish church (possibly because the hardness of granite made it awkward to incorporate such a feature). No visitor can overlook the sumptuous memorial to three shipwrecked Drew brothers and that, with a wall tablet, are only two of the interesting items to be found here. The tablet reads: 'This chapple was repaired in the Mayoralty of Matthew Veale, Gent., anno 1689'.

Mary Newman was born here in a small Tudor house on the steep slope of Culver Street, overlooking the Tamar. She would have seen many fine ships anchored in the river, but did she ever dream that one day she would be the wife of Sir Francis Drake?

To celebrate the millennium a **Town Trail** was created that links the main historical features. By the riverside is a striking mural on the wall of the Union Inn, showing characters from the town's past. A bust of Brunel keeps a watchful eye on his bridge from beside the new bridge over the bypass. The new bridge is decorated with mosaics created by local school children with the assistance of artist Emma Spring.

NORTH
OF SALTASH

Much of Saltash's history has been linked with the villages along the banks of the Tamar. On the A388 Callington Road lies **Carkeel** where an industrial estate offers work in Cornwall for local people who do not want to go to Plymouth. A right-hand turn in the centre of the village – so narrow that it can easily be missed – leads to tree-lined lanes winding round to **Botus Fleming**, set high above the Tamar. A memorial to the Symons family is in the church – an unusual wooden reredos which shows the agricultural nature of the area, with its vines, corn and various fruits.

There is also a memorial brass to one of Cornwall's great engineers, Michael Loam, inventor of the 'man-engine' that saved so many lives in Cornish mines. Born in west Cornwall, he died at Moditonham House where only 12 years before, the Prince of Orange had surrendered Pendennis and Plymouth Castles. During World War II, Moditonham suffered considerable bomb damage, but the National Trust now maintains the little of the building that remains.

CARGREEN
AND HALTON QUAY

Lanes to **Cargreen** are warm with meadow-sweet and bright with purple vetch in summer. Linger beside the quiet quay – a pleasant place to watch the small craft. Walkers may prefer to make a bypass to Landulph church where Theodore Palaeologus was buried. He was descended from the last of the Greek Christian emperors and has achieved later fame as an ancestor of Prince Philip who, with the Queen, visited the tomb in 1962.

A handful of cottages hug Cargreen quay. The village has a lively yacht club and it is hard to realise that this was once Cornwall's Covent Garden. Market gardeners from all over the valley brought their produce here to be ferried across to Devon. Now only sailing boats and birds make the crossing – a walk beside the Tamar at low tide reveals its beauty. It is little wonder that this riverside area is popular with both birdwatchers and naturalists while a marked increase in the number of nurserymen seems to indicate a revival in a former trade.

Motorists climb gently away from Cargreen, past Coombe Lane, where wool used to be collected from local farmers en route to a mill at Liskeard. The turning to the right, after the church, rises high above the valley and ferny lanes give way to open views. **Pentillie Castle**, (not open to the public) overlooking a wooded sweep of the river, can be seen on the right. It was built in 1689 by James Pentillie, a steward to the Coryton family of Cornwall's Newton Ferrers. When Pentillie's great-niece married a Coryton in 1810, Wilkins, who designed London's National Gallery, planned the alterations. Further work was carried out after 1965 and by 1970 the castle was almost the same as the original. Granite pillars from Kit Hill make the front look impressive while a statue of James Pentillie in the centre of the courtyard seems to register approval.

Kit Hill

Kit Hill is an outlying eminence of granite, the summit of Hingston Down where King Egbert defeated Britons and Danes in AD835. The Duchy of Cornwall preserved the 85-foot (26m) stack at the summit and it remains a mining monument to the workers who won tin over so many centuries and who, with Devon men, held their Stannary Parliaments there. In 1985 the Duchy gave Kit Hill to the people of Cornwall to celebrate the birth of Prince William.

On a clear day the views extend to Dartmoor's Hessary Tor 12 miles (20km) away, the Eddystone Lighthouse 23 miles (37km) and west to Bodmin Moor and Roughtor, 15 miles (24km). There are old mine workings among the heather and many people, choosing their weather, enjoy a whole day here. A circular walk is way-marked by granite posts and riders may follow a horse trail. It is an excellent spot for kite flying and bird watching or maybe just a lazy picnic.

Beyond this, narrow lanes climb then dip into the strangely-named Mount Ararat woods before dropping steeply to the peace of **Halton Quay**. The Pentillie fleet ferried Hingston Down granite from here to Devon in the eighteenth century and cargoes of local fruit and flowers down river. Since the quay closed in 1926, bird lovers and fishermen have taken over so that the chapel of St Dominick beside the water is once again a place of quiet.

From here, even narrower lanes lead up past Chapel Farm to the village of **St Dominick** home of the intriguingly named **Who'd Have Thought It Inn** where a warm welcome awaits visitors. Between the inn and Cotehele there is the one remaining cherry orchard of the many which used to supply markets all over the country.

COTHELE

In the next valley lie the mill and riverside buildings of **Cotehele** – the manor on the hill overlooking the Tamar. This romantic medieval house, now a National Trust property and one of the least altered in the country, was built 1485–1627 and constructed around three courts on the foundations of an earlier dwelling. The furniture, tapestries and armour have always been where they are today, but if you wish to make a close inspection of the pictures and textiles, avoid dull days early or late in the season, as certain rooms have no electric light. The valley garden has a restored medieval dovecote and on the walk through the woods to the quay is Richard Edgcumbe's chapel, built by the warring knight as a thanks offering for his survival after declaring against the Crown in 1403.

Cotehele is not a place to hurry away from. The whole area is ideal for a day's pleasure with walks, birdwatching and sometimes salmon fishing to watch. Picnic where you

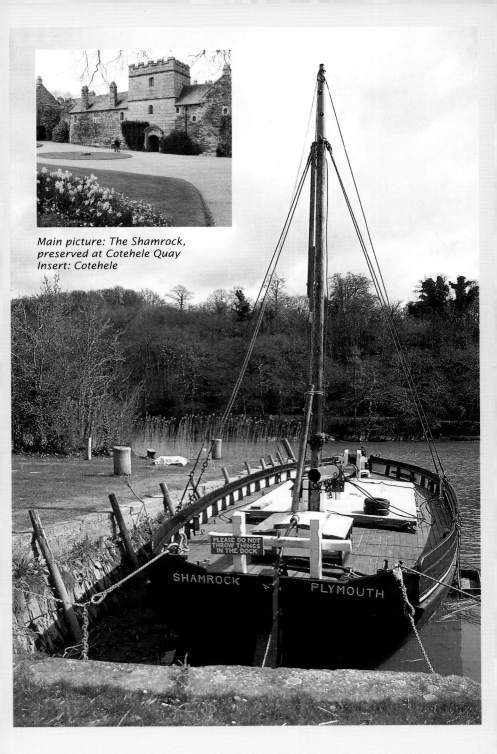

Main picture: The Shamrock,
preserved at Cotehele Quay
Insert: Cotehele

SHAMROCK   PLYMOUTH

PLEASE DO NOT
THROW THINGS
IN THE DOCK

23

will, have refreshments in the old barn or by the river and marvel at the craftsmanship of Shamrock and the skill of those who restored her. She is the last surviving stone-carrying Tamar barge and a grand old lady now available for public charter on a daily basis to interested parties, societies or schools by calling Saltash (01579) 350830. **Cotehele Quay** on the Tamar, with its eighteenth- and nineteenth-century buildings, houses an outstation of the National Maritime Museum and an art and craft gallery. The former public house at Cotehele Quay is now a café and is also open to people not visiting Cotehele House. There is a sign-posted walk from here to Cotehele Mill, which now grinds flour that is on sale to visitors. Here there are exhibitions of old tools displayed in the blacksmith's forge, carpenter's, saddler's and wheelwright's shops.

During summer months a regular passenger ferry service operates between Calstock and Cotehele giving the opportunity for a delightful excursion travelling one way by boat and returning via the riverside footpath. Motorists have to follow a more narrow ferny way to the attractive village of Calstock – another quiet place now but once a busy shipyard. The handsome railway viaduct brought trains to the village but destruction to its shipping. Today pleasure boats make pleasant pictures as they sail past the place where James Goss built the **Garlandstone** which was Britain's last ketch. Most river and fishing ports have always held regattas; Calstock's, which are as famous as

Car Drives

Saltash to Seaton via Torpoint

South of Saltash take the Polbathic road on the B3249 out of St Germans and drive along the A374 towards Sheviock and Torpoint. The river views are delightful and at Sheviock Wood there are picnic areas and well-signed walks. Carry on to Antony where you could stop at the house for a picnic visit but then carry on through to St John village along minor roads, some steep. Join the B3247 in the direction of Portwrinkle, Downderry and Seaton. The coastal views are superb. Turning inland at Seaton a beautiful wooded drive goes to quiet Hessingford and joins the A387 Polbathic road to St Germans and eventually Saltash.

Saltash to Calstock and Kit Hill

To the north of Saltash the road from Calstock Station rises out of the valley and very steeply to Norris Green. Now meander along the lanes through Metherell and Harrowbarrow, note the converted East Cornwall Silver Smelter, to join the A390. Soon after the left turn at that junction take the right-hand B3257 and make your way past historic Hingston Down to Kit Hill Country Park with extensive views. Here is opportune for a picnic before following the B3257 to Kelly Bray when it joins the A388 to nearby Callington and the return to Saltash.

those of Saltash, have recently been revived.

GUNNISLAKE

Gunnislake village climbs to an even steeper slope than Saltash and the road to the New Bridge calls for low gear and good brakes. Before stagecoaches demanded roads and not muddy byways, the approaching paths to the river went straight down the cliff side – a daunting gradient even on horseback. Piers Edgcumbe of Cotehele built this Tamar bridge in 1520 and in 1644 Sir Richard Grenville did his utmost to defend it against the Roundheads. It was then the chief pass into Cornwall, but Sir Richard's efforts were unfortunately in vain. At this point, the Tamar 'tastes' the tide and as maritime trading interests cease, it is appropriate to turn inland again.

Following the A390 westwards you will come to the **Tamar Valley Donkey Park** at St Ann's Chapel, a popular attraction for children with its cuddly animals, donkey rides, woodland walks and play area. The A390 Callington road runs at the foot of **Kit Hill** but make time to leave it and find the B3257 that takes you to the lane leading to the top.

CALLINGTON TO ST MELLION

Before entering Callington, take a minor road on the left signposted 'St Mellion'. A short way down, another lane leads to **Dupath Well**, a handsomely covered spring, the largest of its kind in Cornwall. When the canons of St Germans acquired property, it included 'Theu Path' and they probably had the protective building erected over the holy place.

It remained in their possession until the Dissolution. The name is interesting as it is thought to mean 'The Palm of God' in old Cornish. 'Theu' changing to 'Dew' (God) and 'Path' which is a corruption of 'Palf' (palm of hand) and it then became Dupath as we know it today. Fortunately it was saved from complete disintegration by a rector of South Hill and is now managed by Cornwall County Council

The quiet town of **Callington** was once the centre of a thriving wool industry and possibly it was originally Killiwic where King Arthur had a palace. Pause to visit the museum, unusually housed in the cemetery, and then drive along the short main street, to see a little lane beside the church. This was Tillie Street (now reduced to one cottage), the birthplace of John Knill, St Ives' well known and controversial mayor who will be mentioned again later on.

The Liskeard A390 narrows immediately outside the town and is transformed into country lanes which dip to picturesque **Newbridge**. At this point the River Lynher is spanned by an ancient construction dating from 1478 and the cluster of cottages is typical of a Cornish 'trev' or homestead. The early settlement, however, was once high above on **Cadsonbury**, a prehistoric fort now owned by the National Trust. It is well worth stopping to walk up to it and enjoy the views down the lovely wooded valley.

St Ive (Eve) hamlet sits clean and fresh beside the busy road from Callington to Liskeard. The church is somewhat unusual as it is a Knights Templars' foundation, dating back to

1180. There is more, too, of interest in the compact little village of **Quethiock** (Gwithick) which so many visitors do not know about. Take the narrow lane just opposite the slate-hung Butcher's Arms on the A390 and follow its twists and turns down to the church, content in the protection of the picturesque cottages guarding its history.

The church is one that lovers of brass memorials should not miss. A fine example here is one crafted in 1471 for Roger Kyngdon, his wife and their 16 children. If the church is locked there is a list of key holders' names on the porch. Look out, too, for the Maids' House before you leave. It was built in a new style of architecture not long after 1633 when a charity of poor spinsters was established. Today this remote parish of twisting lanes and secluded farmhouses leads a busy life of its own and one of the highlights is an agricultural show held in mid-July. Here the standards are good and everyone is made welcome.

From Quethiock to **St Mellion**, the lanes dip and curve in almost

Antony House in Springtime

impossible configurations, but in high summer they are cool and delightful. It matters little whether you find the clapper bridge at Bramble Wood or take the way to Pillatonmill and climb out of the deep valley from there – both roads are rarely used. Squire Coryton of Pentillie probably originated the Cherry-Pie Feast in the last century, inviting local school children to a cherry-pie and cream tea on the lawns of his castle. Swings were set up in the 200-year-old lime trees bordering the 1 mile (1.6km) long drive from the road. Everyone enjoyed this event and it was sad when it stopped in 1937. It has however, now been revived and takes place in mid-July at St Mellion Rectory.

St Mellion has another, though very different, interesting point to note. It was the birthplace of John Trevisa (1412), a Cornishman who was eager to promote the use of English. He translated the entire Bible from Latin to English but in so doing was one of the indirect causes of the eventual decline of his native tongue. Today, this village's claim to fame is as one of the UK's leading golf and leisure resorts. The championship course, designed by Jack Nicklaus, caters for all handicaps.

The drive round Saltash covers about 44 miles (71km) but the time cannot be assessed so closely as it would depend on how long the stops were and how deep the investigations into such items as the Kyngdon brasses and the manorial watermill at Cotehele.

SOUTH OF SALTASH

The countryside which lies south of Saltash has quite different attractions from those of the Tamarside villages. A glance at the map shows that this area can be explored in two parts, but only by coming back along the same road. The information in the rest of the chapter covers the Torpoint-Rame peninsula.

TREMATON

Take the road from Saltash where it dips to **Forder** away from the mother church, St Stephen's. After 2 miles (3km) from the town centre there is instant countryside with **Trematon Castle** outlined on the far hill. In the valley, mill buildings and a cluster of old Tudor cottages huddle together watching the traffic climb sharply to the lodge gates of Trematon.

Those who prefer may walk the riverside way and perhaps see the train lumbering slowly round from Saltash after carefully negotiating Brunel's Royal Albert Bridge – the engineering triumph of its time. Today, the high granite shafts and unusual tubular arches give it a strange look, but since its opening in 1859 it has been efficient and safe, the first considerations for a railway bridge.

Train passengers, walkers and motorists all enjoy their brief sight of Trematon Castle with its romantic shape silhouetted against the sky. Possibly the most extensive in Cornwall, it has a well preserved keep which is said to be 'one of the most beautiful examples of the Norman period'. Sited 1 mile (1.6km) south-west of Saltash, it was built either by Earl Mortain or the Valletorts, but is now privately owned. It passed into Duchy hands in the fourteenth century and later figured in a particularly distressing incident when Sir Richard and Lady Grenville were captured by treachery. Beyond the castle, where a road descends to the riverside chapel, a stumpy wayside cross marks the important part once played by this now out-of-the-way place.

Viscountess Boyd of Merton owns **Ince Castle** which stands beside the Lynher. It is situated 5 miles (8km) south-west of Saltash and can be reached at the A38 Stoketon Cross junction which is signed Trematon, Trahan. If you are fortunate enough to be in Cornwall when the grounds are open you can not only wander through ornamental woods, but see the shell house and dovecote. Tea is also available on these occasions.

The architecture resembles that of a French château but the date of construction is probably early seventeenth century. It is believed that at one time the Killigrew owner kept four wives, one in each of the square towers – a picturesque story that matches the building.

ST GERMANS

There is no way for motorists across the Lynher, but the short distance along the A38 to **Tideford** is not unpleasant. This roadside village takes its name from the River Tiddy, quietly flowing down from the high moors of Caradon until it meets the salt water here. Tideford is still frequently spoken of as Tiddyford.

The riverside walk is a pleasant way to reach **St Germans** but motorists have to turn left on to the B3249 to travel the 3 miles (5km) to the historic but now sleepy village of picturesque cottages and flower-filled gardens. At the slope into the

St German's Church

The handsome parish church, formerly Cornwall's ancient cathedral, is away from the traffic, almost hidden among trees. Consecrated in 1261, the building had formerly been of importance as an Augustinian priory and had been the seat of the Cornish bishopric from the close of the tenth to the early eleventh century. Its great west doorway, Cornwall's finest, is a powerful example of Norman architecture and is constructed of elvan stone from Tartan Down near Landrake, while the church's spacious and lofty interior contains numerous features of interest. Since 1974 the diocese has had a bishop suffragan at St Germans.

village notice Sir William Moyle's almshouses. Built in 1538, they were skilfully reconditioned in 1967 at the instigation of the National Association of Almshouses. Driving through this peaceful place today it is hard to believe that St Germans was once a 'rotten borough' which sent two MPs to Westminster.

The Tudor gateway close by leads to **Port Eliot** where the Eliot family have lived for 400 years. It is probably Cornwall's largest private house. Sir Thomas Elyot bought it from Cardinal Wolsey when he was selling monastery lands for Henry VIII. He was known as an astute business man, a skilled ambassador and the first person to compile an English dictionary. But perhaps the best remembered member of this family was Sir John, an MP and vice-admiral of Devon. Unfortunately his interest in maritime affairs proved his undoing as it led him to the Tower and an untimely death. He believed that the king's Bills of Tonnage and Poundage would impose too great a strain on the mercantile community – a group of people with whom he worked closely. His strong feelings in the matter forced him to oppose the new proposals but he paid dearly for doing so.

In 1762, Sir Humphry Repton redesigned the gardens and Sir John Soane made certain architectural alterations which included the addition of a splendid round room, some 40 feet (12m) in diameter. The present Lord Eliot administers all 6,000 acres (2,430 hectares).

The view up river through the thirteen arches of the railway viaduct is a fine sight on a sunny day when seen from St Germans' quay and it is difficult to leave it for the turn to **Polbathic** nearby on the B3249. But once through that village and on to the A374 in the direction of Torpoint there are pleasures of a different kind. A whole stretch of woodland walks and picnic areas beside the St Germans (or Lynher) River, await those wanting to explore the paths to the small village of **Sheviock** and the area around Antony House. It is a part of Cornwall which has been called a miniature kingdom.

ANTONY AND TORPOINT

Antony House was built in the early eighteenth century and is the most distinguished classic house in Cornwall, with its central block of silver-grey Pentewan stone, and wings of red brick joined to the house by colonnades. Now owned by the National Trust it is still very much the home of the Carew-Poles, a fact that adds warmth to its elegance. The 250 acres (101 hectares) of grounds slope gently to the Lynher – both the contents and the house are well worth a visit. An interesting and unusual feature of this property is the Bath House – 800 yards (400m) from the main building and open only by appointment. It was built in 1784 and has recently been repaired.

Antony church which was rededicated in 1259 is a building which should be visited. It is famous for an early brass of Lady Margery Arundell (1420) which is acknowledged to be the most spectacular in the whole of Cornwall.

Torpoint may seem a mere mass of uninteresting buildings after the elegance of Antony House but it does have its own features to offer the visitor. In 1691, William of Orange's

order for the construction of a naval dockyard across the Tamar at Cattewater was followed by such great activity that Torpoint came into existence. According to the comments made by Daniel Defoe, not only did the workmen need homes but the entire operation needed 'yards, dry docks, launches and con-veniences of all kinds for building and repairing of ships'!

The small part of that undertaking that is left today is now private housing and business units, near the Torpoint ferry. This has always been an important crossing and in 1793 the ferryman was obliged to keep three boats for pedestrians as well as a horse boat. His charge for everyone was one penny for the journey there and back. Today, pedestrians travel free from Torpoint but wheeled vehicles have to pay a small charge. Many people use this novel way of commuting to work or school in Plymouth.

Instead of retracing the route use the slightly narrower road out of Torpoint which goes past the shore station of HMS Raleigh before cutting sharply across to **St John**. This is a quiet place of contrast, a delightful medieval cluster of narrow lanes in a fold of hills and cottages that match their surroundings. At low tide, the best way is by the road across the ford at the head of St John's Lake. This is a place to tempt birdwatchers to linger.

MILLBROOK TO RAME HEAD

Walk or drive on to the little town of **Millbrook** but take care to negotiate the narrow, winding lane slowly as you pass fine Georgian

The Copley Arms at Hessenford

houses side by side with humble but picturesque cottages.

The road to **Cremyll** goes first through Maker Heights in a steep climb and looks down on Millbrook as a toy town. Then, from the top of the world, the B3247 slides down to quiet Cremyll, a small group of houses at the crossing to Plymouth named the Passage of Crimela in charters of the thirteenth century. Here is a place that retains its individuality and its old houses while the small, modern, passenger ferry crosses regularly to Plymouth. Watching Drake Island and the shipping in Plymouth Sound keeps Cremyll busy all the year round and there is no objection when visitors park and join in their quiet game.

From here walk into **Mount Edgcumbe Country Park**, 800 acres (324 hectares) of superb parkland, bordered by 10 miles (16km) of magnificent coastline that are open all the year from dawn to dusk with no admission charge. This park is now restored to its Edwardian splendour and the plans have been laid out with such skill that one day is scarcely long enough to encompass everything. From April to September the **Mount Edgcumbe House** and formal gardens, former home of the seventh Earl of Edgcumbe, are open and there are refreshments in the Orangery of the Italian Gardens, with follies and a handsome conservatory not far away.

Walk from here to **Rame Head** – about $2^{1}/_{2}$ miles (4km), skirting the Park and continuing through Maker parish, **Cawsand** and **Kingsand**. There are splendid distant views of Plymouth Breakwater and then across to Heybrook Bay from Penlee Point before arriving at the headland.

Motorists have to climb again to Maker Heights before dropping down narrow lanes to Kingsand and Cawsand Bay at the water's edge. Till 1835 this area did not belong to

Flower Boat Ritual

If a visit to Cornwall coincides with the early May bank holiday stay at Millbrook, near Saltash, because you will be able to see and take part in a centuries-old festival. At some time in mid-morning the Flower-Boat ritual begins. A procession of dancers and singers make their way through the narrow ways of Millbrook, Kingsand and Cawsand, stopping at chosen houses and inns en route. This takes up most of the day, for they carry with them a decorated boat – not a large one but one that is beautified with all the available spring flowers.

The finale is an exciting one and when it grows dark, the boat is launched on the water, usually to the accompaniment of fireworks. This ceremony has been known in Millbrook since the fourteenth century but is thought to be pagan in origin.

The story told by an old inhabitant of Millbrook is an interesting one as it has a particular bearing on the name given to the boat – The Black Prince. It is well known that the son and heir of King Edward III had a great fondness for Trematon Castle, near Saltash, and whenever possible, stayed there for long periods of relaxation.

He had to reach this haven by way of the ferry crossing over the Tamar from Plymouth to Saltash and apparently had a number of craft to choose from. All those in use, however, were showing signs of wear and, according to the ideas of one of the inhabitants, were completely unsuitable to carry royalty. As a result, the Millbrook ferry disappeared one night from its usual moorings only to be seen a short distance away at Saltash. This outrageous theft caused everyone in Millbrook to declare 'war' on their neighbours and, armed with staves and pitchforks, they marched on the offenders.

It was fortunate for all concerned that the Black Prince himself was there at the time for, had he not intervened, there would doubtless have been bloodshed and quite possibly a considerable loss of life. However, when he decreed that the people of Millbrook should have a new ferry – paid for by him, the tension disappeared and the militant villagers returned home quietly. Their gratitude, though, was not a simple matter of a few words of thanks for they then decided that future generations should know about the generosity and kindness of the king's son. So it was agreed that the May Day Flower-Boat would always bear his name, The Black Prince.

An event that probably has the same roots takes place at St Ives on Good Friday – but here it is a less spectacular occasion when model yachts are brought out and sailed. And Cornwall has another story in the same vein, told of the internment of King Geraint. He is said to have been buried in a great tumulus at Carne, above the eastern side of Gerrans Bay on the Roseland Peninsula, after being rowed across the bay in a golden boat with silver oars. This particular royal leader was one of King Arthur's captains in his fifth-century battles against the Saxons and his story sounds more than legend in the light of a recent discovery at Broighter Bay in Ireland's County Derry. This was nothing less than a gold boat with silver oars.

Cornwall and there is still Boundary Cottage standing as a reminder.

Kingsand is very much a sailor's place – the streets twist like an anchor rope in a storm and the cottages cling to the cliff as seamen to the mast in rough weather. Trying to avoid leaning walls and jutting corners, most drivers miss Halfway House and find themselves in and out of Cawsand before they realise it. The **Bellerophon** set out from here under the command of Penryn-born Captain Maitland, who eventually captured Napoléon after his escape from Elba.

Once away from the villages, the road to **Rame** seems to continue for ever and, with land falling away on both sides, gives the strange sensation of driving straight into the sea. But there is a car park beyond the church for those who want to explore the headland. Wander down to the ancient **chapel of St Michael** and wonder at the piety and dedication of the hermits who lived here and kept a light burning to warn ships of the dangerous rocks below. By 1488, however, men were paid for this and they received 4d for 'Keeping of ye bekying'.

SEATON

From here, the road to Seaton keeps close to the cliff top – as does the coastal path and, given fine weather, the views are superb. **Portwrinkle**'s golf course on the cliffs is almost the only sign of life till **Downderry**'s hotels appear. Beyond is **Seaton** – a place of sands and summer enjoyment for those who like crowds. A nearby attraction is the world's first protected breeding colony of Amazon woolly monkeys, the **Monkey Sanctuary**.

The wooded valley which leads from Seaton to **Hessenford** is quiet and magical for lovers of birds and trees. The beauty continues beyond Hessenford until the narrow winding lane opens on to the A38 just east of Tideford, from where it is a short journey back to Saltash.

Before the end of this 40 mile (64km) drive make the short detour into **Landrake**. It was the birth-place of Robert Jeffrye who went to London in the time of Charles Stuart. There he won fame and fortune and became Lord Mayor. He founded the Shoreditch almshouses which are now a museum but did not forget his native village. As well as establishing its first school, Robert Jeffrye also left money to help Landrake's poor. The villagers remembered his generosity and the hall now bears the name of their benefactor.

Hero of Trafalgar

Few people know that a young sailor of Cawsand made history at the Battle of Trafalgar. Lieutenant John Pollard, born in 1784 was a midshipman aboard the **Victory** when Nelson was shot. He later became known as 'Nelson's Avenger' because he shot and killed the enemy sailor who fatally wounded Admiral Nelson.

Walks

Tamar Valley

4$\frac{1}{2}$ miles (7km) • occasionally steep • 2 hours

Map: OS 1:25,000 Explorer Series 108: Lower Tamar Valley and Plymouth

This walk can be enjoyed from Calstock on the Tamar Valley Line, one of the prettiest country branch railway lines, running for 14 miles (22.5km) between Plymouth, Bere Ferrers and Bere Alston in Devon and Calstock and Gunnislake in Cornwall.

Take the train to Calstock Station. Walk downhill to the quay, retrace your steps up the hill for 50 yards (50m) beyond the back of the Tamar Inn and fork left along the lane by the river, under the viaduct which was completed in 1907. The road passes in front of a lime kiln with its characteristic arches and then under a bridge which formerly carried an incline railway. The path turns away from the river at the Danescombe Valley Hotel and branches uphill to the right about 50 yards (50m) further on. Continue up the Danescombe Valley, when the path reaches the road, bear left downhill to the hamlet of Danescombe. Just before the cottages at the bottom of the hill, turn sharp left down a track which takes the walker back along this attractive valley, past the disused and now converted buildings of the Cotehele consols, a former copper and arsenic mine. As the path nears the valley end the route turns right, uphill to Cotehele House. From the house take the road down to Cotehele Quay. Turn back upstream just inside the woods, and follow the path past the chapel to rejoin the route leading back to Danescombe. At the bottom by the marsh turn right for the hotel and follow the riverside road back to Calstock and up to the station.

Rame Head

10 miles (16km) approx • moderate • 4 hours

Map: OS 1:25,000 Explorer Series 108: Lower Tamar Valley and Plymouth

The coastline of Mount Edgcumbe offers wide views over Plymouth Sound and out into the English Channel where the Eddystone Lighthouse can be seen 10 miles (16km) off shore. Some of the most spectacular scenery of the South Cornwall Coastal Footpath may be viewed along the route from Cawsand to Penlee Point. It continues to another point at Rame Head where St Michael's Chapel is situated. Walkers may then continue along Whitsand bay to the caravan site where cars may be parked or return to their original starting point enjoying the views in the opposite direction.

Places to Visit

Saltash

Saltash Heritage Museum
Fore Street
Exhibits depicting history of the area.
☎ (01752) 844846
Open: 2-4pm Wednesday. 10am-4pm Saturday, April to November. July, August and September also open 10am-4pm Thursday and Friday.

Town Heritage Trail
Links historic buildings with the waterside where there are superb views and colourful murals depicting local history.
☎ (01752) 843796
Route is outlined on information boards around the town.

Mary Newman's House
48 Culver Street
Little low Tudor house believed to be the birthplace of Sir Francis Drake's first wife. ☎ (01752) 844846
Entry by prior arrangement

North of Saltash

Cotehele
(National Trust)
St Dominick, beside the Tamar
A romantic medieval house of grey granite, built 1485-1627. One of the best-preserved examples of a squire's house and for centuries home of the Edgcumbes. Beautifully furnished with original tapestries, needlework and armour. Gardens, and art and craft gallery at the quay.
☎ (01579) 351346
Open: 11am-5.00pm (4.30pm in October) daily from April to October.

House, shop and restaurant not open on Fridays.

Cotehele Mill
In woodland near Cotehele house
☎ (01579) 350606
Open: 1-5.30pm (4.30pm in October) daily except Friday, April to October.

Cotehele Museum
The Quay, Cotehele
Branch of National Maritime Museum.
Open: 10am-6pm daily April to October. Small admission charge in honesty box.

Tamar Passenger Ferry
Calstock to Cotehele and return.
☎ (01822) 833331
Runs from late May to early October most weekends and some weekdays in high season.

Cotehele Mill

Places to Visit

Kit Hill
2 miles (3km) NE of Callington
beside the A390
An outlying eminence of granite, the
summit of Hingston Down where
King Egbert defeated Britons and
Danes in AD835. Further
information ☎ (01579) 370030.

Dupath Holy Well
About 1 mile (1.6km) from
Callington between the A388
and A390
This is the largest well building
in Cornwall.

Callington Museum
☎ (01822) 832898
Open: 10am-4pm Friday,
Saturday, Sunday and Bank Holidays,
April to October.

Tamar Valley Donkey Park
St Ann's Chapel, Gunnislake
Donkeys and other animals.
Adventure playground. Café.
☎ (01822) 834072
Open: 10am-5.30pm daily, Easter to
October. November, December and
February to Easter, weekends only.

South of Saltash

St Germans
The church – was the seat of the
Cornish bishopric from the close of
the tenth to the early eleventh
century. Its great feature is the
Norman west door. The almshouses
were built by Sir William Moyle in
1538. They were restored in 1967
through the National Association of
Almshouses.

Antony House (National Trust)
About 15 miles (24km) from Saltash
A Carew-Pole property since the
fifteenth century, but this house was
built in the early eighteenth century.
The Bath House can be seen on
application to the custodian.
Extensive grounds slope to the River
Lynher. Fine paintings are to be seen
in the house.
☎ (01752) 812191
Open: 1.30pm-5.30pm Tuesday,
Wednesday and Thursday. In June,
July and August these times apply to
Sundays also. Open all Bank Holiday
Mondays.

Antony Church
Rededicated in 1259, this church is
mainly remarkable for its spectacular
early brass to Lady Margery Arundell
(1420).

Mount Edgcumbe House
Entrance at Cremyll Ferry
Originally built in 1547–54 for Sir
Richard Edgcumbe but destroyed in
1941 blitz. Rebuilt 1960. Home of
the present earl and open again
since 1988.
☎ (01752) 822236
Open: 11am-4.30pm daily except
Friday and Saturday, from April to
September.

Mount Edgcumbe Country Park
800 acres (324 hectares) of
parkland on magnificent coastline
are open, all year, free admission.

Rame Head
Stretching into the sea beyond
Rame church (St German) with
expansive views east and west.

Ince Castle Gardens & Grounds
5 miles (8km) SW of Saltash,
from A38 at Stoketon Cross take
turn signed Trematon, Trahan.
5 acres (2 hectares) with lawns
and ornamental woods; shell
house and dovecote.
☎ (01752) 842672
Open: on occasional Sundays
in spring and summer.

The Monkey Sanctuary
Nr Looe
Amazon woolley monkeys seen
in garden and tree setting.
Daily talks.
☎ (01503) 262532
Open: 11.00am-4.30pm, Sunday
to Thursday, Easter to the end of
September.

Kernow Mill
Trerulefoot, junction of A374 and
A38. Working watermill housing
craft centre with associated
shopping complex and coffee
shop. See the Cornish National
Tartan. ☎ (01752) 851898
Open: 9.30am-5.30pm Monday
to Saturday, 11am-5pm Sunday
all year.

What to do if it rains

Saltash
• Heritage Museum

Cotehele
• Cotehele Manor
• Cotehele Museum
• Cotehele Mill
• Cotehele Gallery

Torpoint
• Antony House

Callington
• Museum

St Germans
• St Germans' Church

Kingsand
• Mount Edgcumbe House

Seaton
• Murrayton Monkey Sanctuary,

Trerulefoot
• Kernow Mill

Between Saltash and Lostwithiel lies Liskeard, once a prosperous town trading in tin and wool. Minerals from Caradon Hill brought a charter and subsequent wealth in 1240. Stannary privileges followed in 1307, when Liskeard became a coinage town. Later the flourishing wool trade added to the prosperity. The increasing demand for tin in the eighteenth and nineteenth centuries led to the opening of the Liskeard-Looe Canal, which carried ore and stone supplies to the coast for export. Webb's Hotel in the Square was built in 1833 as a coaching inn. It is now being restored to reflect its listed building status and will reopen as offices and restaurant accommodation.

The **Church of St Martin** is the second largest in Cornwall, its history dating from the mid- thirteenth century. Stuart House in Barras Street is attractively slate-hung, as it must have been when

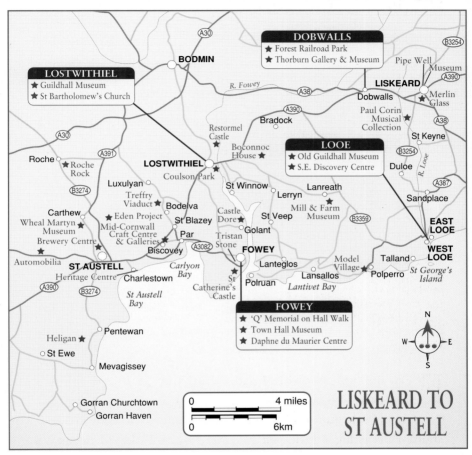

Forest Railroad Park
Thorburn Gallery & Museum
Pipe Well

DOBWALLS

BODMIN

Museum

LOSTWITHIEL
★ Guildhall Museum
★ St Bartholomew's Church

LISKEARD
Dobwalls
Merlin Glass

R. Fowey

Restormel Castle

Bradock

Paul Corin Musical Collection

St Keyne

Roche
★ Roche Rock

LOSTWITHIEL

Boconnoc House ★

LOOE
★ Old Guildhall Museum
★ S.E. Discovery Centre

Duloe

Luxulyan

Coulson Park

St Winnow
Lerryn
Lanreath

Sandplace

Treffry Viaduct ★ Bodelva
Castle Dore ★
St Veep
Mill & Farm Museum

Carthew
Wheal Martyn Museum ★
★ Eden Project
Mid-Cornwall Craft Centre & Galleries

St Blazey
Par
Biscovey

Tristan Stone
Golant

EAST LOOE

WEST LOOE

Automobilia

ST AUSTELL
Heritage Centre
Charlestown

Carlyon Bay

St Catherine's Castle

FOWEY
Lanteglos
Lansallos
Polruan
Lantivet Bay

Model Village
Talland
Polperro
St George's Island

Heligan ★
St Ewe

Pentewan

FOWEY
★ 'Q' Memorial on Hall Walk
★ Town Hall Museum
★ Daphne du Maurier Centre

Mevagissey

Gorran Churchtown
Gorran Haven

0   4 miles
0   6km

LISKEARD TO ST AUSTELL

King Charles stayed there (1644–5). Restored in the early nineties it is now a local arts and heritage centre used for exhibitions and recitals. Traces of the old town linger in and around Well Lane and Market Street where the former Guildhall stands. Next door is Forester House, home of the **Museum** and the TIC. The award-winning building has been beautifully restored with a slate-hung front and was opened in 2002 by Prince Charles. The Pipe Well, originally late sixteenth century, was restored in the early nineteenth century.

Leave the town by the B3254 Looe road, first stopping in Station Road at the old industrial mill that houses **Merlin Glass**. This is the Pavlova Mill which once made gloves exclusively for Pavlova, the dancer.

AROUND LISKEARD; LOOE AND POLPERRO

Beyond Liskeard station follow the sign for St Keyne's Well but turn aside en route and see the **Paul Corin Magnificent Music Machines**. This modern wonder is housed in the family mill deep among lush, narrow lanes beside the River Looe. Spend an hour listening to instruments ranging in size – from the musical box which began it all – to a 20 foot- (6m) high Belgian dance hall organ; an amazing collection to find anywhere but especially in the heart of the Cornish countryside, beside the old Liskeard-Looe Canal.

Two winding ways lead the motorist to Cornwall's most famous well, the longer passing through the hill-high village and church of **St Keyne**. Set below road level where three lanes meet, this beautifully restored well can easily be missed. In the past, newly-married couples always hurried here after their wedding ceremony, believing that the first to drink the water would rule the household.

The lane dips steeply but turn right at Badham's Farm and then take the right fork. There is no signpost here – the map says it leads through Windsor Wood – but visitors who drive along here in spring may be forgiven for thinking that the direction should be 'To Fairyland'. A grass track in the centre of the road tempts cows from their pasture and motorists must wait while they test the quality of the roadway grass, following as the animals make their leisurely way towards the next gate. Ducks, too, use this wooded valley lane and so peaceful is this place that rejoining the B3254 to Duloe seems like finding an unexpected motorway.

In fact, the village of **Duloe** is quiet and attractive, specialising in cottages with country names – fun to list them – but having its own memorable past. The church of St Cuby and St Leonard has a well preserved thirteenth-century tower and interesting associations. Signposted from the main road is a circle of eight stones, 38 feet (12m) in diameter, restored in the nineteenth century.

The B3254 joins the A387 at **Sandplace**. The church of St Wenna at Sandplace, behind a rhododendron screen, is noteworthy for the fine slate memorial to Walter Coode, his wife and their twelve children. The children are represented allegorically as fruits growing out of vines trailing behind their kneeling parents. Also, the walls appear to lean outwards and a tower pinnacle seems to bend out of true. Was the church built like this or was it the scene of devil-worship as portrayed in *Bewnans Meriasek*, one of the Cornish miracle plays? Translated, the lines run:

> *'To my God Jove in his face*
> *I will happily offer a cat:*
> *There can be no better mouser.*
> *I bought it from Morval.*
> *The place where the devil was*
> *anointed.'*

A meal at **Polraen Country House Hotel** would doubtless dispel all witchcraft as would a walk beside the River Looe. Here are birds to watch and old wooden hulks to pass by, left on the mud to rot because ill-luck is believed to come to those who break them up. Looe's golf course is the other side of Morval at Widegates. From there, the B3253 joins the A387 just outside East Looe. The town of **Looe** had a charter as early as 1237 and much of its past is recorded in the **Old Guildhall Museum and Gaol**.

Shark fishing, good sailing and swimming can be enjoyed from the little beach by the banjo pier (so-called because of its shape), which is seen at its best from the cliffs of West Looe. The original bridge was built in 1411, magnificent with thirteen arches and a hermitage chapel, but the present one has only seven arches and was widened in 1960. Before continuing take time to visit the **South East Cornwall Discovery Centre** at the back of the car park at Millpool and learn about both past and present in a free exhibition.

Turn left over the bridge, pass the fourteenth-century St Nicholas church and go up the steep road that leads to Looe Bay. Beyond the rocks lies St George's Island, once a Celtic monastery. It is possible to walk along the coastal path into Polperro from here, but motorists must return to the church and turn left past the 500-year-old inn, The Jolly Sailor.

This narrow, exciting lane to **Talland Bay**, past the Measured Nautical Mile, cannot be hurried. St Tallan church stands proudly at the top of a precipitous hill leading to the beach with its strange pink-grey rocks and grey stony sand. Climb again to Sclerder Abbey, a gracious, peaceful Carmelite monastery near the A387, built by the Trelawny family.

Close by is Trelawne, an ancient house dating back to before the Conquest and once the home of the famous Royalist Bishop Trelawny who inspired the Reverend R S Hawker of Morwenstow to compose *With a Good Sword and a Trusty Hand*, now almost Cornwall's national song. Trelawne was also the place where one of the first therapeutic cures was effected in the early eighteenth century by Dr Jonathan Couch, grandfather of the author Sir A Quiller-Couch. He advised a neurotic young man staying there after a period abroad, to study the habits of the Trelawne rooks daily for a year. The detailed observations he made so absorbed the patient that after 12 months he was completely and permanently cured.

Much of the coast between Talland Bay and Polperro is National Trust property and fine views tend to offset the rough path. Motorists can enter **Polperro** by the A387, but the roads were made for horses and a large car park outside the village marks the place where you must leave your car and continue the journey on foot or by electric buggy. In the summer horsebus rides are available too, a pleasant mode of travel.

Small though the village is, there is a great deal to see – the unspoiled harbour sheltering behind its sturdy wall, the Pilchard Inn where fishermen once had their catch

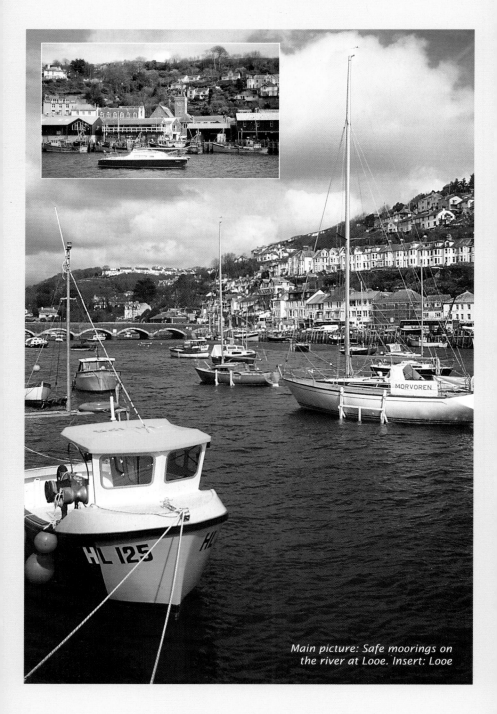

Main picture: Safe moorings on the river at Looe. Insert: Looe

weighed and Couch House where Jonathan Couch was born. But what was Polperro really like before visitors came? The answer is in the **Model Village**, a replica built by local craftsmen and guaranteed to set the imagination working. The history of smuggling in the area is on display at the **Heritage Museum of Smuggling and Fishing.**

Narrow lanes lead to **Lansallos** with its fine church high above Lantivet Bay. Unusual are the 34 carved bench ends, most of them early sixteenth century. Here, too, are some fine slate-carved memorials; and its greatest treasure, Bishop Trelawny's pastoral staff.

To the north, the quiet hamlet of **Lanreath** seems steeped in history – the name recalling a medieval monastery and the handsome Court Barton, once the Tudor manor home of the Grylls family. Perhaps the famous 400-year-old Punch Bowl Inn holds the village secrets for it has been, in turn, court house, coaching inn and smugglers' distribution house. Artist Augustus John stayed there: the unusual inn-sign outside is a reminder of his visit. It is much sought after by holidaymakers who follow Egon Ronay and Ashley Courtenay recommendations. An added attraction is the fine collection of horse brasses, many,

Selected Car Drive

Lostwithiel – Bodinnick Ferry – Luxulyan – St Austell

The first right turn from Lostwithiel on the A390 towards Liskeard will lead you to St Winnow, the waterside church used in the first filming of the Poldark novels. Look across the Fowey River and remember the story of Tristan and Iseult – it happened round here. Return about one and a half miles (2.4km) then drive right to Lerryn – a place of peace and beauty. The Great Wood where this river joins the Fowey was the inspiration of Kenneth Grahame's Wind in the Willows. He wrote much of it while staying with his friend Sir Arthur Quiller-Couch at Fowey. Now drive uphill and down dale to St Veep, Lanteglos Highway and down to Bodinnick Ferry. Daphne du Maurier lived beside that ferry for many years. On the other side, the B3269 goes past the Long Stone (which once marked the burial place of Tristan and Iseult) and joins the A3082 and the A390 for St Blazey Church.

Leave St Blazey Church on the A390 and drive about 800 yards (800m) towards Lostwithiel. Take the left turn to Luxulyan and then the right turn which leads to the glory of the Luxulyan Valley. This beauty spot lies under the Treffry viaduct cum aqueduct built by Joseph Treffry. Follow the Luxulyan sign and enjoy that lovely place. Any of the roads from there will take you through the dreamland of Cornwall's china clay country to Roche. A hermit built a chapel on the top of Roche Rock and lived there for many years. The B3274 in the village will take you through Stenalees to the A391 and St Austell.

doubtless, from places such as the Lanreath Mill across the road, now operating as **Lanreath Farm and Folk Museum,** where the past is literally brought to life, with demonstrations of pasty making, corn dolly work, leather craft and spinning.

On the way back to Liskeard, is the Giant's Hedge, near to where the Lanreath road joins the B3359 (GR SX178574). This prehistoric earthwork was built by the Devil according to legend. After about 2 miles (3.2km), turn right for **Herodsfoot** – walk across country if preferred – and find the delights of Forestry Commission nature trails in Deerpark Wood. In this other world there are holiday cabins deep in the valley overlooking ponds once serving an old gunpowder mill. Sailing, riding and fishing are available for holidaymakers on this self-catering site. To see it at bluebell time is to understand why it won the Civic Trust Award the year after it opened.

Two more award-winning places are signposted at **Dobwalls** on the A38 to Liskeard. A million pound memorial exhibition to Britain's greatest wildlife artist, Archibald Thorburn and a miniature American railroad are run by John Southern and his family. Their enthusiasm for these hobbies has resulted in one of the county's most pleasing attractions. Lovingly displayed in a friendly atmosphere, there is enough here for a day's delight.

LOSTWITHIEL & AROUND

Along the A390 from Liskeard, some 11 miles (17.7km) to the west, is **Lostwithiel**. A quiet, welcoming place, a good touring centre where picturesque ruins and an old church are daily reminders of its importance in history from 1100 when the Normans built **Restormel Castle.** Today the proud shell is well cared for by English Heritage and visitors may picnic here, high above the Looe valley.

The **Guildhall** in Fore Street was built in 1740 and now houses a free museum displaying linen-fold panelling, town insignia and photocopies of the charters. Free parking in the town gives ample opportunity to explore everything – a pottery, antiques, a good bookshop and restaurants. If your pleasure is fishing, birdwatching, walking or simply enjoying the peace of the country, it is all here. Booklets are available to tell you where Coulson Park is and the best way to reach the Duchy Nurseries and an interesting woodland nature trail.

About 4 miles (6.4km) eastwards along the A390, at West Taphouse, a right-hand turn to **Braddock** dips and climbs to the church, a delight in spring but solitary beside woods where historians remember the Civil War. The Battle of Braddock Downs took place in 1643 when Cornishmen put the Parliamentarians to rout and took 1,200 prisoners. Today members of the Cornish branch of the Sealed Knot re-enact this for their own pleasure and that of many onlookers.

Walks

Fowey

10 miles (16km) approx • moderate • 5 hours

Map: OS 1:25,000 Explorer Series 107: St Austell & Liskeard

From Readymoney Cove at Fowey the Coastal Footpath is clearly signed all the way round to Polkerris. It is a very fine walk with views which include Fowey harbour and St Austell Bay. The castle at St Catherine's Point and the outstanding Daymark at Gribbin Head would interest artists and photographers. The way to Polkerris village and refreshment is down through woods. A rest there will enable you to carry on along the upper path which crosses fields to a gate at a road and that is part of the Saints' Way back to Fowey. Turn right on that and soon you reach Tregaminion Church built in 1816 by the Rashleigh family. The Saints' Way is signposted beside the churchyard gate and from there the Cornish symbols should guide you safely back to Readymoney Cove via the Doomsday Manor of Trenant.

Hall Walk, Polruan

4 miles (6.4km) • fairly tough going • 3 hours

Map: OS 1:25,000 Explorer Series 107: St Austell & Liskeard

Park in the long stay car park near Caffa Mill Pill in Fowey. Walk to the ferry and cross to Bodinnick. As you disembark the ferry look up to the right of the slipway where you will see 'Ferryside', the house where Daphne du Maurier once lived. Walk up the road, past the Old Ferry Inn, continue past St John's Church and follow the sign on the right marked 'Hall Walk Polruan'. Continue along the path as it turns east into Pont Pill, cross the cattle grid and follow the path down through the wood. At the bottom turn right, following the sign to Polruan. Descend into the village, turn sharp right down steps, then left at the bottom. The ferry from Polruan Quay runs frequently and will deposit you at Whitehouse Point (Town Quay in winter). Turn back along the Esplanade into Fowey, turn left up Lostwithiel Street and then immediately right along a narrow passage to the church of St Fimbarrus and Place Mansion. Downhill from the church takes you to the water's edge at Town Quay. From here follow the waterside roads back to the car park.

Looe Valley Line

Map: OS 1:25,000 Explorer Series 107: St Austell & Liskeard

This delightful, scenic line from Liskeard to Looe offers the possibility of several fairly gentle walks without the need for a car. There are park and ride facilities at Liskeard station and the combined parking and train ticket offers excellent value. Trains run regularly all year though there are slightly less in the winter. A free information pack available from the Discovery Centre at Looe gives details of 10 walks based on the Looe Valley Line. Each station along the line gives access to interesting places such as St Keyne's well and the village of Duloe with its stone circle and church. Finally from Looe there are magnificent walks along the coast in either direction, as far as Polperro to the west or Seaton to the east for the really energetic, with bus services from both places for the return to Looe.

Road and woodland paths, rich in wildlife, pass close to eighteenth-century **Boconnoc**, a house whose 600 years of history include a brawling duellist, Thomas 'Diamond' Pitt (cousin to Britain's youngest Prime Minister), and a modern event, when camera crews filmed part of Winston Graham's *Poldark* series for television. The house is not open to the public but its park and garden are occasionally. The 'No Thoroughfare' road leads to the church – the key may be borrowed from the nearby estate office. It is small but interesting – more a house chapel, but nevertheless with royal arms, a wall plaque sent to a number of Cornish churches by King Charles II as a token of his thanks for the support of the congregation during the Civil War.

Narrow tree-lined lanes lead to the backwaters of **Couch's Mill** and **Lerryn**, picturesque villages beside the River Lerryn. There are wooded paths on both sides but the one north of Lerryn's sixteenth-century bridge goes to Great Wood and looks seawards along the Fowey. It became the Wild Wood in Kenneth Grahame's *Wind in the Willows*. He discovered it during one of his visits to his friend Sir Arthur Quiller-Couch at Fowey. The path reaches the point jutting into the Fowey and turns upstream to **St Winnow** a lovely, lonely churchtown. The church has one of Cornwall's oldest surviving rood screens, Tudor bench ends and fine windows.

The bridge in the small village of Lerryn

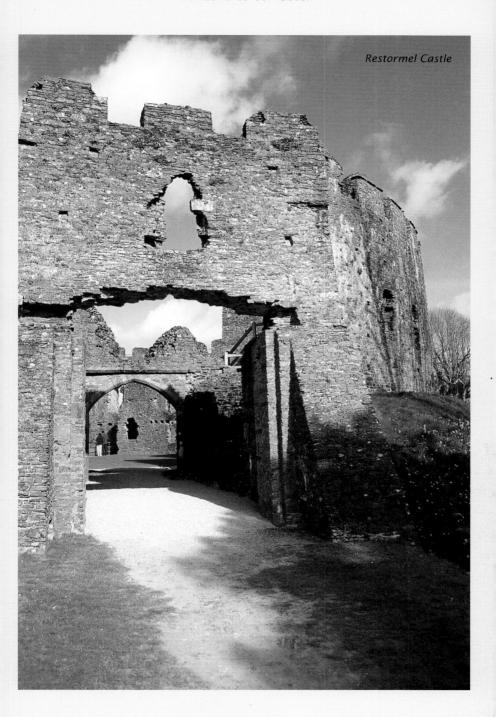

Restormel Castle

History of Lostwithiel

The town was granted a charter of rights and port status in 1190, and a timber bridge was built to mark a crossing point which had existed since the Bronze Age. This was replaced in the fifteenth century by one of granite, still in use today. By 1272, the increasing tin trade required an assay point, so Lostwithiel's Duchy Parliament building incorporated the Stannary Court, the Hall of Exchequer and Exchange as well as the prison. The remains are still to be seen – of particular interest is the cobbled way below a fine stone arch on Fore Street, used by pack animals laden with wool or tin from Bodmin en route for the Stannary Court.

In 1337 Edward III proclaimed his seven-year-old son and heir, Duke of Cornwall. When he came of age he was a just overlord, much concerned with his domain of Restormel and Lostwithiel, which he administered wisely and well and the town prospered with tin, tanning and wool trading. In 1644 Roundhead forces overcame the loyal inhabitants and desecrated **St Bartholomew's church** in a manner clearly described by the diarist Symonds:

'In contempt of Christianity, Religion and the Church they brought a horse to the font, and there, with their kind of ceremonies, did, as they called it, christen the horse and called him by the name of Charles in contempt of his Sacred Majesty.'

It is said, however, that when Essex's men later surrendered, the people of Lostwithiel took their revenge.

But this parish church, dedicated to the patron saint of tanners more than 300 years earlier, overcame its indignities. It is still there now for visitors to admire its unusual features, especially the spire of Breton design added at the same time as the font in the fourteenth century.

IN & AROUND FOWEY

From Lerryn, the road, which is very narrow and between high hedges in places, climbs steeply to **St Veep** church before dipping to **Penpol**. Walkers may follow the river and climb to Haye Farm where National Trust land looks across the River Fowey to Golant. Lanteglos Highway was rightly named as it runs on the spine of this largely unspoilt parish. Before taking the steep road to the Bodinnick ferry for Fowey, make a detour to **Lantivet Bay**. Park the car and walk to Pencarrow Head, where there are fine views east to Rame and west to the Lizard.

Polruan is quaint and very old but has had to give way to Fowey which now claims the first place. In 1066 it was probably the main centre of trade and population at the estuary mouth, but Fowey had a powerful feudal patron to grant and procure necessary privileges

Hall Walk

The 'Q' memorial (a memorial to author Sir Arthur Quiller-Couch 1892-1944) stands looking downriver at Hall Walk, a National Trust property, covering 40 acres (16 hectares) of cliff. A path leaves the road above the Bodinnick ferry, between the houses. It winds along the side of the hill with splendid views across to Fowey and Polruan. At the 'Q' memorial it turns east up a small creek which is crossed by a footbridge at Pont. Thereafter, the path climbs the hill before continuing to Polruan where the Polruan ferry (for foot passengers only) brings you back to Fowey.

You can park at **Bodinnick ferry** (Fowey side) or you may prefer the larger Fowey car park which is also much closer when you leave the Polruan ferry. This is a delightful walk which should not be missed. The paths are best early in the year when they are bright with a variety of spring flowers. Today Bodinnick ferry carries vehicles and has been important since the fourteenth century, forming part of the south coast route from Cremyll.

and this led, over the centuries, to Polruan's decline.

On the Fowey side of the river, coasters can be seen loading their cargoes of china clay – a different scene from the days when the Fowey Gallants sailed away to the siege of Calais in 47 men-o'-war.

June is a good time to visit Fowey. There is room then to wander at leisure through the narrow streets, which twist and turn till one would think that even a cat might lose its way. Every bend brings the past to life again: the **Town Hall Museum**, probably guild chapel then a prison, displays other treasures, the Ship Hotel remembers its days as the Rashleigh's town house (one of the many properties belonging to the family who had been prominent in most Cornish matters for at least 400 years) and even the Fowey Gallants have their name perpetuated by one of the yacht clubs. Fowey seems to offer everything: walks, swimming, sailing, fishing and a wealth of archaeological material close by.

Fowey has literary links with Kenneth Grahame, Leo Walmsley and Sir Arthur Quiller Couch but probably the most well-known is the author of *Rebecca*. The **Daphne du Maurier Literary Centre** offers an insight into her life and work and has features on other local authors. The Daphne du Maurier Festival of Literature and Art is held in May each year in the village.

The coastal path from the town leads past St Catherine's Castle – now ruined – but once one of a chain of south coast forts built by Henry VIII. Gribbin Head is memorable with its huge red and white day mark built in 1842, providing an unmistakable warning for shipping. **Menabilly**, set in the woods behind Polridmouth Cove, and formerly the home of the Rashleigh family, was used as the fictional setting for three of

Above: The King of Prussia Inn, Fowey, named
after a local man with that nickname

Left: The Red Arrows at Fowey Regatta

Daphne du Maurier's novels including *The King's General* and *Rebecca*. It is not open to the public.

Beside the B3269 out of Fowey, is the Longstone or the **Tristan Stone**. Its sixth-century inscription reads *Drustanus Fili Cunomorus* which is translated as 'Tristan, Son of Cunomorus' (the name by which King Mark was known). Historians now think that Castle Dore, the earthwork a short way off was the site of Mark's castle, but facts have not yet verified this and students of Beroul's *Roman de Tristan* continue to puzzle over it.

At Castle Dore, a lane to the right leads to **Golant**, the quiet, sheltered waterside village with more Tristan associations. King Mark and Queen Iseult probably worshipped in the church of St Sampson, as it was near Castle and Lantyan, both connected with them. Today, these names denote farms or similar buildings but the area of **Lantyan Wood** still keeps its secrets of the lovers, silent and watchful beside the River Fowey.

If you park by the riverside to explore the village or visit the adjacent pub, remember the river is tidal. Tristan's duel with Morholt possibly took place there, watched, we are told, by Cornish and Irish on opposite banks, looking like 'holm-gang' (invading Northmen). Is that perhaps how the Holmbush Inn on the A390 at St Austell came by its name?

life to this little port. A harbour was built and waggons took their new loads down to waiting ships until tin-streaming soil and china-clay slurry caused the silting which killed it as a port. Today caravans rest on dunes beside the once prosperous harbour. The latter still contains water despite having no access to the sea these days and is well worth going to see.

Take the Gorran Haven turning from the B3273 to find the **Lost Gardens of Heligan,** a unique collection of gardens within a garden and a joy that no visitor should miss. Formerly the seat of the Tremayne family the estate had been buried for years under unchecked growth of ivy and bramble, laurels and fallen timber. It has largely being revealed and restored in the manner of the great nineteenth-century horticulturists.

ST AUSTELL

ECC International – the giant producer of Cornwall's kaolin, has its headquarters at **St Austell** in the heart of the 'mountains'. It is a pleasant place with old buildings, quietly enjoying the life of a medieval village in the church-town away from the new shopping precinct and rumbling white clay lorries. Modern interests thrive at the **Arts Centre and Theatre**. The B3273 leads to **Pentewan** where stone from Duchy quarries was in great demand for rebuilding churches during the fifteenth century.

William Cookworthy's discovery of china clay at Carloggas in the eighteenth century brought new

Charlestown

Traditional Food

With so much to see and do in Cornwall healthy appetites are very much the order of the day. What better then, than to sample the many traditional foods that can be found here. Seafood is wonderful from crabs, lobsters and shellfish to mackerel, pilchard and sole. Every harbour and cove will have at least a couple of boats bringing in fresh catches and specialist fish restaurants abound.

According to some people, the only food associated with Cornwall is a pasty. That is certainly not correct but few know that there can be at least ten fillings to this healthy 'convenience food', the traditional one being best steak, potato, onion, salt and pepper. Originally baked for the miners to take to the depths of the mine for their mid-day meal, the pasty could have a savoury filling at one end and a sweet one at the other. The crimped edge was there for the miner to hold his pasty with his arsenic stained hands. The crust was then discarded to appease the mine spirits, if you take the romantic view, or to avoid arsenic poisoning if you are a realist. Whichever way you look at it a delicious all-in-one meal was invented that is still enjoyed today.

Others however are eager to taste the clotted or scalded creams, made differently from cream produced in Devonshire. Queen Elizabeth I learnt about it from her sailors but probably did not know that it had to be eaten with splits – not scones. Not often met is a teatime delicacy named thunder and lightning, splits spread with golden syrup and topped with clotted cream. The word clotted comes down from 'clout', a thick piece

A minimum of half a day will be needed to explore all the features and stout footwear is advised if a walk around the 'Lost Valley', the 'Jungle' and the farmland are to be included. There are 80 acres (32 hectares) of pleasure grounds, which include a large collection of rare sub-tropical shrubs, walled gardens, grotto, kitchen garden (smell the seaweed used as fertiliser) and ravine fernery. Heligan is more than just a lovely garden however. The aim is to explore man's relationship with the land, the food we eat and the modern environment; to look back at how things were done in the past and look forward to how they may be done in the future.

Farmland adjacent to the gardens has been acquired and there is a herd of cattle and a flock of sheep. Visitors will have the opportunity to learn about the yearly cycle on the farm and taste the results in the restaurant where Heligan beef and lamb will be served along with fresh fruit and vegetables from the gardens. The most recent addition is a farm shop in the car park selling local produce. All of this is achieved with consideration to the local wildlife, trees and plants and of leather. So the cream served with your tea should be like a thick crust (or leather) not a semi-solid cream.

Dairy produce used to be plentiful in Cornwall and junket was a popular dessert. In traditional households today junket topped with cream is one of the May Day customs still observed. Look too for Cornish cheeses, made on the farm.

According to local tradition saffron cake should only be eaten indoors. Rarely found outside Cornwall this is a yeast bun delicately flavoured and coloured with saffron, obtained from the stigmas of the crocus flower. Heavy or 'hevva' cake is quite different, made from flour, sugar, butter/lard, currants and cream and scored in a fish-net pattern.

Star-Gazey pie must surely be unique. Pilchards are baked in a pastry crust with the heads projecting from a hole in the centre. Traditionally this pie is eaten on 23 December in Mousehole to celebrate Tom Bawcock's Eve.

Beer drinkers will appreciate Hick's Special Draught, a traditional cask beer from St Austell Brewery. The Brewery was established in 1851 by Walter Hicks and the family name continues to this day in this excellent beer.

Good eating places are everywhere, offering local Cornish produce – new potatoes, fresh vegetables, seafood, strawberries, cream and meat – to give the best of both old and new regional specialities. Make the next visit a food tasting one and add to it by drinking local beer, Cornish mead or wine from one of the vineries.

by managing the land in the most environmentally sustainable way.

Returning towards St Austell a footpath goes part of the way to Black Head but joins the road where the cliff becomes too sheer for walkers. Views across St Austell Bay to Gribbin Head have a touch of mystery about them for the water shimmers with the constant presence of china clay slurry and the effects are strange and ethereal. Little wonder that Cornwall's famous historian, Dr A L Rowse, chose to live at Trenarren on Gerrans Point.

Charles Rashleigh began to develop the port of **Charlestown** for tin in 1791 and it continued to prosper with the growth of the china clay industry. Then J T Treffry of Fowey constructed the port of Par which rivalled both Pentewan and Charlestown, and it is still the main china clay port for smaller vessels. Today the **Heritage Centre** recreates the heyday of this once thriving port with consummate skill. The little beach is a pleasant place for fishing, bathing and sailing. Only 800 yards (800m) along the cliff path is **Carlyon Bay** offering added attractions – the Cornish Leisure World and Polkyth

First Postal System

Beside the A390 Ralph Allen was born in a cottage only a few yards along the road towards St Blazey and a small plaque on the wall marks the place. Not many visitors to Cornwall realise that well over a hundred years before Rowland Hill invented the Penny Post, Allen had devised the first real postal system in the country.

Recreation Centre providing everything from table tennis to opera.

There is little of architectural interest in this area, but up the hill past Allen's birthplace is the Mid-Cornwall Craft Centre and Galleries at **Biscovey**. First class goods for sale are well displayed and it is also possible to take part in art and craft courses. It is well worth a visit.

At the top of the hill notice the Four Lords Inn – probably a unique name. The sign is attractive, depicting Elizabethan nobles in costume. The building marks the common meeting point of estates belonging to Edgcumbe, Raslleigh, Carlyon and Treffry – all local landowners and hence the name. Continue down the next hill to **St Blazey**. The church dedicated to St Blaize stands slightly above the Cornish Arms at the bottom of that same hill. St Blaize is not a Cornish saint's name, but in medieval times wool was as important as tin in this area and he is the patron saint of wool-combers in the town that was once a port. Beside the Pack Horse Inn, a short distance

The figurehead at the Rashleigh Arms, Polkerris

The silted up harbour of Pentewan

away, a solid building standing four square to the road was the wool market. Now neither tin nor wool finds its way here, and by the traffic lights only the Shell House remains as an interesting reminder of St Blazey's great days as a port.

Par is its replacement perhaps, the port reclaimed from the sea by Joseph Austen who became Joseph Treffry. His finest achievement was the massive viaduct across the Lux-ulyan Valley, unbelievably beautiful in bluebell time. A left-hand turn before the St Blazey level crossing, then first right, leads to one of Cornwall's loveliest places, with walks through the woods in

plenty. Even the viaduct does not detract from Luxulyan's beauty and standing proud still, though unused, this rail, road and water bridge seems almost part of the woodland scene.

The narrow lane winds to **Luxulyan** village, up and up between stone-littered fields: undoubted ploughing hazards but no disturbance to Channel Island cattle happy with the grass rich in minerals from the granite below. Overlooking Tregarden quarry, source of its building stone, Luxulyan's church centres the handsome cottages, all built to endure.

55

Everywhere beyond are white 'mountains' and at **Roche** (pronounced like 'poach') the scene is unparalleled. In this village the Rock (a rocky outcrop with a ruined chapel) rises like a mute guardian.

Nearby is **St Dennis**, its church set within an Iron Age encampment. The A391, off the B3374 at Stenalees, leads to **Carthew**. Here is **Wheal Martyn China Clay Museum**, a unique open-air museum based on a restored clay pit. Displays, artifacts, books, pottery and slide programme add to the interest with new exhibitions being added all the time. A short walk guides you past old slurry pits, waterwheels and much else, describing how the clay was obtained for this Cornish industry, which is still important today.

On the other side of the A391 the road leads to the **Eden Project.** Set in a 37-acre (15 hectare) former china clay pit, 197 ft (60m) deep, this unique 'global garden for the 21st century' aims to tell the story of mankind's dependence on plants while demonstrating the opportunities for a sustainable future. Once at the edge of the pit the eyes are immediately drawn to the two huge biomes – greenhouses resembling giant bubbles made of hexagons covered in transparent foil.

The larger of the two, big enough to house the Tower of London, is the humid tropics biome, where plants from the rain forests grow. These huge plants, grouped by region of origin, show Man's almost total dependence on plants in many of these areas. Plants provide not just food but shelter and clothing, fuel and tools. Look for the 'ancient welly' and see how cocoa pods grow. A small coffee plantation is thriving and it is hoped that soon Eden coffee will be available.

The slightly smaller warm temperate biome illustrates similar principles but in a totally different environment. Here it is cooler and drier and the plants smaller but the range of uses which man makes of them is just as diverse. Throughout both biomes there are art works that complement the scientific information.

Outside the themes are continued but with plants that will grow in the Cornish climate. There are useful plants, clever plants, plants for taste, plants for crops and plants for healing and much, much more. This is a place to spend the whole day, taking breaks to absorb what you have seen as you go along. A lot of walking is involved but there is a land train to transport visitors around the site and wheelchairs are available free of charge on a first come, first served basis. Parking is not a problem and buses convey people from car park to visitor centre. There is so much here to learn and to entertain, backed up by friendly staff and excellent facilities all run in as environmentally friendly a way as possible.

Places to Visit

IN & AROUND LISKEARD

Liskeard Museum
Pike Street
☎ (01579) 346087
Open: 11am-4pm Monday to Friday;
11am-1.30pm Saturday.

Merlin Glass
Pavlova Mill, Station Road
☎ (01579) 342399
Gallery shop open Monday to Friday
9.15am-5.30pm. Saturday 9.15am-
12.30pm.

Paul Corin Magnificent Music Machines
St Keyne Station, just off B3254
Amazing collection of mechanical
musical instruments.
☎ (01579) 343108
Playing daily 10.30am-5pm, Good
Friday till end of October.

Lynher Farms and Dairies
Netherton, Upton Cross, about 5
miles (8km) north of Liskeard
Cheese making, rare animals, nature
trails, shop and tea room. The home
of Cornish Yarg cheese with a
distinctive nettle covering.
☎ (01579) 362244
Open: 10am-5pm Monday to Friday,
10am-2pm Saturday, March to
October.

Town Museum
East Looe
☎ (01503) 263709
Open: 11.30am-4.30pm Sunday to
Friday, Easter week and from late-
May Bank Holiday to the end of
September.

SE Cornwall Discovery Centre
Millpool, West Looe
Ideas for what to see and do in
south-east Cornwall from displays,
exhibitions and video presentation.
☎ (01503) 262777
Open: March to Christmas,
daily except Saturdays.

Land of Legend and Model Village
Polperro
Miniature replica of old Polperro.
Model railway. Stories of legends
and superstitions from Cornwall's
past.
☎ (01503) 272378
Open: 10am-6pm daily, April to
October; 10am-8.30pm in July and
August.

Lanreath Folk and Farm Museum
Churchtown, Lanreath
Exhibits of vintage tractors and
implements, granite cider press and
old farmhouse kitchen. Pets' corner,
cream teas.
☎ (01503) 220321
Open: 11am-5pm daily except
Saturday, Easter to end of
October.10am-6pm, June to
September.

Porfell Animal Land
Nr Lanreath
Wildlife park and sanctuary for
exotic species and farmyard animals.
Tea room, picnic area, woodland
walks.
☎ (01503) 220211
www.Porfellanimalland.co.uk
Open: 10am-6pm daily Good Friday
to October.11am-4pm weekends and
school holidays from 27 December
to Good Friday.

Places to Visit

Dobwalls Family Adventure Park, Miniature Railroad and Thorburn Gallery
Half a mile (1km) north of the A38 through Dobwalls
Unique award-winning collection of wildlife paintings. Also Forest Railroad Park (both under management of John Southern). Based on the American railroad – film shows and models.
☎ (01579) 320325
www.dobwallsadventurepark.co.uk
Open: low season 10.30am-5pm; high season 10am-5.30pm; daily April to September. Weekends and half term only in October.

Charlestown's historic harbour

IN & AROUND LOSTWITHIEL

Restormel Castle
(English Heritage)
1¹/₂ miles (2.4km) north of Lostwithiel
Impressive remains of twelfth-century castle above River Fowey. Has connections with the Black Prince.
☎ (01208) 872687
Open: 10am-6pm daily, April to September. 10am-5pm daily, during October.

Guildhall Museum
Fore Street, Lostwithiel
Built 1740, this has linenfold panelling, town insignia and photocopies of the charters.
☎ (01208) 872079
Open: 10.30am-12.30pm and 2.30-4.30pm Monday to Saturday, April to end September.

Boconnoc
North of Couch's Mill
Eighteenth-century house and beautiful gardens. Park and gardens only open to public on occasional Sundays in May.

IN & AROUND FOWEY

'Q' Memorial on Hall Walk
Granite monolith facing down River Fowey, at a spot beloved by Sir Arthur Quiller-Couch.

Town Hall Museum
Trafalgar Square
Town history exhibits. Possibly guild chapel, later prison.
☎ (01726) 833513

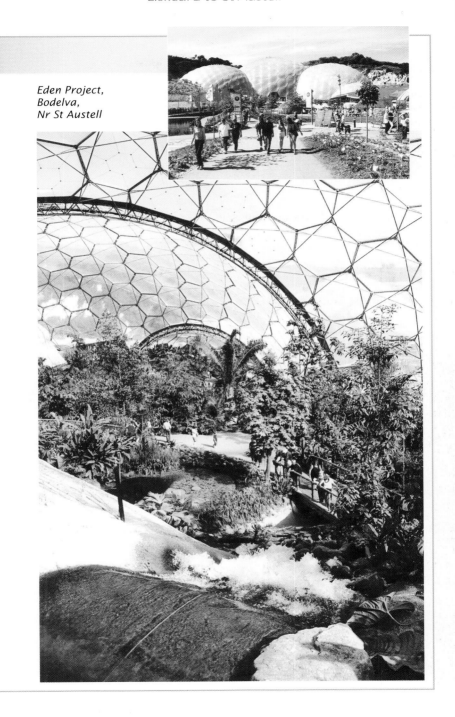

Eden Project,
Bodelva,
Nr St Austell

Places to Visit

Open: May to September 10am-5pm
Monday to Friday.

St Catherine's Castle
Three-quarters of a mile (1.2km)
south-west of Fowey towards Gribbin
Remains of Henry VIII's harbour fort.
Good views

IN & AROUND
ST AUSTELL

Automobilia
St Stephen, on the A3058
☎ (01726) 823092
Open: 10am-4pm April, May and
October daily except Saturdays.
10am-6pm June to September daily.

Brewery Visitor Centre
☎ (01726) 66022
Guided tours by appointment.
Visitor centre and shop.
Open 9.30-4.30pm Monday to
Friday.

The Lost Gardens of Heligan
Pentewan, St Austell
Beautifully restored Victorian
gardens. Large areas suitable for
disabled people. Plant sales. Tea
room. Picnic area.
☎ (01726) 845100
www.heligan.com
Open: 10am-6pm main season, 5pm
in winter daily. Allow at least half a
day for a visit.

Shipwreck, Rescue and Heritage Centre
Charlestown
Recreation of village life, display
about shipwrecks including many
artefacts recovered from the seabed,
hands-on exhibition of lifeboat and
rescue equipment and much, much
more.
☎ (01726) 69897
Open: 10am-5pm (6pm in high
season), daily March to November.

Cornish Leisure World
Crinnis Beach, Carlyon Bay
4.8km (3ml) E of St Austell
1 1/4 miles (2km) of sandy beach,
with restaurants, outdoor attractions,
miniature railway, nightclub.

Wheal Martyn China Clay Museum
Carthew
Unique open-air industrial
archaeology museum based on
restored clay works (dating from
about 1880), with water-wheels, etc,
demonstrating this important Cornish
industry.
☎ (01726) 850362
www.wheal.martyn.com
Open: 10am-6pm daily, all year.

Mid-Cornwall Craft Centre and Galleries
Biscovey A390
Fine collection of craft and painting
in skilfully converted school.

Eden Project
Bodelva, Nr St Austell
Exploration of Man's relationships
with plants.
☎ (01726) 811911,
www.edenproject.com
Open: 10am-6pm daily, March to
October; 10am-4.30pm, November
to February.

What to do if it rains

Liskeard
- Church of St Martin
- Museum

St Keyne
- Paul Corin's Magnificent Music Machine

Looe
- Town Museum
- Discovery Centre

Polperro
- Land of Legend and Model Village
- Smuggling Museum

Lanreath
- Folk and farm museum

Dobwalls
- Adventure park
- Miniature railways, museum and art gallery

Lostwithiel
- St Bartholomew's Church
- Guildhall museum

Fowey
- Town museum
- Daphne du Maurier Centre

Bodelva
- Eden Project

Carthew
- Wheal Martyn China
- Clay Museum

St Austell
- Brewery visitor centre
- Polkyth Recreation Centre

Biscovey
- Mid Cornwall Galleries

Charlestown
- Heritage Centre

St Stephen
(St Austell)
- Automobilia

TRURO

The exact meaning of the name Truro is uncertain, though of the suggested 'settlement near water', 'three roads' and 'three rivers', possibly the last is the most feasible. The 'three rivers' were the Allen, Kenwyn and a third, long lost under Tregolls Road where the A39 enters the city from the east.

About 2,500 years ago, the first inhabitants settled here on the ridge above the water. Celts then established themselves, but not till 1140 was there any building of importance. This was a Norman castle, but only the name remains, as Castle Hill, the site of the new Crown Court.

The tin trade brought wealth to Truro and it was one of the earliest stannary towns to hold a charter, which was granted by Edward I in 1307. King John built a Coinage Hall in 1200 but this was demolished in the early nineteenth century. The Black Death (1348) halved the population, causing such poverty that the government

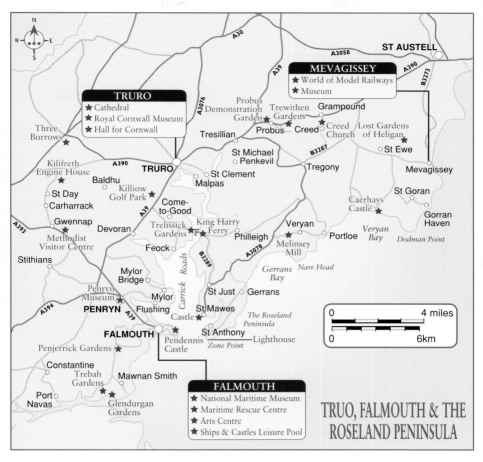

TRUO, FALMOUTH & THE ROSELAND PENINSULA

remitted all taxes. During the Civil War, Prince Charles and Royalist troops were quartered here, and for a while Truro was also the temporary home of the Royal Mint.

In the eighteenth century, the town was as fashionable as Bath, and among the cultural activities were a Philharmonic Society, Library and Book Society.

Many gracious buildings were erected. The **Assembly Rooms** by

the cathedral has a fine façade worthy of attention, as does Ralph Allen Daniell's Mansion House in Prince's Street. He was nephew to Ralph Allen of St Blazey (see Chapter 2), and wealthy enough to use Bath stone and have the oak specially carved by craftsmen from the local French prisoner of war camp. The date 1792 is engraved on the roof. Merchants like William Lemon built elegant houses on both sides of Lemon Street, named after him, and looking down on them is a monument to Richard Lander. He discovered the source of the River Niger and, in 1830, was the first holder of the Royal Geographical Society's Gold Medal.

The ordinary houses, too, are worth more than a passing glance. Look for strangely shaped roofs, old porticos, decorated façades, narrow, pointed windows and emotive names like Tanyard Court, Tippett's Backlet, Pydar Street and Coombes Lane – recalling the great days of Truro's wool trade. St Nicholas Street may not seem unusual, but here the merchants' houses and warehouses were cheek by jowl with the Guildhall of St Nicholas, probably extending across Boscawen Street down to

Lemon Quay itself. The present car park is where ships anchored while waiting for their cargoes. Today at the Quay, across the A39, pleasure boats berth in the summer and run weekday boat trips down the Fal.

Most Cornish towns have narrow passages between houses. These are 'opes' – pronounced 'ops'. Truro is no exception and Squeezeguts Alley is perhaps the smallest and most awkward; Cathedral Lane is another 'ope'.

There is much to see in the **Royal Cornwall Museum** (founded in 1818). On display is a wide variety of material connected with life in the region since earliest times; the mineral section is unusually fine. Temporary exhibitions of art works from the museum's collection and visiting artists are usually on

---

Truro Cathedral

The Prince of Wales laid the foundation stone on 20 May 1880. It was the first to be built in Britain since St Paul's. Truro, however, had become a city in 1877 when Bishop Benson was enthroned in St Mary's parish church. This was later demolished, except for the south aisle, which was incorporated into the new building.

The three-spired towers are interesting in their dedications. The central one (Victoria) was given in 1901 as a memorial to the Queen's life, and nine years later, another local benefactor gave the two western towers – Edward and Alexandra. Altogether an unusual building, its Gothic style gives the city a continental look. Its Willis organ is famous and interesting features include memorials to 'Q' (Sir Arthur Quiller-Couch the essayist), the missionary Henry Martyn, and the Robartes family. Notice the Bath stone reredos representing Christ's sacrifice, the window showing John Wesley preaching at Gwennap Pit and the painting Cornubia by John Miller.

The first bishop, Edward White Benson originated the service of Nine Lessons and Carols here in 1880 and after serving in Truro for seven years he was translated to Canterbury. There is also a cathedral bookshop for books and souvenirs and the Chapter House where you can get refreshments.

Walks

Trefusis Point

7 miles (11km) • easy • 3 hours

Map: OS 1:25,000 Explorer Series 105: Falmouth and Mevagissey

Cross to Flushing on the ferry from Falmouth then turn right off the quay. The road runs through a village of picturesque houses built for the nobility and packet captains. Follow it round bearing left at the next jetty and carry straight on to the end of the tarmac area. Right here leads to a small, usually quiet beach but walkers carry on left where the path winds round the point, giving fine views of Falmouth Harbour. Nearing Mylor Yacht Harbour and the Ganges Restaurant the views across the Fal are of the Roseland Peninsula. There is a chance to see Mylor Church, quiet and beautiful, before walking up to follow the road down again to Flushing and the ferry.

St Clement

5 miles (8km) • easy • 3 hours

Map: OS 1:25,000 Explorer Series 105: Falmouth and Mevagissey

Leave the Trafalgar roundabout in Truro where the A39 goes up Tregolls road and take the turning signposted St Clement. Almost at once turn right up Trennick Lane through the grounds of Truro School and continue up the road for about half a mile with the Truro River below, until it reaches a farm called Trennick. Keeping left, take the track straight ahead – it's muddy sometimes! At the valley bottom cross the footbridge and go up the other side. Follow the footpath to St Clement Parish Hall, turn right down into St Clement hamlet where the church is 'guarded' by picturesque thatched cottages and public toilets are to be found nearby. Go down to the water, enjoy a picnic, wander along beside the river to Tresillian and the ancient Wheal Inn for refreshment before returning to Truro. Alternatively, leave St Clement Church and take the road uphill for Truro.

Place to Portscatho/Gerrans

7$\frac{1}{2}$ miles (12km) • easy • 3 hours

Map: OS 1:25,000 Explorer Series 105: Falmouth and Mevagissey

The best way to reach Place is on the ferry across the lovely Percuil River from St Mawes which links with the Falmouth-St Mawes ferry. At Place Quay the path is signposted to Bohortha. Pass through the hamlet and turn right at the road junction, then almost immediately turn left across the field and left again on to the coast path above Porthbeor beach. Walk along the coast as far as Towan beach and continue along the coast path to Portscatho, an attractive village, then walk up the hill to Gerrans Church and turn left following the signs to the car park. Carry on along the lane passing through Posteague and coming out at Porth. Turn right in Porth, following the path alongside Porth Creek and the Percuil River back to Place.

display. A café is open daily.

The **Hall for Cornwall** is a first class entertainment venue in Truro offering everything from classical music to pantomime, one-man shows and lectures to plays, opera and popular music plus restaurant and coffee shop. Outdoor entertainment can be found during the summer in Victoria Gardens where there are band concerts, jazz and special children's entertainment.

Both Victoria Gardens, and Boscawen Park along the bank of the river, offer peaceful havens after exploring the City centre.

EAST OF TRURO

From the Trafalgar roundabout, a road running past Radio Cornwall, the BBC's first purpose-built local radio station, follows the river to **Malpas** (Mopus).

At the end of the road there is a footpath to **St Clement**. Photographers love the old church and thatched cottages – the slate-hung upper room over the lych-gate provides added interest. From here one of the Duchy's loveliest creekside paths leads to Pencalenick, where the A39 is rejoined for **Tresillian**. At the far end of this long village is the uniquely thatched Wheel Inn. Here history was made when the Civil War ended and the Royalist Lord Hopton capitulated to Fairfax after surrendering at the bridge. Fairfax Road beside the water com-memorates the occasion.

You will need more than a day to explore the **Veryan** area and to visit some of the interesting places on the way. Follow the road, the A390, out of Tresillian and take the exit to **Probus**, which is now a quiet village but was once an educational centre. Now only its collegiate church and a road name, College Close, are left as reminders. The fine church tower is Cornwall's highest, at $123^1/_2$ feet (37.6m), lovely with its finely carved granite. Recently restored and replaced outside the church is an attractive lamp standard erected to celebrate Queen Victoria's Diamond Jubilee. Just past the village is **Cornwall's Demonstration Garden and Arboretum**. Keen gardeners can learn much there but it also has interesting displays and layouts in beautiful surroundings to delight the amateur. It is open throughout the year.

Atlantic Crossing

The tannery at Grampound, sadly now closed, is the place which provided skin for the hull and sails of Tim Severin's curragh *St Brendan*, which weathered a force eight gale and crossed the Atlantic safely in 1976. Surely this was ample proof of the theory of the author-historian captain who believed that St Brendan made the same crossing a good thousand years before Columbus – in an identical craft.

About 3 miles (5km) beyond lies **Grampound**, quietly at peace beside the rushing traffic, deceptively different from the bustling port of Norman times when the sea brought ships there.

When silting began, a bridge over the Fal was built at that point and the town was given the name Grandpont – known in 1299 as the Borough of Ponsmur, its Celtic name. Eventually maritime trading ended and the town declined slowly into the present peaceful village.

The second turning on the right, up the hill out of Grampound, winds narrowly to **St Ewe**, beautiful

Mevagissey

and almost unspoilt. The church, enclosed by trees, has old stocks inside – both merit a close look.

After Kestle is **Mevagissey**, one of the Duchy's oldest fishing ports. Its narrow streets and quaint shops, up the hills or by the quays, make it a captivating place. Watch the gulls and the fishing boats or go fishing. If it rains, there are always the **World of Model Railways** and the **Museum** to enjoy. Park on the harbour quays and move for a while into a miniature world that has been featured on television. There is enjoyment here for the whole family.

The road south to **Porthmellon** hugs the cliff before dipping down to the cove famous for Percy Mitchell – the self-taught boat designer. He started his shipyard in 1924 and constructed everything from a 7-foot (2m) dinghy to vessels of over 30 tons. An artist in wood, he built the *Windstar* for Sir Philip Hunloke, Sailing Master to the Queen's father as well as various boats for the Admiralty. Drive out with care along the narrow winding road – summer traffic can be dangerous here.

The coastal path to **Gorran Haven** passes Chapel Point – another place associated with Tristan. He was imprisoned in the chapel but leapt from a window to the safety of a rocky ledge – so the story goes. Views here are reward enough for walkers, even the inland lanes do not compare. Gorran Haven itself is unexpectedly small but opens out into a wide bay. Above, at **Gorran Churchtown**, Anne Treneer was born. Her book, *Schoolhouse in the Wind*, is an excellent autobiography, which breathes the delights of Cornwall in the early 1920s when for her, Falmouth was a distant romantic seaport. She writes of the enchanting bareness of Cornwall and tells how she would walk to Dodman Point and 'look into the sparkling intoxicating space'.

Dodman Point, this 'noblest of Cornish headlands' is a well preserved Iron Age fort with baulk ditch and rampart. It has been National Trust property since 1919 and this impressive structure can be viewed all round from the circular walk that starts and ends at the Penare car park. At the extreme point is a huge granite cross, erected in 1896 as a mark for seamen by the Vicar of Caerhays. After dedicating the cross he kept a night's vigil beneath it, praying for the souls of shipwrecked mariners. This same promontory fascinated Sir Arthur Quiller-Couch and he used it in his first book *Dead Man's Rock*.

William Gregor

He was born not far from Creed in 1761. During his incumbency of the parish, he discovered titanium in black sand sent to him from Manaccan. It has been called manaccanite and gregorite but is now universally accepted as titanium. In the secluded church there is a photograph of a titanium bowl and also a portrait of William Gregor.

Hemmick Beach has only a narrow lane beside the water. It is quiet here and there is more than one stretch of sand. Perilous lanes lead to it, so first gear is essential to get to **Porthluney Cove**. There is a large car park here and looking down over the beach, is John Nash's Gothic **Caerhays Castle**, built in 1808 for J B Trevanion. A fairytale place, it is scorned by some but loved by all when the rhododendrons are in bloom.

The Grampound road, after climbing past Caerhays church and Tubb's Mill, turns right along more narrow winding lanes to **Creed**. From the Tregony road out of Creed the right-hand turn goes over the Fal to Golden Mill and Manor. This is a privately owned farm but it is possible to drive as far as the main building without trespassing. The great barn on the left still has the fine windows and sturdy walls of a medieval hall.

In 1577, Francis Tregian and his family lived here and offered shelter to Cuthbert Mayne (canonised in 1974). As they were known recusants their property was searched, Mayne was discovered and executed, while Francis Tregian was condemned to a long period of imprisonment. Somehow he survived it all, went abroad and died there in 1608. There are elegant memorials in Probus church to the Tregians and the Wolvedons (Golden is the Cornish mutation of this name).

A different kind of country house is at **Trewithen**, nearby on the A390. It was the seventeenth-century home of the Hawkins family and 20 acres (8 hectares) of its grounds are now internationally famous as Trewithen Gardens, which are open to the public on summer afternoons. Shrubs are always on sale here.

THE ROSELAND PENINSULA AROUND VERYAN

The **Roseland Peninsula** includes the west side of Veryan Bay and Gerrans Bay, involving a long but very lovely drive. Take the A3078 where it turns off the A39 between Tresillian and Probus. It crosses the **Tregony** bridge where the left turn leads up to the now quiet village with its wide central street. This was once a bustling port and had a castle, a medieval market and a thriving wool factory. Even when the river silted up and trade declined, it was still a society meeting place. In the late nineteenth century, the learned Powder Book Club held meetings there for the improvement of local ladies, but no such excitements now remain.

Little is left of former glories except the fourteenth-century church of **St Cuby** with its slate tower and the handsome seventeenth-century clock tower that was rebuilt in 1895. Tregony is now a place of the past, recalling when ships unloaded ceramics, glass and wine then sailed away with leather, wool and tin.

From Tregony, high-banked, narrow lanes lead to **Portholland**, a harbour of two coves, east and west. There is a fine cliff path to **Portloe** but motorists lose the view temporarily as the road takes the

Above: Gorran Haven
Below: St Just-in-Roseland Churchyard

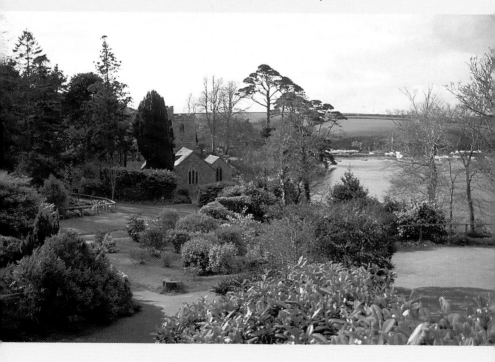

inland route to this tiny port more used to horse and pony transport than motorised traffic. Parking halfway down the steep hill to the beach avoids unpleasant turns, but visitors to the comfortable seven-teenth-century Lugger Inn, will find a park beside it. This village loses the sun very quickly, lying in the shadow of Jacka and Manare Points, but it is a pleasant place in the sunshine.

Walking opportunities

The National Trust owns land here, as well as a considerable area along the cliff to **Nare Head**, where there is a viewing platform with a ramp for wheelchairs. One of the Trust walks is round the point from Caragloose to Camels Cove. At Kiberick Cove there is a small car park and a footpath to the secluded beach. Another walk from the same parking place is down the valley to Paradoe Cove beyond the Nare, returning via that fine headland – one of the least frequented in Cornwall.

Veryan is well known but still relatively unspoilt. The reasons for its fame are the unique round-houses at each end of the village. Some say that a local vicar built them to keep the devil out and away from his daughters. Whatever the reason, the white, thatched cottages have a charm all their own. Pause a while at the New Inn where the food is good and the welcome warm. An interesting art gallery at the north end is worth visiting. Inside the church, with its unusual dedication to St Symphorian, lies Admiral Kempe, notable for sailing round the world with Cook and scaling Quebec Heights with General Wolfe.

Returning towards the A3078, about 880 yard (800m) out of Veryan, lies **Melinsey Mill**. This is a sixteenth-century water mill featuring a twelve foot-high, overshot wheel, on the site of a much earlier mill dating from 1210. Last used in 1928 it was discovered derelict but intact and has been fully restored. It is now open as a working museum and tea rooms.

From close by there is a walk down the lovely wooded valley to **Pendower Beach**, another National Trust property. A disused lime-kiln is an interesting feature of this pleasant place. The great tumulus (Cornwall's largest) at nearby Carne Beacon is said to be the burial mound of King Geraint who built Dingerin Castle where the Gerrans road leaves the A3078. It is believed that his tribesmen rowed his body, in a golden boat with silver oars, across the bay to be burned and buried at Carne.

The spire of the church at **Gerrans** village is a landmark from both sea and land. From here is a walk of about 4 miles (6.4km) along the coastpath to St Anthony Head, the eastern arm of Falmouth harbour. This superb route offers unsurpassed panoramic views on every side until reaching Zone Point and the lighthouse, built in 1808 for J B Trevanion, which is

Walk to a place of legend

There is a splendid and easy coastal walk round Zone Point to **Place**. Behind the privately owned manor is the church of St Anthony, wrapped in legend. Tradition says that this was once a Celtic monastery whose history is written between the two rows of dog teeth on the south door. A rough translation of it is that Christ visited this peninsula when his uncle, Joseph of Arimathea, came to trade for tin. When they were off St Anthony Head, a storm blew up and they sheltered in the little bay below Place Manor. While making the ship seaworthy again, they camped here, leaving a shrine behind them. Some years afterwards a church was built on that site. Apart from any legend, here is quiet beauty and a good place to picnic looking over to St Mawes.

open to visitors. The headland has been fortified since Napoleonic days. It was under military occupation during World War II and then bought by the National Trust in 1959. There is wheelchair access to the viewpoint.

A delightful walk from Bohortha Farm to picturesque **Froe** overlooks the River Percuil and, at the head of Froe inlet, the water almost makes this headland an island. The journey back to Truro along the A3078 and A39 is about 20 miles (32km), but there are views of the Carrick Roads for most of the way, which make the distance worthwhile.

THE ROSELAND PENINSULA AROUND ST MAWES

The last exploration of the Roseland Peninsula is shorter and could last either an afternoon or a day. From Tresillian on the A390 follow the road to **St Michael Penkevil** – a handful of cottages round the church with the great gates of **Tregothnan** proclaiming it as private property. In 1319, the church was an important arch-presbytery (a college with four chaplains). An interesting feature is the second altar on the upper floor of the tower, an old tradition in churches dedicated to St Michael. Leaving the churchtown, take the first lane on the right through beautiful **Lamorran Woods** which lead to **Ruan Lanihorne**. This is a haven for birdwatchers and there is also a 4 mile (6.4km) walk beside the river, where ships once sailed to Tregony.

There are walks to **Philleigh** where the old Rectory, a fine early Georgian house with an elegant slate-hung façade is worthy of more than a passing glance. Set nearby in Cornish elms is the church with its unusual dedication to St Filius.

Resist the temptation to drive straight to King Harry Ferry – leave that until later – but watch the last times of sailing! Go on to **St Just-in-Roseland** where the church, in its creekside setting of tropical trees, is possibly unrivalled for beauty of position. At the water's edge of St Just Pool ships' figureheads or specialised work for the QEII used to be crafted.

The A3078 eventually reaches St Mawes Castle and drops down into the village to follow the harbour round for the return journey. **St Mawes** is a sheltered place and a yachting paradise, particularly for the wealthy.

St Mawes Castle

The castle, cared for by English Heritage, is a round tower, built by Henry VIII and probably enlarged by his son Edward in 1550. Its name is believed to have come from the hermit, St Mawes, St Mauditus or St Mause who effected cures with the water from a holy well. It is small but interesting with ample parking. The grounds are pleasant – an ideal place to picnic and watch the various activities on the Carrick Roads.

On the way back to King Harry Ferry, make a detour to **Turnaware Point**. Here, in late summer, Cornwall's best blackberries grow abundantly. It also has historical interest as it was one of the places in Cornwall from which American troops sailed for Normandy in 1944.

Nearby, at the water's edge, **Tolverne's** thatched smuggler's cottage is interesting for its history and good for its cream teas. Contraband was delivered in the past, but today be prepared for a surprise as large ships are anchored here. They are laid up, some full of cargo that could not be sold and some for lack of work, and all seem too large for such a narrow stretch of river. Keep an eye open along the lane to the cottage for plaques that indicate where various parts of the American troop encampment were. A ferry links Tolverne with Falmouth.

Ruined Tolverne chapel was built by Henry VI, who also established the crossing nearby to Trelissick, known as the **King Harry Ferry**. Tales of Henry VIII riding with Ann Boleyn across this reach on their honeymoon, may be romantic but they are not true. The latest ferry, launched in 1974, glides smoothly across the Fal to **Trelissick**, another delightful National Trust property. The Trust has made a nature trail round the grounds. The gardens are open to the public from March to October, but the house is not open.

The thatched Punch Bowl and Ladle Inn at **Penelewey** dates from the eleventh century and is probably the only one with such a name. Cowlands Creek and Coombe are worth a detour to enjoy the birds, the creekside walks and the famous Kea plums.

The lane joins the A39 Falmouth to Truro road at **Calenick**, once the site of Cornwall's chief smelting house. All that remains of it is the handsome clock tower on the slate-hung Bridge House.

WEST OF TRURO

The great men of Truro made fortunes in tin during the eight-

Above: St Mawes Castle

Right: Cannons, St Mawes

eenth and nineteenth centuries, but it had been 'streamed' in the surrounding districts long before Truro became an important trading centre, so it is interesting to look at those old mining areas. The Truro to Falmouth A39 road down Arch Hill, goes under the track of a railway before climbing the hill to Playing Place – once the site of a theatre-in-the-round. At the Playing Place roundabout is the entrance to the 18-hole parkland golf course of Killiow which has a floodlit golf driving range.

Carnon Downs looks like a bungalow suburb, but hides much mining history. Its much-needed by-pass is now complete and at the roundabout take the left-hand exit for **Come-to-Good**, a misleading name which has quite a different meaning. The thatched Quaker Meeting House of 1710 is called after its location *Cwm-ty-quite* – Cornish for 'the House of the Coombe in the Woods,' appropriate for this attractive building still in use.

Feock church has an interesting lych-gate with a slate-hung upper storey and expensive properties beyond the village straggling down to Restronguet Point beside the Carrick Roads. Before Tudor times a passenger ferry, which functioned at the turn of this century, took travellers from Truro through Mylor to Penryn and Falmouth.

At **Point**, Restronguet Creek is joined by the Carnon River, a bird sanctuary and a place of beauty. Once it was a prosperous mining port with a smuggling reputation

74

Pandora Inn

Across the narrow water from Feock is the thatched Pandora Inn. Originally called The Ship, it was renamed when its captain returned from sailing with Bligh of the *Bounty* to capture the mutineers. On the return voyage, the vessel – the *Pandora* – foundered and though its captain brought home some prisoners he was dismissed from the service. He then bought this inn and named it after his lost ship.

as well. Tin has been streamed in the Carnon River since the days of pre-history, and in the Middle Ages, ore for export from the inland mines was brought here on mules and horses. In 1826 the Redruth and Chacewater Railway opened, the stretch from Devoran to Point still retaining horse-drawn wagons: part of this track can still be seen. Great schooners from Scandinavia anchored there, unloading timber that was taken on barges to Perran Wharf. The Norway Inn is a reminder of those days. There are still bollards and wooden wharves at **Devoran** and the old weighbridge gate remains

Bottom left: In the grounds of Melinsey Mill Bottom right: Trelissick Gardens

at the junction where the Bissoe road leaves the A39.

Beyond the Norway Inn, a road winds away to Perranwell and opposite are the buildings of Perran Foundry (1799) recalling the days when the Fox family established an industrial site there. The machinery was of high quality and many European nations bought it.

Turn right over the railway bridge at **Perranwell** and drive along Grenna Lane. There you will overlook the Carnon Valley and perhaps imagine what it was like when mining was at its peak. Then beyond Perranwell and Frogpool, **Gwennap** village lies in peaceful beech woods, deceptively quiet now, yet once the heart of a region which yielded more copper and tin than any other place in the old world. Gwennap Pit is not in the village, but is near **Busveal**, reached by turning off the A393 Falmouth to Redruth road at the Fox and Hounds, one of the many inns where a service is held and produce auctioned for charity at harvest time.

The road twists and climbs above the derelict expanse of the now silent mines: Crofthandy, Goon Gumpus, Creegbrawse, Tolgullow and others with Celtic names. The men who worked there often died young and left widows with families. Others fell ill and were unable to work. Wesley's message from the Pit and elsewhere brought hope to these people because, as he wrote, 'The more I conversed with the believers in Cornwall, the more I am convinced that they have sustained great loss for want of hearing the doctrine of Christian Perfection clearly and strongly enforced.'

Gwennap Pit was probably formed by the collapse of underground mining excavations. In 1806, circular terraces were cut for seating and since 1807, an annual service has been held there on Whit Mondays. Wesley writes of preaching in a hollow capable of containing many thousands of people. Gwennap Pit is certainly large and was central and ideal for his purpose whether it held hundreds or thousands. A museum of Cornish Methodism was opened near here in 1982.

Carharrack is a village of mining memories but **St Day** has a different story to tell. Prosperous mine owners and captains lived there but perhaps its real place in Cornwall's history is its role as one of the resting places for pilgrims en route to St Michael's Mount. Today, living precariously over a honey-comb of mines, it welcomes modern pilgrims to the St Day Walsingham Festival in September.

Killifreth engine house, beside the B3298 St Day-Scorrier road, is undoubtedly one of the most impressive industrial buildings remaining. It is near **Scorrier** where John Williams, the mining entrepreneur, built his fine mansion. At nearby **Chacewater**, formerly Chasewater, there are memories of Cornwall's first true railway. About 2 miles (3km) north-east along the A30 is **Blackwater**, the birthplace of John Passmore Edwards who built reading rooms and institutes for all workers, especially miners. His Reading Room there stands beside the main road; and almost every town in Cornwall owes its library to him. Altogether he was responsible for 53 benefactions from Newlyn to Dundee.

This section of the A30 has three important tumuli beside it, Two Burrows, Three Burrows and Four Burrows and one of the Midsummer Eve Bonfire ceremonies by members of the Old Cornwall Society usually takes place at the last of these.

From the A390 at Chacewater, minor roads lead to Baldhu (Black Mine) and Wheal Jane Mine, re-opened in 1970 as a modern mining complex but now closed. Visit **Baldhu Church** where churchyard memorials tell of the overseas journeys miners undertook to find work and there is a handsome stone commemorating **Billy Bray**. He is buried there but a small chapel nearby was actually built by this preaching miner. The surrounding area is one where mineral enthusiasts can explore ochre pits, arsenic works and similar remains. From here to Truro by way of the winding lanes of Penweathers there are walks and picnic places.

PENRYN AND FALMOUTH

Before going to Penryn and Falmouth, turn left from the A39 immediately after the Norway Inn. This leads to **Mylor**, a village much sought after by yachtsmen. The steep lane that winds away from the traffic is known locally as 'Craft and Danger', an interesting corruption of *croft an D'Angers* (D'Angers' fields). This must have

described it in 1154 when that uncultivated hillside belonged to the Norman from Angers who owned the barton of Crueglew (the enclosed land by the prehistoric barrow).

The wealthy mining engineer, William Lemon of Breage, bought the estate in 1749 (then called Carclew) and the house became one of the cultural centres of Cornwall. The Lemons were great benefactors to the people of Mylor: Sir Charles bought the workhouse, converted it into a school and maintained it for years. Fire unfortunately destroyed the manor house but Carclew Gardens are occasionally open to the public. The Lemon name died out and became Tremayne, but is perpetuated in the village in the Lemon Arms and Lemon Hill.

Mylor Bridge is at the head of the creek though the original settlement was the churchtown at its mouth 1 mile (1.6km) away. In the mid-nineteenth century the buildings by the pier were known as *HMS Ganges*, at that time the Royal Navy's only shore-based training centre and hospital. The ship, however, was anchored at St Just Pool across the Carrick Roads. Today it is a yachting centre but the restaurant there still bears the old name.

The writer **Howard Spring** found this creek so enchanting that he moved here in 1939 and used it as the background for his bestselling novel *All the Day Long*. The walk round Trefusis Point has views of Falmouth Bay which some say is the finest natural harbour in the world.

The walk ends at **Flushing**,

St Mylor Church

Almost hidden in trees, beside the water at Mylor Churchtown, stands **St Mylor Church**. It is a picturesque building with a separate bell tower and Cornwall's tallest cross, embedded in the ground at the south door. One of the churchyard epitaphs is unusual and visitors are always told to read about **Joseph Crapp**, a shipwright who died 'ye 26th of November 1770, aged 43 years.' His death is graphically described:

Alas friend Joseph
His end was almost sudden
As though a mandate came
Express from heaven
His foot, it slip and he did fall
*Help, help he cries, and that
was all.*

Another gravestone is 'To the Memory of the Warriors, Women and Children, who on their return to England from the coast of Spain; unhappily perished in the Wreck of the *Queen Transport*, on Trefusis Point, Jan 14, 1814', just one of the many ships wrecked off the Cornish coast. Inside, the carved wood of the pulpit is believed to have come from Armada wrecks but the choir screen recalls more recent events. It was given in memory of those drowned in 1966 when an overloaded local pleasure boat capsized.

meeting the road from Mylor. Its Celtic name was Nankersey, but when Dutch engineers arrived to build Falmouth's quays, they settled here and changed the name as a reminder of their homeland. The cottages cling to the waterside, the village is reputed to have the mildest climate in the country and flowers bloom all the year round as if endorsing that claim. In the nineteenth century, the great days of packet-ships, it was a fashionable place to live. Lord Exmouth was born here and Lord Buckingham dined and wined with other society notables. Today sailors are there for pleasure, not national business, as were those men of former days.

No bus runs from here and the ferry across to Falmouth is the quickest way out of the village. At the head of the river is **Penryn**, reached either by a waterside path or inland road. These ways meet at the bottom of the steep hill beside St Gluvias, the parish church of Penryn. A place to visit is the **Town Hall Museum**. It was once the gaol but now houses a variety of interesting items connected with Penryn's history.

The town, in fact, grew from a settlement on the hill across the river. It has an interesting history, part splendid, part sad, but cherishes hopes for the future. Founded as a borough in 1216, it was granted a charter in 1236 and saw the rise and fall of Glasney collegiate church from 1265 to 1549. This establishment was a centre for religious instruction (renowned throughout Europe), growing in importance as Penryn's trade increased.

The closure of Glasney, at the Dissolution however, followed by the unexpected rise of Falmouth at the mouth of the river, led to a decline from which Penryn has never really recovered. But in 1977 its unique medieval character was recognised as rare, and Government grants were given to save old buildings, so bringing a conservation programme into being. As a result, the town whose granite is to be seen in buildings as different as London's Thames Embankment, Singapore harbour and Fastnet Lighthouse, is fast becoming a tourist attraction.

In Tudor times, the Fal River saw more shipping than any other port in the kingdom and Henry VIII, concerned about possible Spanish attacks, had Pendennis Castle built.

It commands **Falmouth**'s best views: on one side, the holiday beaches, on the other, the docks and the town.

In the coaching days, the Greenbank Hotel was important. In the early years of this century, Kenneth Grahame began his *Wind in the Willows* here – proof of this is framed in the lobby – while Florence Nightingale's signature can be found in the old register. Down High Street – much changed since a disastrous fire in the last century – and to the left, is the Prince of Wales Pier where the Flushing ferry disembarks its passengers. It is also the berth for numerous pleasure boats.

The Moor lies above Market Strand and deceives most people with its name. From the bottom of Jacob's Ladder – 111 steps – boatmen used to ferry people over and moor outside the Seven Stars. This small building (dated 1610) is where generations of innkeepers have drawn beer from the wood, a tradition carried on today.

The granite obelisk in the centre of the Moor in Falmouth is a memorial to men of the packet service when 'Falmouth for Orders' was the command obeyed by all captains of these ships. For over 250 years, the packets carried mail, cargoes and passengers to many parts of the world. In 1833 a wagon loaded with bullion from a packet-ship, left Killigrew Street on Monday and was in London by Saturday.

Walking through the town is a casual affair, traffic usually gives priority to pedestrians. In Church Street is the **Falmouth Arts Centre**,

Richard Trevithick (1771-1833)

The son of a mining engineer, he followed his own ways even while he was at school, paying little attention to lessons because he was absorbed in his own diagrams and calculations. He would not even learn to spell yet could produce the correct answer to any mathematical problem six times faster than any adult. When he left school officially, Trevithick refused to have anything to do with the mine administration affairs in his father's office and wandered about the underground workings, examining and studying everything. The miners appreciated his knowledge of the machinery and his skill as a wrestler made him a popular figure.

His invention – the high-pressure engine – so impressed the wealthy Cornishman, Davies Gilbert (later President of The Royal Society) that they grew to be close friends. On Christmas Eve 1801 Trevithick frightened the local people with his 'puffing devil', which carried ten or more passengers even uphill (the model he made in 1797 is now in the Science Museum in London). Two years later he took a similar engine to London but had to bring it home because of financial difficulties.

There is no room here to tell more about the extraordinary career of this great man except to say that his high pressure locomotive predated Stephenson's *Rocket* by 12 years. Among his other inventions were the blast pipe, a ship propeller, screw propeller and central heating, yet the government flatly refused him any remuneration for his brilliant work. In desperation he turned to the New World but there met similar ups and downs of fortune.

Eventually he went to London and died while working at Dartford in Kent. Because of his penniless state he was buried in an unmarked grave but there is a tablet to his memory in the parish church, and windows in Westminster Abbey record his main achievements. His statue outside Camborne Library faces the street where he first put his theories into practice.

where in 1833 the Fox family of Quakers established the Poly-technic Society and reading rooms, setting a trend later followed throughout the country. At the far end of the town is the **Georgian Custom House**, handsome with its Greek Doric columns and fine façade. Beside and below the King's Pipe – a chimney where contraband tobacco was burnt – is an inter-esting reminder of the manner in which contraband tobacco used to be destroyed.

Dominating the harbourside is the new **National Maritime Museum Cornwall**, opened in 2002. This innovatively designed building, using granite, slate and green oak boarding, holds a fascinating collection of boats. Through unique and interactive displays visitors learn how boats are shaped by the part they play in people's lives. Entering the first gallery, three storeys high, visitors experience audio-visual displays of life on and by the sea while viewing boats suspended in this great space. Smaller galleries tell of Cornwall's maritime heritage and of the ways that people use boats for work and pleasure.

The top of the lookout tower gives wonderful views over the harbour and of the boats moored on the pontoon outside. At the base of the tower visitors are five metres below high tide level and can see passing fish or the rise and fall of the tide. Move on through another tall gallery of famous craft to see boatbuilders at work, learn about navigation and metereology and finally put all that information into practice by sailing a radio-controlled boat in the large indoor pool designed for the purpose. A café and shop complete an unmissable day out for the whole family even the irredeemable landlubber. It is even possible to arrive by boat as a park and float system has been set up. Park just outside Falmouth and take the special ferry to the Museum.

The view over the docks from Castle Drive is one no visitor should miss. With the background of Trefusis Point and the Roseland Peninsula, this busy area is probably unique and there are hopes for a prosperous future as business people appreciate its potential.

Pendennis Castle is a well preserved defence built by Henry VIII in 1539–43, shortly after the Little Dennis blockhouse below it.

Founders of Falmouth

Opposite Arwenack House is the waterside granite obelisk erected in 1738 by Martin Lister Killigrew as a memorial to his wife's family. They had lived at Arwenack and founded Falmouth, which evolved from Sir Walter Raleigh's plan to develop the harbour. He had stayed at Arwenack with the Killigrews and urged them to press forward with the project. By 1613, in spite of objections from Penryn, the town's identity had been formed and Falmouth was born.

Later Elizabeth I had it enlarged but it was besieged successfully by Fairfax during the Civil War. Now owned and cared for by English Heritage its exhibitions and displays are well worth a visit. Nearby is the modern **Ships and Castles Leisure Pool** offering water fun for all the family.

Pendennis Point is ideal for a coastguard station and one of the most modern, the **Maritime Rescue Co-ordination Centre**, was opened in 1981 by Prince Charles. In 1982 it was the first centre in the eastern Atlantic to answer calls in the Marisat satellite system. Here officials co-ordinate search and rescue round the coastline of Great Britain and Northern Ireland.

Round the headland, the road leads to Castle Beach, Gyllyngvase and beyond to Swanpool and Maenporth. These are beautiful beaches with sands and rock pools to keep children happy for the whole holiday. Swanpool – as its name implies – is something else as well; rowing boats and canoes often share the waters with a variety of birds.

Take the road out of Falmouth that leads past the hospital to **Budock,** its church and the village of **Budock Water**. The church was the mother church of Falmouth and had its origins as the centre of a religious community in the sixth century. An alternative route out of Falmouth leads to **Mabe** with its church high above the Argal and College Reservoirs. Look down from the Penryn-Constantine road (B3291) and pause to walk or fish.

The way to **Mawnan Smith** passes **Penjerrick Gardens,** a Fox property now opened to the public. Springtime is best for a visit here – then the flowering shrubs are a mass of colour. From the beaches the coast path goes to Rosemullion Head but motorists are restricted

Full page & opposite page bottom left & right: Pendennis Castle, Falmouth

Opposite page top: The Old Barracks, Pendennis Castle

to the road, which ends at Mawnan church. It was built on an Iron Age site, the tower warning seamen that they were near the dreaded Manacle Rocks. Over the lych-gate an inscription in Cornish reads: *Da thym ythyn nesse the Thu* which means 'It is good for me to draw nigh unto the Lord'. Inside is a wide variety of colourful tapestry kneelers, those of the choir are patterned with medieval tunes.

Round the headland lies **Durgan**, a tiny village reached either by cliff path or road by way of Mawnan Smith. It consists of a handful of cottages, just beside the small beach. There is no sand here, but safe bathing and an ideal place for wind-surfing. This area, together with **Glendurgan**, is National Trust property. Although the house is occupied by members of the Fox family and is not open to the public, the valley garden may be visited. It is a garden of great beauty with fine trees and shrubs, walled and water gardens; a wooded valley runs down to Durgan on the Helford River.

Nearby is another place of delight beside the Helford River. **Trebah Gardens** are dramatic, uniquely beautiful and a friendly paradise for children and families. It is open all the year round and

dogs are allowed provided they are kept on their leads.

Port Navas and **Polwheveral Creeks** between here and Constantine are rivals in beauty but the former has an added interest, being the site of the Royal Duchy Oyster Farm. There are no cliff walks here but tracks lead to the Merthen earthworks. **Constantine** church, high in the village has seen continuous worship since the fifth century and is worth visiting for its brasses and 200 embroidered kneelers. It may be locked but the key is at a nearby cottage.

On the right of the lanes to **Stithians** is the Rosemanowes Quarry where successful hot dry rock experiments have been carried out by the Camborne School of Mines. This village hides its church behind a screen of trees.

From here a secondary road climbs to overlook the village of **Ponsanooth** and Kennal Vale where at one time gunpowder was manufactured at Kennal Mills. Gunpowder was an important part of industrial mining. Woollen mills were here, too, forming the basis of carpet manufacture and cloth exports. Sadly, now the river has all but dried up and could not possibly support the 39 waterwheels it did when Magdalen

Feast Day

St Stythian's Feast and Agricultural Show, are held in the second week in July. Second only to the Royal Cornwall Show, it was first held in 1834 to stimulate competition between local farmers at a time when agriculture was at a very low ebb.

(Maudlin) Mine and the Perran Foundry were at peak production. These mine workings are hidden beneath undergrowth by the viaduct over the lane leaving Ponsanooth at the school and dropping to the A39 at Stickenbridge. A public footpath passes close by but there is little to show the world the tinworks that were old in Tudor times.

The A39 is at the bottom of Magdalen Lane, named after a Tudor chapel. To the right lies Falmouth, to the left, Carnon Downs and Truro.

Selected Car Drives

Truro to Porthluney Cove and Caerhays Castle

Leave Truro on the A39 for St Austell but after Tresillian at the roundabout take the turn for Tregony. Through the village, after admiring the clock tower, you will be on the B3287. About 3 miles (4.8km) on there is a right turn to St Ewe and so on through High Lanes to Porthluney Cove. This has a car park and a wonderful view of Caerhays Castle where the gardens are open in springtime. A steep hill leads up to Tubbs Mill and eventually across the B3287 to Creed and Grampound, which is on the A390 for your return to Truro.

Truro to Gwennap and Trelissick

On the A390 west out of Truro is a lane that falls away to Penweathers, a twist of countryside which you can follow to Baldhu Church, built for miners who soon were forced to emigrate to find work. Beyond there is Billy Bray's Chapel, a place of great interest. The lanes lead to the little villages of Chacewater, St Day and Carharrack with its Methodist Museum. Gwennap Pit is at nearby Busveal from where you should take the lanes through Frogpool, Perranarworthal to find the A39 Falmouth to Truro road. The valley of trees is beautiful at all times of the year as you drive towards Truro. Before taking the hill road across the Carnon River causeway at the end of the valley turn right and wander beside the Carnon River to Point and out of Penpol to join the B3289 where a right turn leads to Trelissick with its Barn Restaurant, shop and gardens. You may be tempted to cross the Fal on the King Harry Ferry for St Just and Veryan's Round Houses but another alternative is to drive to Playing Place and join the A39 to Truro. If you still have time to spare turn right at the bottom of the hill. That lane will take you to Calenick and Coombe. In season there are Kea plums in plenty at Coombe and tranquillity at any time. The drive back to Truro means retracing the road but these lanes are so lovely that it will be a pleasure.

Places to Visit

TRURO

Truro Cathedral
Designed in Gothic style by J L Pearson, constructed 1880–1910, cleverly incorporating part of the former parish church. Monuments to 'Q' and missionary Henry Martyn, a stained glass window of John Wesley at Gwennap. West porch niches facing High Cross have figures of kings and bishops. Look out for the beautifully carved memorial to one of the Robartes family of Lanhydrock who died in the Great War.
☎ (01872) 276782
www.trurocathedral.org.uk

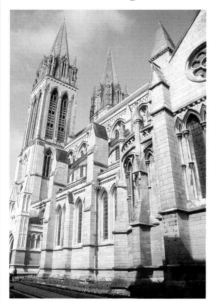

Truro Cathedral

The Royal Cornwall Museum
River Street
Founded 1818, this museum exhibits Cornish history, has a library of Cornish books for members and an interesting art gallery. Seasonal displays of special interest.
☎ (01872) 272205
Open: 10am-5pm except Sundays and Bank Holidays.

Hall for Cornwall
Back Quay, Truro
Spectacular arts and entertainment centre offering something for everyone. Occasional antiques fairs and flea markets during the daytime. 'Stars Restaurant' and coffee bar.
☎ (01872) 262466
www.hallforcornwall.co.uk

Boat Trips to Falmouth
Town Quay, Truro
Take a one hour trip from the centre of Truro to Falmouth, sailing the full length of the Fal river. When tides do not permit sailing from Truro departure will be from Malpas, a short way down the river. A bus connection from Truro to Malpas is included in the ticket price.
Enterprise Boats ☎ (01326) 374241.

EAST OF TRURO

Probus Demonstration Garden and Arboretum
Probus, Truro
7-acre (2.8 hectare) horticultural education and advice centre.
☎ (01726) 883868
www.probusgardens.org.uk
Open: 10am-4pm Monday to Friday, January to March; 10am-5pm daily, April to October.

World of Model Railways
Mevagissey
An unusual attraction offering a

miniature world of nearly 50 trains. Collection of model locomotives and rolling stock. Children's layout at floor level. Model shop. Wheelchair access.
☎ (01726) 842457
www.model-railway.co.uk
Open: From 10am-5pm daily, March to October. Winter, week-ends only and occasional school holidays. Telephone for details.

Mevagissey Museum
East Quay
☎ (01726) 843568. Open Easter to October, Weekdays 11am-5pm, Sundays 2-5pm.

Dodman Point
Given to National Trust in 1919; a well preserved Iron Age fort with baulk, ditch and rampart, crosses the neck of the headland. Granite cross, erected as mark for seamen.

Caerhays Castle Gardens
A picturesque mansion built by John Nash for J.B. Trevanion (1808). Early spring displays of shrubs are fine, especially camellias, magnolias and rhododendrons.
☎ (01872) 501310
Gardens open 11am-4pm, Monday to Friday plus occasional Sundays, mid-March to mid-May.

Creed Church
1 mile (1.6km) from Grampound
Rebuilt in 1734 and retaining some of its wagon roof. Portrait of William Gregor and photograph of a titanium bowl near organ.

Trewithen Gardens
Grampound Road, near Truro
Privately owned, 30 acres (12 hectares), internationally famous for rare shrubs such as camellias and rhododendrons of special species. Plants for sale on summer afternoons.
☎ (01726) 883647
Open: 10am-4.30pm Monday to Saturday, 1 March to 30 September. Sundays in April and May only.

WEST OF TRURO

Gwennap Pit and Methodist Museum
2 miles south-east of Redruth
On Whit Monday, Methodists come here for a celebratory service.
☎ (01209) 82081
Open: 10am-12.30am and 2-4.30pm, Monday to Friday, Spring Bank Holiday to September.

Methodist Museum
Carharrack
☎ (01209) 820381
Open by appointment only.

Killifreth Engine House
Beside the B3298 St Day-Scorrier road
Impressive industrial building.

Two, Three & Four Burrows
Important prehistoric tumuli. Beside the narrow road south of B3277; beside A30 at junction of A30 and A390; beside A30 about 2 miles (3.2km) east of above.

ON AND AROUND THE ROSELAND PENINSULA

Melinsey Mill
Nr Veryan
Working museum and tea rooms in a restored water mill.
Open: 10am-5.30pm, April to September, Tuesday to Sunday.

Places to Visit

St Mawes Castle

Described as Henry VIII's most decorative fort. Colourful gardens and lawns to the sea. Unusual clover-leaf plan produced by a central tower with three semi-circular bastions. English Heritage special events during summer.

☎ (01326) 270526

Open: 10am-6pm April to October daily and 10am-4pm November to March daily, closed 1-2pm in winter.

Trelissick (National Trust)

Gardens only but they have fine shrubs and nature trails. Shop and barn restaurant.

☎ (01872) 862090

Open: 10.30am-5.30pm daily, mid-February to October. Sundays not open until 12.30pm. Woodland walks, all year daily.

PENRYN & FALMOUTH

Penryn Town Hall & Museum

Standing centrally on Penryn's spine road, it houses offices and museum of local history.

☎ (01326) 372158

Open: 10am-4pm, Monday to Friday all year. Opening times may vary as staffed by volunteers, check with Town Hall ☎ (01326) 373086.

Falmouth Art Gallery

Municipal Buildings, The Moor, Falmouth

Permanent collection includes 19th and early 20th-century paintings, prints and drawings. Regular temporary exhibitions. Shop area, access for disabled. ☎ (01326) 313863

Open: All year, Monday to Saturday 10am-5pm, free admission.

National Maritime Museum Cornwall

Discovery Quay

How boats and people interact for work and leisure; stunning displays; interactive exhibits; café and shop.

☎ 01326 313388

www.nmmc.co.uk

Pendennis Castle

Falmouth

Museum, discovery centre, displays of coastal defence armament and access to former secret installations. Regular special events from April to October.

☎ (01326) 316594

Open: 10am-6pm April to September (open 9am July and August), 10am-5pm in October, 10am-4pm November to March, daily.

The Maritime Rescue Co-ordination Centre

Pendennis Point

Purpose-built coastguard station opened in 1981. Officials co-ordinate search and rescue round coastline of Great Britain and Northern Ireland. A limited number of visitors are welcome, but please telephone beforehand.

☎ (01326) 310800 (office hours)

Ships and Castles Leisure Pool

Castle Drive, Pendennis Headland

Modern leisure pool with wave machine, 230-foot (70m) flume, river run, water geysers, spa pools, fitness suite, solariums, café.

☎ (01326) 212129

Penjerrick Gardens
1 mile (1.6km) S of Budock Vean
Large garden created by the Fox
family featuring rhododendrons,
camellias, bamboos, tree ferns and
magnificent trees. ☎ (01872) 870105
Open: 1.30-4.30pm, March to
September, Wednesday, Friday and
Sunday.

Glendurgan Gardens (National Trust)
Valley gardens of great beauty – best
seen in spring for flowering shrubs.
Runs to Durgan village on Helford
River. ☎ (01326) 250906
Open: 10.30am-5.30pm, late
February to October. Closed on
Sundays and Mondays, Good Friday.

Argal and College Reservoirs
B3291 Penryn-Constantine
Pleasant recreational areas, ideal for
walking.

Duchy of Cornwall Oyster Farm
Port Navas
☎ (01326) 340210
Buy oysters and mussels. Picnic
outside.

Trebah Gardens
Mawnan Smith, Falmouth
Magnificent 25-acre (10 hectare)
garden cascades down a wooded
ravine to a private beach (open to
visitors to the garden). Special events
programme including children's
activities, plant sales, coffee shop.
☎ (01326) 250448 Open: 10.30am-
6.30pm, daily all year.

What to do if it rains

Truro
• Cathedral
• Royal Cornwall Museum

Mevagissey
• World of Model Railways
• Museum

Veryan
• Melinsey Mill

St Mawes
• Castle

Trelissick
• Shop and art and craft
  exhibitions

Carharrack
• Methodist Museum

Penryn
• Museum

Falmouth
• Pendennis Castle
• National Maritime Museum
  Cornwall
• Falmouth Art Gallery
• Maritime Rescue and
  Co-ordination Centre
• Ships and Castles
  Leisure Pool

About halfway between Truro and Penzance is historic Helston where on May 8 each year, the past takes over as old houses and twisting streets echo with Flora Day celebrations – once a pagan welcome to spring.

Legend links Flora Day with St Michael and the devil, who tore the lid off hell in a final effort to defeat the saint. An inaccurate aim sent the stone away and till 1783 it was to be seen embedded in the courtyard of The Angel Hotel. This is an attractive building with parts dating from the sixteenth century. At the end of the seventeenth century it was the town house of Cornwall's great statesman, Sidney Godolphin and later it became the Excise House. This included the Assembly Rooms with a minstrels' gallery. Great celebrations followed and the townsfolk adopted the saint as their patron. Whatever the truth, this annual event is worth seeing, particularly the noon dance, when couples in morning dress pick up the words of the song played by a local band and dance literally 'in and out of the houses'.

HELSTON

Helston's 1305 charter ruled that tinners should bring their mineral here for coinage or testing. Below the old Grammar School where Charles Kingsley was educated, Coinagehall Street is an echo of medieval days. The church at the back of the town is behind the **Guildhall** and **the Museum**.

Portreath

B3300

A30

Navax Point

B3301   Cornish Beam
School of   Engines   **REDRUTH**
Mines   Cornwall Centre and Museum
Museum   Pool
Carn   William
Trevithick's   **CAMBORNE**   Brea   Murdoch's
Cottage   House
Penponds   A393   A39

HAYLE   A30
Shire Horse Farm
& Carriage Museum

Nine Maidens &   Stithians
Hangman's Barrow

B3302   *Stithians
Reservoir*

Leedstown   B3280

Godolphin   B3303   Carnkie   A39
House
Godolphin   **FALMOUTH**
Cross   Wendron   A394
Goldsithney   Tregonning   Poldark Mine
Sithney   Trevarno Gardens
A394   Breage   **HELSTON**   Constantine
*Cudden   Flambards   Cornish Seal   Port   Trebah   Mawnan
Point*   Sanctuary   Navas   Gardens   Smith
Rinsey Head   Praa Sands   Gweek   Durgan
Trewavas Head   B3304   Culdrose   Mawgan   Helford   St Anthony
Porthleven   Viewing   Manaccan
Loe   Centre
Pool   Trelowarren
House

HELSTON

★ Angel Hotel
★ Museum
★ Guildhall
★ Creftow (Cornish Crafts)

A3083   Goonhilly   Porthoustock
Gunwalloe   Earth   St Keverne
Marconi   Station
Poldhu   War Memorial   B3293   Roskilly's
Marconi Centre   Mullion   B3294
Mullion Cove   Coverack

Black Head

St Ruan
Cadgwith
Grade
*Kynance   Lizard
Cove*   Lizard Wireless Station
Lizard Lighthouse
Lizard Point

HELSTON & THE
LIZARD PENINSULA

0   4 miles

0   6km

Walks

Helford River/Gillan Creek

5 miles (8km) • easy • two and a half hours

Map: OS 1:25,000 Explorer Series 103: The Lizard, Falmouth and Helston

This walk starts at the picturesque village of Helford which can be reached by road (parking available near the church) or by ferry (hourly foot passenger service available from Helford Passage from Easter to the end of October). It extends for 5 miles (8km) along the edge of the Helford, through the tiny waterside hamlet of St Anthony in Meneage to Dennis Head. Your return journey takes you along Gillan Creek to Manaccan. In Manaccan, go through the churchyard (a 200-year-old fig tree grows from the church wall), turn past the school and follow the footpath marked to Helford where you will find refreshment.

NB Dogs are not allowed on the section of the path that runs through the Bosahan Estate. This section is a permissive path by courtesy of the Bosahan Estate.

Lizard to Mullion

9 miles (15km) • strenuous in places • 4 hours

Map: OS 1:25,000 Explorer Series 103: The Lizard, Falmouth and Helston

A spectacularly beautiful walk, well worth the effort and offering stunning coastline views and a wealth of wildlife interest. The walk passes through lowland Britain's largest National Nature Reserve. Public transport can be combined with your walk allowing you not only to leave your car behind but to avoid retracing your footsteps.

At Mullion, park in the car park to the north of the church. From here you can catch the bus to Lizard village green. Walk down to the Most Southerly Point and follow the coast path west in front of the Wave Crest Café. The path takes you past beautiful Kynance Cove to the Rill from which point spectacular views of the coast are afforded. It was from here that the first sighting of the Spanish Armada heading for Britain occurred in 1588. When you reach Mullion Cove, follow the road uphill back into the village. Do not forget to visit the fifteenth-century church, with some of the finest carving in Cornwall.

Neither of these should be missed, particularly the latter with its emphasis on the former crafts and industries which flourished in and around Helston during the nineteenth and early twentieth centuries. It has a good display of folk history, which includes Henry Trengrouse's life-saving rocket – invented after the Anson shipwreck on Loe Bar. Modern crafts are found opposite the museum in the **Creftow Gallery,** where the artists and crafts people of modern day West Cornwall display their products. Fresh fish and craft shops in Meneage Street are of above average quality.

In contrast to the bustle of Helston's streets a 3-mile (5km) drive northwards along the B3302 will take you to the turning for **Trevarno Estate and Gardens.** Here is an oasis of peace and tranquility combining mature woodland landscapes with formal gardens. The history of the estate dates back to 1296, when it acquired its name from Randolphus de Trevarno and it has been developed continuously over the intervening 700 years. Restoration is still being carried on today with something new to delight frequent visitors on each occasion including the **National Museum of Gardening.**

TO THE WEST OF HELSTON

Porthleven is the birthplace of Guy Gibson, 'Dambusters' hero, and a road bears his name. It is a good place for tea after wandering through its narrow streets and visiting Breageside by the harbour. This was once the heart of a thriving port – note the picturesque store built originally to hold some 7,000 tons of china clay.

Off the A394 to Penzance, running almost parallel with the coast, several lanes lead to headlands and byways. **Trewavas Head** (Joseph Trewavas received Cornwall's first VC in 1856) and

nearby **Rinsey Head** are ideal for picnics. Part of the area and the car park belong to the National Trust, who have partly restored the engine house and chimney of a disused copper mine, Wheal Prosper.

Praa (Pray) Sands, a caravanners' haven, has a silver mile of dunes and safe beaches. Motorists can drive on to the privately-owned Acton Castle where Sandor Vegh began his Masterclasses. This unusual place was built at the end of the eighteenth century for John Stackhouse who originated sea-weed studies here. There are footpaths only for **Cudden Point** with its unusual view of St Michael's Mount. Walkers will enjoy Prussia Cove and Betsy's Cove, both haunts of John Carter, eighteenth-century smuggler and self-styled 'King of Prussia'.

The great inland mining area is reached via **Goldsithney,** a busy place in coaching days, now a quiet village. St Hilary Church, Goldsithney dates from 1854 but the tower dates from the thirteenth century, while an inscribed stone in the churchyard is probably sixth-century. The unusual pictures on the inside walls are reminders of the despoliation of the church in the 1930s when violent protests were made against the vicar, Fr Bernard Walke who had introduced Anglo-Catholic services. It was originally whitewashed and served as a landmark for ships in St Ives and Mounts Bay. Its broached spire is one of the few in Cornwall.

Annual Events & Festivals

Throughout Cornwall there is a busy programme of events and festivals all year, some ancient and traditional, some of more modern origin but all providing fun and entertainment for visitors and local residents alike. Surfing festivals and championships are held regularly at Newquay and other watersports events at many of the beaches and harbours in the area. Art exhibitions are held in the various galleries in the region while agricultural shows are a constant feature of the summer calendar, as are flower festivals in spring and summer. Music, drama, literature, traditional ceremonies, sailing, windsurfing, carnivals and air displays, all are catered for. Details can be found in the local press and in the Tourist Information Centres. The following are a few to look out for:

February
- **Hurling** Columb Major, traditional street ball game

March
- **St Piran's Day** (5th) Cornwall's patron saint
- **Festival of Spring Gardens** (to end of May)

April
- **Trevithick Day**, Camborne

May
- **Obby Oss procession**, Padstow
- **Flora Day**, Helston (8th)
- **Gwennap Feast**, Methodist service at Gwennap Pit
- **Minack Theatre season** (until September)
- **Daphne du Maurier Festival of Arts and Literature**, Fowey and St Austell
- **Wesley Day**, Wesley's Cottage, Trewint

June
- **Murdoch Weekend**, Redruth
- **Golowan Festival**, Penzance Includes Mazey Eve and Mazey Day
- **Royal Cornwall Show**, Wadebridge
- **Midsummer Eve** bonfires throughout Cornwall starting at Chapel Carn Brea near Land's End
- **Truro Jazz Festival**

July
- **RNAS Culdrose Air Day**
- **Camborne Show**
- **Bodmin Riding and Heritage Day**

August
- **Bude Jazz Festival**
- **Falmouth Regatta**
- **Newlyn Fish Festival**
- **Fowey Regatta**

September
- **Cornish Gorsedd**, various venues
- **Crying the Neck** – several places
- **St Ives Festival of Music and the Arts**
- **Helston Harvest Fair**

October
- **Falmouth Oyster and Fresh Seafood Festival**
- **Lowender Peran**, Perranporth Celtic dance and music

November
- **Camborne Music Festival**

December
- **Tom Bawcock's Eve**, Mousehole

Main photograph: Porthleven
Insert: Kynance Cove

Loe Pool

The B3304 passes the boating pool on the Porthleven Road but walkers and ornithologists will want to explore the grounds of seventeenth-century Penrose beside **Loe Pool**, Cornwall's largest lake. Owned by the Rogers family since 1770, it is the main feature of their gift to the National Trust in 1974 – some 1,600 acres (648 hectares) altogether, the largest from Cornwall. A condition of this gift, that it be kept as a place of quiet beauty, makes it excellent for bird-watching. The house itself is not open. There is easy parking at the two entrances and the 6 mile (9.6km) walk taking in Loe Bar Sands will probably mean a rambling day and a picnic. The Loe is a long shingle bank dividing the freshwater lake from the sea.

Off the B3280, a turn to the village of **Godolphin Cross** comes after the hamlets of **Relubbus** and **Bosence**, both busy, lively places in Roman times. Relubbus had the tide at its feet and Roman remains at Bosence prove its trading capabilities. Deep in woodland lies **Godolphin**, a house that deserves a book to itself. This fifteenth-century mansion, was built with wealth from nearby mines. Sir Sidney Godolphin, Elizabeth I's great High Treasurer, and the famed Godolphin Arab stallion are only part of the history associated with this property.

The whole area of Godolphin and Tregonning is ideal for walks and picnics are made more pleasant by easy roadside parking. Chief Conin's dwelling, **Tregonning**, is a hill of ancient settlements and of more recent interest for William Cookworthy's discovery of china clay there in 1746. His subsequent findings at Carloggas near St Austell eventually led to the formation of Cornwall's china clay industry. The white 'signal' house was used to send messages to the ships defending Britain against Napoleon.

Before returning to Helston, stop at **Breage** (pronounced like 'vague') church. It has Margaret Godolphin's coffin plate, a Roman milestone and some fine murals among its other features.

NORTH TO CAMBORNE AND REDRUTH

Three miles (5km) north of Helston, along the B3297, is **Wendron** and the **Poldark Mine**. Here you can go safely underground and experience for yourself something of the past. Tin lodes, working machinery, and even dripping water help to recreate the mining age, with some of Richard Trevithick's instruments on display. Ample picnic space inside or out is available and there are entertainments for the children. Allow plenty of time here.

North once more, the bleak **Carnmenellis Moor** emphasises the mining atmosphere and a short climb to Hangman's Barrow and the Nine Maidens stone circle adds still more. This, too, is a place of many walks. Nearby, **Stithians Reservoir** is a must for ornithologists and yachtsmen but they should first obtain permission from South West Water.

The village of **Carnkie**'s disused engine houses have a melancholy beauty best viewed from the centre of the village and then in panorama from **Carn Brea**. Here is another place to visit whether you are artist, historian, birdlover or gourmet. Come when gorse and heather are out, explore the top of the Brea, where you can sit and relax and, while admiring the view, perhaps wonder about the Neolithic families who once lived here. The 90-foot (27m) granite monolith is a memorial to Francis, Lord de Dunstanville and Basset of Tehidy, erected in 1837. Then find the path downhill to **St Euny**, Redruth Churchtown.

Nearby Reswythen Bridge was made unstable in 1301 by the mining operations of Ralph Wenna and John de Treveyngy and their goods were confiscated to pay for the damage. In **Redruth** itself, in Cross Street, William Murdoch used his invention of gaslight for the first time in 1792. Murdoch House has been restored as a memorial to him and is a centre for the Cornish Global Migration Programme. It is possible to show the house though there are no Murdoch artefacts on view. Redruth has a number of interesting old buildings, which can be seen by following the three town trails.

The **Old Cornwall Society Museum** on Penryn Street tells the history of the town and numerous temporary exhibitions are held there. In the newly refurbished Old Post Office building on Alma Place is the **Cornwall Centre**. This houses the Cornish Studies Library and a well-stocked visitor centre. Through the building and down the stairs that connect with Market Way are the 58 panels of the Tregellas Tapestry, each beautifully embroidered with a different aspect of Cornish history.

Sir Richard Tangye

Sir Richard Tangye (1833-1905) born at nearby **Illogan** became a national benefactor and a brilliant engineer. He instituted the Saturday half-holiday and also built machinery to raise Cleopatra's Needle on the London Embankment. He was inspired by a fellow-countryman, the neglected genius, Richard Trevithick (1771–1833).

Pool has a fine Leisure Centre and it is a good place to spend a day enjoying sport or relaxing – sometimes plays are performed here, too. The leisure centre almost closed in 2000 but was rescued by an enormous community effort. It is now run by a charitable trust and has a unique attraction – an indoor surf training centre.

Beside the main road at Pool are the **Cornish Mines and Engines.** On the south side of the road is a huge, restored Cornish beam engine, while just north of this is the **Industrial Discovery Centre**

Cadgwith Cove

Selected Car Drives

The Lizard Peninsula

From Helston take the A394 Penryn road to Trewennack where you will see a right-hand turn to Gweek. These lanes wander down to that little village at the head of the Helford River and you could pause there to visit the Seal Sanctuary. At the end of the village turn sharp left by a thatched cottage and follow the wooded lanes through Mawgan to Garras by Trelowarren on the B3293. Turn off immediately after the lodge entrance to that estate on your left and wander at leisure to Newtown, St Martin and Manaccan. Consult your map and watch for Helford village with the old Shipwright's Arms and you will see Frenchman's Creek signposted on the way. A short drive from here is St Anthony and Dennis Head beside Gillan Harbour. The lane from this peaceful place is very steep but beyond the cove of Porthallow is St Keverne, attractive and historical as you will see on the plaque on the church wall. The B3293 from here will take you past Goonhilly Satellite Earth Station back to Helston. As you approach Culdrose watch for a lane on the left to Gunwalloe. As you drive down the lane into the village look out for the thatched cottage on the right where a plaque notes the time that Compton Mackenzie spent here in 1908–9, another Cornish literary connection. Go through the village with its very ancient church and Halzephron Inn to the **Halzephron Herb Farm** to find a shop full of herbal products where there is generous free sampling and a warm welcome. Return to the A3083 and so to Helston.

Helston – Tregonning – Godolphin

Leave Helston on the A394 towards Penzance and follow it to Ashton, turning right for Breage church before reaching Ashton. In the centre of the village a right turn to Balwest will take you below the little-known Tregonning Hill. A drive or walk to the top will give you wonderful views over Mounts Bay and place you in history because Cookworthy discovered china clay on this hill. A short distance ahead is Godolphin Cross, and the Manor which is not far from Townshend on the B3280. A right turn here goes to Leedstown and Praze-an-Beeble with its right turn to Nancegollan on the B3303 to Helston. It is also possible to wander round the narrower lanes within this small rectangle of B roads and still not get lost.

Right: St Keverne Church

and another great beam engine, currently undergoing restoration. The engines raised copper ore and men to the surface, and pumped water out of the workings. These two engines are now in the care of the National Trust.

It is worth pausing for a while in Camborne to explore the town trail and see the fine architecture of many of the old municipal buildings there. The internationally famous **Camborne School of Mines**, housing a museum, is on the A3047, while just off the B3303 at **Penponds** is the cottage – now National Trust – where Trevithick lived for a great part of his life and perfected most of his inventions.

Barriper (from Beau Repaire) road was once part of the pilgrims' route to St Michael's Mount and the whole area is so peaceful that it is difficult to imagine it as a prosperous industrial locality. The un-Cornish name of **Leedstown** is a reminder of the time in 1740 when the youngest daughter of mining magnate Sir Francis Godolphin married the Duke of Leeds.

William Oliver lived at Truthall, a fine privately-owned manor in **Sithney** parish. He later moved to Bath and made famous the biscuits that bear his name and portrait, Bath Olivers. The church has a fine collection of glass medallions believed to be thirteenth century.

THE LIZARD PENINSULA, EASTERN SIDE

From Helston, the **Lizard Peninsula** can be explored by turning off the A394 Falmouth road past Trewennack to **Gweek**. Pleasant high-hedged lanes lead to Boskenwyn Downs and open on to a straight road probably constructed by the Romans to take tin from Grumbla to the port. Gweek's unusual name comes from the Latin Vicus which confirms the Roman presence. Since very early times the valleys all round have been streamed for tin, and careful observers may still discover ancient tin moulds built into the quay walls. In 1201 Gweek was important enough to warrant a merchant guild as well as burgess privileges.

The creek is now silted up but beside it is the **Cornish Seal Sanctuary**; the Marine Animal Rescue Centre. It was established in 1958 and is the largest in Europe. Over the years the objectives of this conservation centre have been expanded and it now cares for all marine animals. It also shows how everyone can help.

The B3292 to St Keverne runs between a thatched tollhouse and the water – a pretty road affording occasional glimpses of the creek and walks through the woods. But a narrower primrose-clad lane on the far side of the house offers rewards for brave motorists. It is narrow and steep, winding up past an ancient earthwork, dipping through beech and elm woods before crossing the B3293 to wander up and down into the valley where **Mawgan-in-Meneage** lies. The whole parish of Monks (Meneage or Menaig seems to come from Cornish managh or monk) is full of beauty and history – its church provides something of both. Look for the seventeenth-century sundial, a dog door and an unusual brass memorial to the unknown Hannibal Basset with the words 'Shall we all die'.

Keep to the Manaccan road through wooded lanes until a signpost to Kestle is reached. This lane leads to the unbelievably beautiful haven of **Frenchman's Creek**, which Daphne du Maurier saw, loved and made famous in her book of the same name. It has rightly been described as a place of 'distinct, eerie charm', and access to it is close by the farm. Over 35 acres (14 hectares) along the south bank are National Trust property and footpaths go to Tremayne Quay and Helford.

Motorists should return to the Manaccan road for **Helford** to see its thatched beauty. Stop at the old Shipwrights' Arms and cross the river at Monks' Passage to the Ferryboat Inn. Cars, other than exempted vehicles, are not allowed in Helford village between mid-March and the end of October, during the hours of 10am-6pm. There is a car park above the village on the Manaccan side but it is quite a steep descent to the village.

The road to **Manaccan** is a delight. So is the village, perched saucily on a hillside. The centuries-old New Inn provides a wide variety of good food – beside a log fire. Geologists will remember that William Gregor discovered titanium from here and all should note that ill luck befalls those who pick figs from the tree in the church wall. Few, however, may know that

Bligh of the Bounty came here to survey for the Admiralty, was mistaken for a French spy and promptly arrested.

St Anthony church on the beach at **Gillan** harbour is as beautiful as its surroundings. This was a busy port in medieval times, with ships sailing to Southampton loaded with fish, fish oil, hides, slate and tin. Today, the charm of this quiet corner of the Lizard lies in its remoteness and not in trade. The lonely village across the water is protected by a difficult access road so walkers may follow the coastal path, as motorists have to turn inland again.

St Keverne lies a little south of Manaccan and its church, about 1 mile (1.5km) inland from Manacle Point, has reminders of shipwrecks and has rightly been called the 'church of heartbreak'. A plaque on the churchyard wall is in memory of Michael Josef an Gof, the blacksmith who led the Cornish army to Blackheath with Thomas Flamank of Bodmin. This was the first rebellion of 1497 and he paid for this fight with his life. However, before his grim death at London's Tyburn, he told the crowd that both his name and fame would not be forgotten. His words came true for his memory and deed lives still in the hearts of all Cornishmen.

Just outside St Keverne is the Tudor farmstead of Tregellast Barton, a small traditional Cornish dairy farm. Here the famous **Roskilly's** ice cream is made and the farm is open to visitors. As far as possible everything offered in the restaurant is made on the premises and Cornish produce, much of it from the farm is sold in the shop. See the cows being milked in the late afternoon and take a walk around the farm to visit the wildlife habitats that have been created.

At this point some may wish to return to Helston, wandering quietly through the narrow lanes. If so, look for **Trelowarren**, between the villages of **St Martin's** and **Garras**. For 500 years it has been home to the Vyvyan family and the handsome house is now used for conferences and retreats. One of the most secluded caravan parks in Cornwall takes a small part of the extensive grounds and a cluster of former barns and outhouses have their own attractions. A small pottery and an excellent restaurant will tempt most people while others may like to buy Trelowarren herb plants or visit one of the variety of craft exhibitions held throughout the summer.

THE LIZARD PENINSULA, WESTERN SIDE

There is even more to see and enjoy on the western side of the Lizard so allow plenty of time for this. Immediately outside Helston, along the A3803, is the Royal Naval Air Station at **Culdrose**. It is Europe's largest helicopter base established well over forty years ago. Good views of air traffic may be obtained from its public viewing area and subject to operational commitments, visitors can enjoy guided tours of the base.

A very different kind of entertainment is to be found just off that same road in the **Cornwall Aero Park** and **Flambards Victorian Village**. All-weather family amusements are set out here and include a life-size layout model of the London blitz.

The B3293 from here will lead you to **Goonhilly Downs** and the startling sight of a group of futuristic-looking dishes. This is the **Goonhilly Satellite Earth Station**, where the enormous aerials turn to the sky like creatures of science fiction. They were sited in this particular area because only the depth of granite found here was strong enough to bear the weight of these impressive structures. July 1997 saw the first 35 years of these satellite communications. The first commercially funded satellite was known as Telstar. There is a very fine centre for visitors. Here you can study working models of both dishes and satellites, enjoy the well presented audio-visual explanation of the mystery of modern telecommunications and try the interactive exhibits of the very latest technology, even send an email into outer space.

About 4 miles (6.4km) farther along the B3294 is **Coverack**, a picturesque village, still mainly Cornish in character, with an appeal for those who enjoy sea views and a safe beach. The local lifeboat station is a particular place of interest.

There are numerous cliff walks in this area, the one leading to **Kennack Sands** ends in a safe beach for swimming in fine weather. The motorist, however, must return to the B3293 and turn left at Traboe

Cross in order to reach the National Trust **Poltesco Cove**. It is reached by scrambling down beside a trout stream, but is well worth the effort, and for energetic walkers, there are nature trails to follow.

Cadgwith is a very 'picture-postcard' village, which is a little sad because it has lost most of its former fishing activities, although it still attracts artists and photographers. Serpentine can be found around these parts, and inland from Cadgwith, great blocks of it can be seen in the church towers of **St Ruan** and **Grade** – the latter to be found at the end of a cart track.

Marconi conducted some of his pioneering wireless experiments for the **Lizard Wireless Station** at Bass Point overlooking Housel Bay. It was here that on 23 January 1901 he received a communication from the Isle of Wight, which proved that wireless signals could travel well over the horizon. Replicas of the original equipment are now on view here. In earlier times the Lloyds' signal station was based here. Ships would semaphore details of their cargo to the shore and these could then be relayed to the ship's master well before the ship itself reached the Port of London.

All the cliff walks round here offer spectacular views at **Lizard Point** but the motorist has to go inland a short way from Landewednack and Grade to reach **Lizard village** which is little more than a cluster of souvenir shops with serpentine goods in great variety. At the end of the road is a lifeboat station, open for viewing when not in service, and Britain's most southerly beacon with interesting historical points to note. It was from here, about 400 years ago, in the summer of 1588, that the ships of the Spanish Armada were first sighted.

The **lighthouse** is now automatically controlled but guided tours are offered over the summer, subject to operational requirements. A youth hostel is now established in the buildings next door.

Cliff walkers will have no problem in finding the lovely places along the western coast of the Lizard Peninsula – **Kynance**, **Mullion** and **Gunwalloe** – before the return to Helston. Perhaps this is one of Cornwall's finest cliff walks because, not only are there attractive villages to see en route, but all the time there is a view of St Michael's Mount, topped by its fairytale castle and looking different at every turn.

Motorists will need to watch for signpost directions along the Lizard-Helston A3083, watching particularly for the turn to Cury and Poldhu where Guglielmo Marconi's Memorial stands on the cliffs of **Poldhu Cove**. This stands near the site from where, on 12 December 1901, the first wireless communication was sent across the Atlantic to Marconi in Newfoundland, just eleven months after the earlier Isle of Wight transmission. Exactly 100 years later the **Marconi Centre** was opened at this spot to celebrate the event, exploring Marconi's place in history. So wireless telegraphy was born here

103

and, in time, played a vital part in World War I. It is also interesting to note that the coaxial cable, which is an integral feature of every home television installation, was devised in the course of research done at Poldhu.

So, although the Lizard Peninsula may seem small in relation to the rest of Cornwall it has been, and will continue to be, responsible for events that make vital contributions to the progress of world science. A thought to remember on the return to Helston.

Rare flowers and plants

From July to October the barren downs that surround the Earth Station are brilliant with white-pink and deep lilac Cornish heather which is only found on the Lizard Peninsula. A walk round the adjoining National Nature Reserve affords the chance to see some of the Lizard's unique flora. However do not be fooled by the colourful succulent growing over many of the walls and cliffs at the Lizard point. This is the hottentot fig and is not native but an introduced plant that has taken over. The National Trust is trying to eliminate it to restore the natural flora in that area.

History of the Lizard Light

The first guiding light on this headland was built in 1619 by Sir John Killigrew of Falmouth who needed money and planned to collect the dues from passing ships. So many vessels passed by without paying, however, that he was forced to give up his scheme as it was too expensive to maintain. In the mid-eighteenth century, two towers were built here to house a coal-fired warning light, but that produced so many problems that the idea was abandoned until oil lamps were installed in 1812. 1840 saw the first fog signals, and in 1878, a steam-driven generator powered two electric arc lamps, which gave good service until 1903 when they were replaced by a single 12 million candlepower beam. The light that shines from the Lizard today is one of the most powerful in the world.

Places to Visit

IN & AROUND HELSTON

Creftow (Cornish Crafts)
Helston
☎ (01326) 572848
Open: 10am-5pm Monday to
Saturday, Easter to Christmas. Closed
on Wednesdays between Christmas
and the following Easter.

Guildhall
Coinagehall Street
In 1576 a market house was built
here and it incorporated the Town
Hall. The classical structure seen
today, when erected in 1837-8, also
had a corn market in part of the
building, so carrying on the purpose
of the original.

Museum
In the former Market House in
Church Street.
It was built in 1837-8 and was
composed of two buildings, one
selling butter and eggs, the other
meat.
☎ (01326) 564027
Open: 10am-1pm, Monday to
Saturday; open till 4pm late May
bank holiday week, late July to early
September and 1–20 December.

Trevarno Estate and Gardens
Off B3302 north from Helston
Beautiful formal Victorian and
Georgian gardens with collections of
rare shrubs and trees. Woodland
walks, a gardening museum,
fountain garden, conservatory, hand-
made soap workshop, pottery and
bee centre all add to the pleasure of
a visit. Refreshments available.

☎ (01326) 574274
Open: 10.30am-5pm, all year.

Poldark Mine
Wendron
A real mine to explore. Another
world of tunnels, chambers and
caves where old machinery is at
work. Also museum of mining
ephemera, picnic areas and
undercover amusements for children.
☎ (01326) 573173
Open 10am-5.30pm Sunday to
Friday, Easter to October, open
Saturday in high season.

WEST OF HELSTON

Loe Pool (National Trust)
2 miles (3.2km) S of Helston
This freshwater lake is an unusual
example of the 'drowned valleys'
occurring in Devon and Cornwall.
The Loe Bar formed by accumulated
shingle from the Atlantic has
dammed the former estuary, which
made the port of Helston. A 6-mile
(9.6km) footpath runs round it. Small
car parks at various points, make it
ideal for a day's outing.

St Hilary Church
Near Goldsithney
On an ancient Celtic site. Despoiled
in 1932 but it remains open for those
who want to see its treasures.

Godolphin House
Breage
Fifteenth-century mansion, standing
3 miles (4.8km) from Mounts Bay on
the lower slopes of Godolphin Hill.
Tin mines provided the family
fortune.
☎ (01736) 763194

Places to Visit

www.godolphinhouse.com
Open: Easter to end of September.
11am–5pm Thursday and Friday.
2–5pm Sunday. Plus Tuesdays in
July and August and all bank
holiday Mondays.

Tregonning Hill
Ashton
A place of pre-history with Bronze
Age barrows and fortified 'rounds'.
The site of St Breaca's Celtic
settlement, later the church at
Breage. Today a good picnic place
with walks and wide views to St
Michael's Mount and beyond.

IN & AROUND
REDRUTH

Nine Maidens/Hangman's Barrow
Near junction of B3297 Wendron
road and B3280 Praze-an-Beeble to
Redruth road
Megalithic standing stones.

Stithians Reservoir
A centre for birdwatching, water
sports and natural trout fishing.
For permits apply to the SWWA
(see Fact File).

Shire Horse Farm and Carriage Museum
Redruth
☎ (01209) 713606
Open: 10.30am-5pm April to
October daily except Saturday. In
October –Sunday, Tuesday and
Thursday only.

William Murdoch's House
Not far from the Buller's Arms this
renowned house is tucked away
in a Redruth back street. House only,
no museum.

☎ (01209) 215736
Open: 10am–1pm, Monday
to Thursday.

Old Cornwall Society Museum
Penryn Street
Local history and heritage
☎ (01209) 215084
Open 10am–4pm, Wednesday
to Friday.

Cornwall Centre
Alma Place
Cornish Studies Library, visitor
information, Tregellas Tapestry.
☎ (01209) 216760
Open: 10am–6pm, Monday to
Friday; 10am–4pm Saturday.

Cornish Mines and Engines
Agar Road, Pool (National Trust)
Cornwall Industrial Discovery Centre
at Taylor's Shaft with exhibition and
nearby fully restored pumping
engine house with its enormous 90
inch cylinder. Across the road is
Mitchell's winder, a splendid
working winding engine built in
1887.
☎ (01209) 315027
Open: Discovery Centre, 11am-5pm
Sunday to Friday plus bank holiday
Saturdays, April to October.

Camborne School of Mines Museum and Art Gallery
On the A3047 midway between
Camborne and Redruth
Internationally famous School of
Mines houses a fine collection of
minerals and rocks from Cornwall
and many other parts of the world.
Art gallery has shows all year for
local artists.
☎ (01209) 714866

www.ex.ac.uk/csm
Open: 10am-4pm Monday to Friday all year.

Carn Brae Leisure Centre
Station Road, Pool
Swimming pool, sports, sauna, indoor surf training.

Richard Trevithick's Cottage
Lower Penponds, Camborne
Residence of Richard Trevithick the Cornish engineer. Trevithick room full of memorabilia.
☎ (01209) 612154
Open: 2-5pm Wednesdays from April to end of October by courtesy of the occupiers. (National Trust)

Crowan Reservoirs
Beside the B3280 Redruth-Hayle road.

THE LIZARD PENINSULA

Cornish Seal Sanctuary
Gweek
Started in 1958, now devoted to seal rescue and care. Baby seals are in the hospital from September to March, but others are always on view. Two safari trains are available for transport from the car park to the main points beside the lovely Gweek River.

Top: Lizard Lighthouse
Middle: Goonhilly Earth Station
Bottom: Coverack

Places to Visit

☎ (01326) 221361
www.sealsanctuary.co.uk
Open: 9am-5pm daily except
Christmas Day. (9am-4pm in winter).

Roskilly's
Tregellast Barton, St Keverne
Working farm plus woodland walk,
farm shop and restaurant.
☎ (01326) 280479
www.roskillys.co.uk
Open: from 10am daily during the
summer, weekends only in the
winter.

Trelowarren
Mawgan-in-Meneage
Woodland walks open 10am–6pm
daily, April to September. The chapel
may be open during daylight hours if
not in use by the Trelowarren
Christian Fellowship. Plant nursery
and courtyard open all year.
☎ (01326) 221224
www.trelowarren.co.uk
Restaurant
☎ (01326) 221595
Open 10.30am–12 noon coffee;
12noon–2.15pm lunch; 3–5pm
cream teas in high season only;
7–9.30pm dinner, limited opening
in winter; open on Mondays only
in high season.

Cornwall Crafts Association
Trelowarren
Temporary exhibitions, local crafts
on sale.
☎(01326) 221567
Open: daily, March to the end of
October.

Trelowarren Pottery
Reduction fired stoneware pottery
and handwoven rugs from Nic and
Jackie Harrison
☎ (01326) 221583
Open 11am–5pm daily.

Royal Naval Air Station
Culdrose
This is beside the A3083 Helston-
Lizard road. It is one of Europe's
largest stations and machines are
always on standby. Public viewing
enclosure is close to the B3291,
tours available.
☎ (01326) 565085
Open: 9.15am–5pm, Monday to
Friday, April to October.

**Cornwall Aero Park and
Flambards Victorian Village**
Flambards, nr Helston
Aeroplanes, life-size Victorian
village. Also 'Britain in the Blitz' –
recreation of a wartime street.
Children's attractions and rides.
☎ (01326) 573404
www.flambards.co.uk
Open: 10am-5pm April to October,
daily in high season, closed
Mondays and Fridays in early
October.

Goonhilly Satellite Earth Station
Beside the B3293. There is a public
viewing enclosure and a new visitor
centre with unique multimedia
visitor experience and interactive
displays.
☎ (0800) 679593
www.goonhilly.bt.com
Open: 10am-5pm (6pm in high
season) mid-February to New Year
weekend, daily. Closed on Monday

February, March, November and December.

Lizard Lighthouse
☎ (01736) 360077
Open: 11am-5pm Sunday to Thursday, April to August; also Fridays in July and August. Operational restrictions may apply.

Marconi sites:

Lizard Wireless Station
Bass point (National Trust)
☎ (01326) 290384
www.lizardwireless.org
Open: regularly throughout the year.

The Marconi Centre
Poldhu
☎ (01326) 241656
www.mulliononline.com
Open: regularly throughout the year.

Memorial
Poldhu
The first radio signals across the Atlantic were sent from here by Guglielmo Marconi. Spot marked by a small Art Deco obelisk just south of Poldhu Bay, behind the Poldhu residential home.

Halzephron Herb Farm
Gunwalloe
Herb products of all kinds plus advice and help.
☎ (01326) 240652
www.halzherb.com
Open: 11am–4pm Monday to Saturday, mid-February to December.

What to do if it rains

Camborne
- School of Mines Museum
- Richard Trevithick's Cottage

Helston
- Museum, local history
- Creftow, craft centre
- Flambards Village Theme Park
- Goonhilly Satellite Earth Station, Nr Helston
- Godolphin House, early Tudor manor
- Trevarno Estate, museum and pottery

Mawgan-in-Meneage
- Trelowarren Craft Centre

Pool
- Carn Brae Leisure Centre
- Cornish beam engines and Cornish Industrial Heritage Centre

Redruth
- Shire Horse Farm and Carriage Museum
- Cornwall Centre Museum

Wendron
- Poldark Mine, underground mine

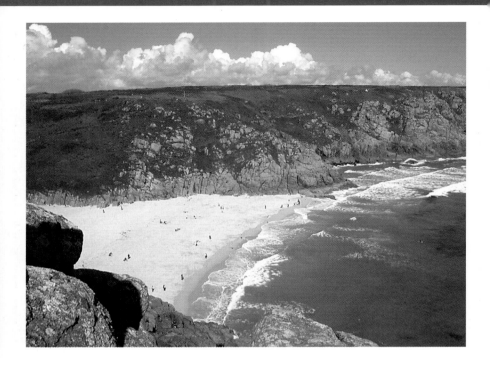

Travellers have always thought of Penzance as the place of journey's end. It is certainly the rail terminus in the west but the locals say that it is in fact where Cornwall begins. Before exploring the area of West Penwith (*Penwyth* is the Cornish for extremity) to discover the truth of this statement, there is much to enjoy in the town of Penzance itself, for it is a place of surprises.

PENZANCE

Beautiful still, with its high, stone-stepped pavement is Market Jew Street, the main thoroughfare that greets pedestrians, motorists and rail travellers who have left the station at the bottom of the hill. The long road leads to the handsome granite Town Hall, before which stands the statue of Sir Humphry Davy.

Opposite page: Porthcurno Beach

Left: Botallack Mine

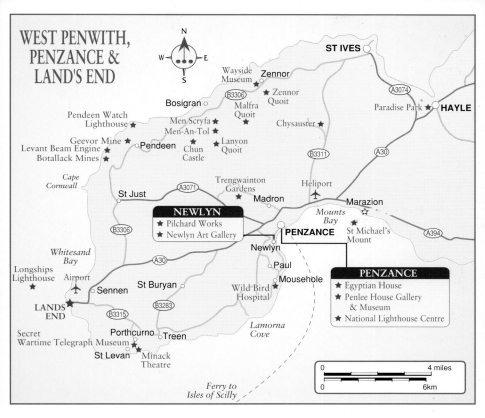

WEST PENWITH, PENZANCE & LAND'S END

N
W E
S

ST IVES

Wayside Museum

Zennor

★ Zennor Quoit

Bosigran ○

B3306

Malfra Quoit ★

Paradise Park ★ HAYLE

A3074

Pendeen Watch Lighthouse ★

Men Scryfa ★
Men-An-Tol ★

Chysauster ★

Geevor Mine ★
Levant Beam Engine ★
Botallack Mines ★

○ Pendeen

Chun Castle

★ Lanyon Quoit

B3311

A30

Cape Cornwall

St Just ○

A3071

Trengwainton Gardens

Madron

Heliport

Marazion

☆

Mounts Bay

NEWLYN
★ Pilchard Works
★ Newlyn Art Gallery

PENZANCE

St Michael's Mount ★

B3306

Newlyn

Whitesand Bay

A30

Paul

A394

Longships Lighthouse ★

Airport

St Buryan ○

○ Mousehole

PENZANCE
★ Egyptian House
★ Penlee House Gallery & Museum
★ National Lighthouse Centre

Sennen

Wild Bird Hospital ★

B3283

LANDS END ★

B3315

Lamorna Cove

Secret Wartime Telegraph Museum ★

Porthcurno ○ Treen

St Levan ○ Minack Theatre

Ferry to Isles of Scilly

0 ———— 4 miles
0 ———— 6km

Sir Humphry Davy

He was born in a house near to his statue and there, too, began the experiments which eventually brought him fame. He was knighted in 1812 for his contributions to science and was later created baronet for his invention of the miner's safety lamp. It is perhaps not surprising that Davy, one of the foremost European chemists of the nineteenth century, was the one who realised and encouraged the talents of Michael Faraday. Davy's wide range of interests also touched on poetry, as well as the natural sciences. President of The Royal Society at 41, founder of the Athenaeum Club and the London Zoo, this man of Penzance was worthy to be called a genius.

The road behind the former town hall, now the Market Hall, turns left towards the harbour and the Barbican complex down Chapel Street. This once bustled with mule trains laden with their copper ore for ships' cargoes. Now it is a backwater of memories, many of them lingering in the Union Hotel where the Battle of Trafalgar victory was first announced from the minstrel's gallery. Local fishermen had learnt it from the ship racing up-channel to Falmouth with the news. Such was local pride in this 'first' that Penzance men made the Nelson banner (now in Madron church) which has ever since been carried in procession on the Sunday nearest to Trafalgar Day. At the back of this historic building there is the shell of a Georgian theatre, opened in 1789. Here miners sought relaxation in the performances of Edmund Keen, Grossmith and other well known actors.

Number 25 Chapel Street claims different honours. It was the **home of Maria Branwell** who married in Yorkshire and became mother to Charlotte, Emily, Anne and Branwell Brontë. She never lost her love for Cornwall, remembering it even on her death bed when she begged the nurse to raise her up so that she could watch her clear the grate because 'she did it as it was done in Cornwall.' The house is not open to the public.

The Landmark Trust's **Egyptian House** with its flamboyant façade, also in Chapel Street, is of unusual interest. There are many side ways and shop-lined lanes to explore in this most western of Cornish towns

and each has something to offer.

Not far away is the **Penlee House Art Gallery and Museum** in Morrab Road – a place of many treasures standing in subtropical gardens where camellias bloom at Christmas above the long promenade stretching from Newlyn to the memorial at the end of Chapel Street.

Returning to the harbour to enjoy the comings and goings, the **Lighthouse Centre** will be found on Wharfe Road. Housed in the old buoy store that was also used to dress the granite blocks for the construction of the Wolf Rock lighthouse, displays tell the story of the lighthouse keepers whose job is no more now that all lights are automated.

Madron village is very close to Penzance on the B3312. It is high over the port and has a huddle of cottages pleasantly grouped near the church, which is named after a sixth-century holy man from Brittany, Maddern. It is the mother church of Penzance and, acknowledged to be one of Cornwall's finest, is well worth a visit. The pew ends are unusually fine, there is the Nelson banner (mentioned earlier) and the great bell from the famous Ding-Dong Mine, whose ruined engine house is silhouetted starkly on the high land ridge behind the village.

The lovely **Trengwainton Gardens**, a National Trust property, lie beside the A3071 below Madron. There has been a house here since the sixteenth century, but it is now privately owned. In 1814, Rose Price, the son of a rich West Indian sugar planter, bought

Walks

St Just-in-Penwith

3-4 miles (5-6km) • fairly strenuous • $1\frac{1}{2}$-2 hours.

Map: OS 1:25,000 Explorer Series 102: Land's End, Penzance and St Ives.

Start at St Just-in-Penwith at the large car park. Take the footpath beside the churchyard gate across the town square. On reaching the road at Nancherrow Farm, follow the narrow path on the left that runs down the narrow Nancherrow or Kenidjack Valley to the sea. Notice the huge waterwheel pit at the seaward end. Follow the coastal footpath signposted up to the right and enjoy dramatic cliff scenery and some of the most famous ruined mine engine houses in the world, ie Botallack and Levant. From the latter place a narrow road almost 1 mile (1.5km) long leads inland to Trewellard village where you can get refreshments and catch a bus back to St Just.

St Michael's Way

12 miles (19km) • easy • 5 hours.

Map: OS 1:25,000 Explorer Series 102: Land's End, Penzance and St Ives.

Part of the European network of ways followed by pilgrims travelling to the shrine of St James of Compostela, this leaves the church of St Uny at Lelant, near Hayle on the north coast, and carries across the narrow 'waist' of land to St Michael's Mount. It is signposted all the way, marked with a stylistic shell based on the Council of Europe's sign for pilgrim ways.

Lamorna

12-15 miles (19-24km) • some strenuous • all day.

Map: OS 1:25,000 Explorer Series 102: Land's End, Penzance and St Ives.

The magnificent scenery in this part of Cornwall can be enjoyed by those who like cliffs and the sea. The South West Coastal Footpath is clearly marked by Acorn signposts. Start at Mousehole and follow the route to Lamorna where there is rest and refreshment. On to the National Trust's Penberth Cove and round to the Logan Rock from where the lovely sights of Porthcurno can be viewed – the beach, the strangely blue sea and the unique Minack Theatre. Footpaths inland lead to Treen, Tresidder and St Buryan where doubtless a bus will take the weary walker to Penzance.

The National Trust's Egyptian House

the house and estate and began to develop it along the lines seen today. He enlarged the original house, gave it a granite façade, built the lodge, planned the walled gardens and planted the magnificent woods of beech and sycamore which are so greatly admired today.

EAST TO ST MICHAEL'S MOUNT

From Penzance, the road follows the vast, magnificent sweep of Mount's Bay past the Heliport (for the Isles of Scilly) and Long Rock to **Marazion**. This place is a delight, with its view of St Michael's Mount (acknowledged to be the earliest identifiable place in Britain). Its golden sands and safe bathing are ideal for children while the marshes nearby attract bird-watchers. Marazion was a thriving port as long ago as the Bronze Age as it was on one of the main overland routes for merchants taking Irish gold to Brittany.

Ordnance Survey maps mark **Long Rock** just offshore and the houses along the main road take their name from it. Legend relates that St Michael appeared to some hermits, supposedly on a large rock, which has ever since been known as St Michael's Chair, while history tells us that it was Edward

Wishing Well

A short distance away is Madron's famous wishing well. Those who care to walk about half a mile (800m) down a damp ferny lane will probably see rags hanging from the surrounding bushes –offerings still made to St Maddern, possibly for happiness in love or simply to placate the invisible spirits and hope for their protection.

the Confessor who established a Benedictine chapel on **St Michael's Mount**. The monks' domestic buildings are now incorporated in the fourteenth-century castle on the rock summit but the abbot's kitchen is well preserved and stands apart.

Even grey skies cannot dim the magical quality of the Mount, which was given by Lord St Levan to the National Trust in 1954. His son, the fourth baron, now lives here. Visitors reach it by foot across a causeway or ferry from Marazion. Apart from the situation of this spectacular retreat, there is interest here for all. The harbour and village may always be visited, but visitors should check for opening days of the castle beforehand.

Meaning of a name

Marazion is usually interpreted as meaning 'Little Market' but probably 'Small Sea' is a better meaning of the interesting name: 'mara' meaning sea and 'zion' comes from *vyghan* or small. The latter describes perfectly the narrow strip of water between the village and the Mount, which can perhaps be seen to better advantage from the higher villages inland.

St Michael's Mount

Historic past

It would be easy to spend a whole day on St Michael's Mount thinking of the past: perhaps of 1497 when Perkin Warbeck left his wife on the Mount to make an abortive claim for England's throne, or of 1549 when the owners of the castle were involved in the Prayer Book Rebellion. Later in 1642–3 the future King Charles II was given sanctuary en route for the Isles of Scilly – a plaque proclaiming this is on the wall of a house in Marazion.

WEST
TO LANDS END

Brenda Wootton who was Cornwall's popular folk singer, has a song called *My Yesterday Town*. It is about **Newlyn** where she was born and looks back sadly to former times when it was an important fishing harbour before artists and visitors poured in to intrude on the intimacy of its community life. Then it was a village with five bridges, five pubs, one church and cottages tip-tilting down the hill to the sea, their livelihood, their joy and their sorrow. Fishing is still very much part of life in Newlyn as can be seen by visiting the **Pilchard Works,** an award winning heritage museum telling the history of pilchard fishing in Cornwall.

Memories of sadness are still retained in the name Mount Misery, high above the bay. This was where anxious wives and sweethearts watched during storms, fearful that their men might not return. The fisherman's world is no longer the same, but the charm of the old cottages remains and there is still the fine quality of clear light which later on attracted Stanhope Forbes and other artists who exhibited in the Newlyn Orion Art Gallery donated by Passmore Edwards. Eden Phillpotts, the prolific novelist, began his career while staying in this area.

The name **Penlee** reverberated round the land like the tolling of a funeral bell at the end of 1981 when storms off this coast caused a lifeboat tragedy. Penlee Point is on the coast road to **Mousehole** (Mouzel), the prettiest fishing village according to many visitors, and which, with Penzance and Newlyn, was burned by the Spaniards in July 1595 and almost destroyed. Its delightful cluster of cottages hugging the harbour appeals to artists, photographers and most holidaymakers. Others enjoy visiting the **Bird Hospital** on Raginnis Hill, founded by the Yglesias sisters, now a registered charity.

The village of **Paul** clusters round its church, another guide for shipping. The church is high above Mousehole and on the churchyard wall is a memorial to Dolly Pentreath whom some consider to be the last traditional speaker of Cornish. She was buried there under her married name of Jeffery in 1777.

Only 2 miles (3.2km) along the cliff path, but further by road past the Roman encampment of Castallack, lies the fertile and lovely **Lamorna Valley**. A bubbling trout stream and colourful gardens tempt visitors down to the little harbour or cove, justly known as one of Cornwall's loveliest, enticing them to linger. The artist Samuel John Birch could not leave, added Lamorna to his name, and gained fame as S J Lamorna Birch R A. The 10-mile (16km) cliff walk from here to Land's End is one that should not be hurried as there are flowers, birds and views sufficient to satisfy everyone.

Above Lamorna Cove, past Trewoofe (Troove) is **Boleigh**, site of the last battle between the Cornish and the English, which took place in AD935. To celebrate his victory, King Athelstan gave a charter to found a collegiate church at **St Buryan**. The two immense megaliths known as 'the Pipers' are believed to have been erected by the king as peace stones to seal the treaty.

Selected Car Drives

Newlyn, Mousehole, Porthcurno and Land's End

Leave Penzance station and follow the road along the coast, round Cornwall's only promenade into Newlyn and on to Mousehole. A steep hill up to Raginnis and a right turn at the next junction will take you to the B3315. A little over 2 miles (3km) along a minor road on the left is signed to Lamorna. That romantic steep lane is worth the climb down. Returning to the B3315 notice the Merry Maidens standing stones. After a short distance take the minor road to St Buryan, enjoy the village and join the B3283 on to Porthcurno where everything is lovely: a magical blue sea and Minack open air theatre which has to be seen to be believed. Return up the same steep hill out of Porthcurno but turn left at the top to Land's End joining the A30 before stopping at the complex there. This road returns to Penzance.

St Just and the north Penwith coast

Leave Penzance on the A30 towards Land's End but at Castle Horneck take a right turn to the A3071. It opens out to ancient moorland where the small fields remain as they were in ancient times. The little granite village of St Just sits solidly against the storms but leave it for the B3306 and detour to Botallack for a glimpse of majestic old engine houses clinging to the cliff edge. This B3306 follows the coast all the way round to St Ives where the A3074 will lead you to the A30 and Penzance again. On the coast road is the isolated Zennor Wayside Museum and a church with tales of a mermaid. Numerous lanes lead inland to the moors and it is worthwhile driving along them to see Chun Castle, Men Scryfa and Lanyon Quoit, knowing that you can return to the safety of the B3306 at any time.

Marconi's romance

Few people know the story of how the famous Marconi met and fell in love with Betty Paynter on the Lamorna cliffs. She was then the fifteen-year-old daughter of Colonel Paynter of nearby Boskenna House, but the vast difference in age did not stop the engineer. He installed a radio receiver in her schoolroom at home, sent diamond bracelets to her at school and sailed his yacht into Bournemouth almost every weekend in the hope of a meeting; a story in the best romantic tradition, but one that did not end according to the Cinderella pattern. After three years of fun and friendship, the schoolgirl, then grown up, realised that the love was all on his side and refused him for the last time.

St Buryan is a handsome church of the late fifteenth century with a fine rood screen and a 92-foot (28m) granite tower. Further along the B3283 lies the village of **Treen**, once the heart of a busy tin-streaming area now only a cluster of houses in the beautiful wooded valley leading to the National Trust properties of Penberth Cove and part of Treryn Dinas. The cove is a reminder, perhaps, of the way of life once common in many Cornish fishing communities where wives and children grew violets and narcissi for the London market – now you can buy wines there. The old trade developed considerably after the opening of Brunel's Royal Albert Bridge in 1859. The valley, cove and headland passed to the National Trust in 1957, many of the small gardens are still cultivated and inshore fishermen are as active as their forefathers were.

The fine jagged headland of **Treryn** (Treen) **Dinas** forms one side of **Porthcurno**, a bay of startling blues and greens with the **Minack Open-air Theatre** on its other side. Treryn Fort consists of 36 acres (14.5 hectares) and incorporates a complex of defensive ditches dating from the Iron Age. Here is the famous Logan Rock, once moved ill-advisedly by Oliver Goldsmith's nephew for a prank. It weighs 66 tons and the over-enthusiastic young man had to replace it at his own expense. Space is limited on this headland so visitors must leave their cars above the bridge over the stream and walk the last quarter of a mile (400m).

Motorists who leave the B3315 to drive to **Porthcurno Beach** and on to the Minack Theatre must be prepared for narrow and winding lanes. The road passes the former Cable and Wireless Training School before the car park nearest to the beach. The building is now the **Porthcurno Wartime Telegraph Museum** housed in a series of tunnels built in 1941 to protect the telegraph station during World War II.

Theatre-goers have to drive up the steep road beyond to reach their destination, but it is a place not to be missed. It is unique. In 1932, Miss Rowena Cade and her gardener began the task of creating an amphitheatre out of the natural rock on the cliff edge for a performance of *The Tempest*. Stone seats now replace the original grassy ledges, sound and lighting and dressing-room accommodation are of the best, but the original magic remains. The theatre is open all day for visitors but those who are fortunate enough to attend a per-

Newlyn

formance see it at its very best. No matter what the play or the players, the setting makes every performance one of individual delight – the sight of the moon rising over the backcloth of ocean is a never-to-be-forgotten experience.

The church of **St Levan** and its holy well lies beyond the Minack, and there the road stops, so motorists must return to the B3315 for **Land's End**. The walk along the coast from here would take most people about two and a half hours. On a fine day the views are unrivalled. Here is another place for a whole day's exploration;

photographers, botanists, poets and holidaymakers of all ages will find something here to please them. Longships Lighthouse lies due west of the last group of rocks while 7 or 8 miles (11 or 12km) beyond is Wolf Rock. This was the place used by Trinity House for their experiments in airlifting supplies to lighthouse crews. The results were completely successful.

Also at Land's End is one of Cornwall's most varied family attractions with exhibitions, visitor centre, discovery trail, RSPB hide, shops and restaurants. It takes a day to see them all.

Land's End

NORTH OF LAND'S END

About a mile (1.5km) to the north lies **Sennen**, near the Mayon and Trevescan Cliffs, both National Trust properties. Mayon Cliff is topped with a good example of a Cornish cliff castle (Mayon meaning *maen* or stone) with sheer drops to the sea and a view of basking sharks cruising off the rocks in summer. Above Sennen Cove, which continues on to Whitesand Bay, is the ancient church of St Sennen, the westernmost church in Britain. It is small and low, as befits its site and was re-consecrated in 1440.

Before the village of **Crows-an-Wra** (Witch's Cross) several paths leave the main road and climb to **Chapel Carn Brea,** which also belongs to the National Trust. It is the first and last hill in Britain and is reputed to have the widest sea view from the mainland of the British Isles. Two Bronze Age barrows and the remains of a medieval chapel dedicated to St Michael may be seen after a gentle climb to the top, where in 1907, one of Cornwall's largest Bronze Age urns was found (it is now in the Truro Museum).

The whole area is good for picnics and walks and for exploring the many antiquities in the locality. Nearby **Sancreed** church is worth looking at. There is a good rood screen, original barrel roofing and five crosses in the churchyard. One, which has lilies on it, is said to be noteworthy. Half hidden in trees in a field close by is the Sancreed holy well and baptistry possessing an exceptional air of mystery and sanctity.

The road runs past Drift Reservoir to join the A30. It is a pleasant place for walks and picnics as old mingles with new here, for **Drift** village is mentioned in Cornwall's best known folk tale – John of Chyannor. He left Treen when mining was at a low ebb and went to look for work in the east. That to him was not land overseas, but a farm a few kilometres (miles) east of Marazion. This particular story is especially interesting as it names all the places John visited in his wanderings, something which does not often occur in folk tales.

Deep in the valley of Buryas Bridge there is a cross inscribed with symbols of the Cretan mysteries – another link with the

Prayer for sunshine

Today at Carn Brea (not to be confused with Carn Brea at Redruth) members of St Just Old Cornwall Society light the first in the chain of forty bonfires which illuminate Cornwall on Midsummer Eve from Land's End to the Tamar. This is a particularly festive occasion. Songs and prayers (usually in Cornish) accompany the 'sacrifice' of herbs and flowers thrown in the flames by the Lady of the Flowers to propitiate the sun god, a plea, shared by all visitors, for summer sunshine.

strange past of West Penwith. These insignia appear to relate to the famous Cretan labyrinth where the Minotaur lurked, but no-one has yet provided a real explanation for the designs.

THE PENWITH COAST

To see the best of the northern part of this peninsula follow the A3071 out of Penzance. It passes **Castle Horneck** shortly after leaving the edge of the town, a splendid place for a youth hostel and once the home of the Levelis or Lovell family. They owned much of the land in this area in early medieval times and were greatly involved in the Crusades. A well-known Cornish Christmas song, *The Mistletoe Bough*, is based on a tragic incident in the Lovell family. A young bride hid from her husband in an old oak chest and was entombed there, trapped by an unseen spring lock.

The countryside around **St Just** is almost other-worldly; its small fields and dry-stone walls bringing to mind the first men who ever settled here many centuries ago. The tower of the church though low, can be seen from quite a distance as it has stood in granite solidity since the fifteenth century. Near the clock tower a grassy arena is used today for the ceremony of choosing St Just's Carnival Queen. It is, in fact, a *plen-an-gwary* (Cornish for 'playing place') where medieval mystery plays were performed.

From St Just explore the Penwith coast starting from Cape Cornwall Street which leads from the Square to **Cape Cornwall**, now a National Trust property. Many people find it pleasant to spend a day here, taking advantage of the numerous walks, picnic places and advantageous locations for birdwatching. The towering nineteenth-century chimney at the summit of Cape Cornwall is a reminder of the many mines once busy in this district. There is an extensive view from this height although Priest's Cove to the south is probably hidden. It was once a medieval landing beach but now has a different character, and is very popular with local swimmers.

Beyond Land's End is the Longships Lighthouse while in the other direction are the picturesque cliff-edge ruins of the Three Crowns Mine at **Botallack**. The coastal path, like the road, goes towards **Trewellard**, an old mining village with a unique church. The Reverend Robert Aitken designed it himself and by 1851 it was finished, built entirely by the local miners. Some may think little of the plain, bleak place of worship but no-one can deny that it suits the surroundings and reflects the comfortless life which was the lot of most people who lived at Trewellard in those days.

Pendeen Manor, an attractive sixteenth-century farmhouse, was the birthplace of Dr Borlase, the father of Cornish archaeology. In the yard there is a fogou or underground passage which runs for 23 feet (7m) in one direction and 33 feet (10m) in another. At the angle of these is another chamber. There has been much speculation as to the original use

Above:
Lamorna Cove

Left:
Trewellard, Levant
Steam Engine

Below:
Botallack Mine

Opposite page:
Levant Steam
Engine

Three Crowns Mine

In 1865, the Prince and Princess of Wales (later King Edward VII and Queen Alexandra) came here and descended the mine. This profitable mine caught the imagination because it produced riches from beneath the very sea bed itself. Tunnels 7ft by 4ft (2m by 1m) were cut into a rich copper lode and men worked there each day at a depth of 1,360 feet (415m) below sea level and half a mile (800m) from shore. When the quarterly accounts were produced, owners and mine managers would celebrate their gains with a feast at the Count House.

of these constructions – Cornwall has several of them. Archaeologists have not yet been able to agree on a satisfactory reason for their existence so no-one can say whether the fogous were built for storage, defence or even primitive housing. The most recent thought on the subject is that they might have been designed for worship.

Past the manor, the road leads to **Pendeen Watch**, a lighthouse open to the public. Perched on a cliff edge, it is surrounded by open land where there are birds and flowers in plenty. Also at **Pendeen**, is the spectacularly-situated **Geevor Mine**, which once yielded both tin and copper. It was registered as a limited company in 1911 and incorporated the old mines of Wheal Stennack and the ill-fated Levant. Tragedy struck in the latter in 1919 when the man-engine, carrying its full complement of men and boys to the surface, broke, crashed in ruins to the bottom of the shaft and killed 31 miners. The deeper workings were then abandoned, work ceased altogether from 1930 and the sea took possession of them.

Fortunately the Cornish Engine Preservation Society (now the Trevithick Society) saved the beam engine in 1935 and in 1967 handed it to the National Trust. They then restored both engine and engine house, a fascinating reminder of the prosperous times of 1870 when the area supported about 20 mines. The **Levant Steam Engine** is now open to the public for most of the year and volunteers from the

Penwith Antiquities

Penwith is an area full of ancient sites and many legends exist which have been told from generation to generation. Ludgvan (Lugian) is a quiet churchtown set well above Mount's Bay amidst narrow, twisting lanes. Dr William Borlase, born at Pendeen in 1695, was village rector for 52 years and published several books including *The Natural History of Cornwall* in 1758, 31 years before Gilbert White's well-known *Natural History of Selborne*. This energetic clergyman was the first archaeologist to detail the heritage of Beaker Age monuments and his work in this field is still unsurpassed.

From the steep B3309 below the church towards Crowlas, just east of Penzance, the second lane on the left leads to the exciting Penwith countryside, studied by Borlase. A lane curves round the foot of **Trencrom Hill** (SW 518362) a hill fort with fine views over the narrowest part of Cornwall and forming part of the granite backbone of West Penwith with well preserved Iron Age remains at the summit. The soil here is good and Channel Island herds thrive in the area. The site was given to the National Trust by Colonel G L Tyringham of Lelant in memory of the men and women of Cornwall who gave their lives in the two World Wars. It consists of 64 acres (26 hectares) of gorse-covered hill, overlooking an expanse of both land and sea, that is ideal for views, walks and picnics.

Here are numerous well-preserved antiquities – an Iron Age stone-walled hill fort enclosing several hut circles. Legend says that Giant Trecobben used to throw 'pebbles' at his brother Cormorran who lived on the Mount: the gigantic Bowl Rock beside the Lelant-Towednack road to the north, given to the Trust in 1962, has the notice 'thrown by a giant'!

Further along that same road is **Trink** – once reputed to be the home of another giant but now a delightful place for holidaymakers. North-east from here, a turning off the B3311 leads to lonely **Towednack** church. A strange story lingers in its history which is remembered on 28 April when the Towednack Cuckoo Feast used to be celebrated. Here the event recalls the time when a local farmer caught a cuckoo which flew from a log he was burning during a party. Perhaps the villagers hoped to hold and preserve the spirit of spring in this way. (Most Cornish churches hold their feasts to commemorate the arrival of their patron saint.)

The way to **Castle-an-Dinas** and **Chysauster** is down the Nancledra valley where tin has been streamed since earliest times. The former is one of the chain of hill forts across the country, the latter (along a pleasant lane off the B3311, two and a half miles/4km NW of Gulval) probably one of the best preserved beehive hut circles in Great Britain. It was an Iron Age village from about the second century BC to the third century AD and consists now of a series of stone houses, each containing a number of rooms. Partial excavations have been made here and the walls of the buildings are still clearly visible.

Chysauster is an English Heritage site with set opening times and a charge for entry. Open: 10am-6pm or dusk daily March to October; ☎ (01736) 61889

Not far away at the head of the Trevaylor valley, towering over the Penwith

Peninsula is **Mulfra Quoit**. This close group of standing stones on the site of an ancient settlement at Mulfra Hill, gives substantial evidence to the theory of ancient ley lines. Three of the four original uprights still stand and support a partially displaced capstone. Traces of a circular barrow about 40 feet (12m) in diameter, the original covering of the chamber, can be seen.

Also in the same area is the **Men-an-Tol**, a fascinating monument with numerous legends. In 1749 Dr Borlase learnt that local people still crept through the hole to cure their rheumatism, while children who suffered from rickets were passed through it at certain times of the year. Sir Norman Lockyer wrote that this megalith was an astronomical instrument for the observation of certain sunrises and sunsets.

Close by are the **Men Scryfa** (3 miles/4.8km NW of Madron) an 8 foot-(2.4m) tall inscribed stone and the **Nine Maidens Stone Circle**. Were these stones really girls who had danced on the Sabbath and had been turned to stone for their sin? That is what the legend says. The Men Scryfa, however, is thought to be closer to reality. *Rialobranus Cunovali Fili* is the Roman inscription and could be translated as 'Son of Chief Royal Raven'. Some think it was the grave of a giant warrior, others consider it another ley marker and there are those who think it could be the gravestone of the noble Rialobran (Royal Raven) who lived between the fifth and sixth centuries BC on nearby Carn Galver.

Beside the lonely secondary road which runs from Morvah to Madron about 4 miles (6.4km) NW of Penzance stands **Lanyon Quoit** – probably Cornwall's most famous monument and the only known example of the remains of a long barrow. A huge granite capstone (18 x 9ft) on three upright stones it was originally 90 feet (27m) long, its capstone so high that Dr Borlase rode his horse under it. It was re-erected by public subscription in 1824 after a violent storm (1815) broke one of its four stone supports and this accounts for the present lower height.

Another group of stones – the **Merry Maidens** stand alongside the B3315 Newlyn-Treen road. This is the best known stone circle and consists of nineteen stones, the whole being about 75 feet (23m) in diameter and is one of the places where the Cornish Gorsedd is sometimes held. This gathering is an annual event at which new bards are admitted to the Gorsedd, or College of Bards, an organisation unique to Celtic communities enshrining their common cultural heritage

Carn Euny near Sancreed, 4 miles (6.4km) west of Penzance is an ancient Iron Age village now cared for by English Heritage. The remains are said to rival those of Chysauster and there is the added attraction of a fine 60 foot-(18m) long fougou or underground chamber. The Blind Fiddler Stone – source of many legends – stands beside the A30, and down a farm lane opposite is Boscawen-noon, an isolated stone circle with a central heel stone or altar. Henry Jenner, who revived the Cornish Gorsedd in 1928, chose this place for its first assembly.

Each of these sites, created by the ancient Cornish people, will reward visitors with a special atmosphere and sense of history.

Trevithick Society run the engine in steam regularly.

Geevor, a working mine until 1990, is now a preserved mining site offering underground tours and a museum to tell the tale of how local people fought to win the minerals from hundreds of feet underground and out under the sea. For many other mines only their ruins remain, picturesque and sad, along the cliffs, slowly but surely weathering away.

From here to Zennor, the coast road is particularly interesting, especially at **Bosigran** beyond Morvah on the National Trust cliffs. These are wild and exposed but man has learnt how to survive here from prehistoric times, sheltering his crops and animals in tiny fields surrounded by their stone hedges which remain from the Iron Age. The adventurous will probably enjoy the circular walk westwards from Porthmeor Cove to the Iron Age ruins of Bosigran Castle, along the spur path and back to Porthmeor Cove along the main road.

The village of **Porthmeor** is missed by most people who, not unnaturally, are eager to reach Zennor. It is, however, worth asking at Borthpennis for permission to cross the private land and look at the Iron Age village courtyard house here. It is similar in many respects to Chysauster but in addition has its own fortification and gatehouse and is one of the best of the numerous ancient monuments scattered on the downs above the B3306.

Today, **Zennor** is a picturesque miniature village lying in the slight shelter of Trewey Hill. It has, however, a long and interesting history. Isolated as it was by the natural features of land and sea, Zennor remained almost inaccessible for centuries, which is why the presence of the past is still so strong in and around it. The small fields of middle and late Bronze Age settlements are still to be seen at Trewey and Wicca. Some tools and farm implements used for agricultural work down the years are among the exhibits in the small **Wayside Museum**, close to the car park. Whether mining is quite as old as farming here no-one knows, but it is said that tin-streaming has thoroughly worked almost every area of the Foage valley. Tools used for this are another feature of the museum.

Both these industries were quite local but Zennor's stone-workers

Climbing connections

Adjoining Bosigran is more Trust property with a rather special history. Here, during World War II, commandos trained (the western side of the valley is, in fact, named 'Commando Ridge'). Here, too, Lord John Hunt and Sherpa Tensing climbed together to celebrate the tenth anniversary of the ascent of Everest. Never before had Tensing seen the sea and it was his first experience of cliff climbing. Cars can be parked by the road here and access to the coast is by the spur path past the Climbers' Club hut.

were once famous far beyond their homes. Tradition tells that the granite for St Ives' church was brought by sea from here, boats sometimes having to wait for weeks in order to take advantage of a spell of rare fine weather. Great cubes of Zennor rock were also used in the construction of Falmouth harbour and some also went to London for pavement edging.

The square church tower is not high but stands as a clear marker of the centre of Zennor life. On the outside wall of the church just inside the gate is John Davey's memorial stone. He was a man of history who died in 1891 and was said to have been the last one to speak the traditional Cornish language – more than a century later than Dolly Pentreath, mentioned earlier. There are only two old bench ends in the church but one of them is especially interesting. It portrays a finely carved mermaid and recalls the story of the beautiful sea-creature whose charms were the downfall of Matthew Trewhella. Opposite is the Tinner's Arms, so old that its origins are unknown.

Behind the inn the path, which runs parallel to a trout stream flowing into Pendour (Mermaid) Cove, leads down to Zennor Head. This is part of the 84 acres (34 hectares) owned by the National Trust along the cliff, enabling walkers to enjoy the delights of thyme-scented springy turf all the way to Wicca Pool, an Anglo-Saxon name, so out of place in this essentially Cornish area.

There is a great deal to see in this little valley: another Logan Stone, Zennor Quoit, Giant's Rock and the very fine views from the gorse-covered slopes. Little wonder that D H Lawrence loved it here and that Virginia Woolf, who spent childhood summers in St Ives, wrote that Cornwall's cliffs and seas had endowed her with riches beyond price.

The quickest way back to Penzance by car is up Trewey Hill, climbing away from Zennor and on to moorland that tempts many to a last walk and picnic above the magnificent cliffs of Penwith's north coast.

The Tinners' Way

This ancient trackway – in Cornish, *Forth an Stenoryon* – runs from St Just to St Ives. Only recently has the Tinners' Way been brought to the notice of the public, the person responsible being a past Grand Bard, Hugh Miners (a Grand Bard is the elected titular head of the College of Bards in each of the Celtic countries). For the experience of a lifetime join a night group at the full moon nearest to Midsummer Day and you will always remember your walk in the steps of the tin traders.

No-one knows the exact age of this moorland path but it was certainly used by tinners more than 2,000 years ago while ornaments and ingots made by Bronze Age goldsmiths found close to the trackway go back another 1,500 years. Stone axes, which had been quarried from the Kenidjack cliff, have been discovered throughout southern Britain and such discoveries lead to the logical conclusion that West Penwith's Tinners' Way was originally part of a nationwide network for trade in Neolithic times.

To explore the area yourself, take an Ordnance Survey map and walk the route on your own. Although it consists mainly of rough tracks and paths, no part of it is particularly difficult and when you reach the harbour at St Ives you will have the satisfaction of knowing that you have travelled over many centuries of history. Begin by walking down the church path away from St Just until Nancherrow Bridge where the way turns up towards Carn Kenidjack. This is often called the 'Hooting Carn' and is associated with many tales of haunting but as you climb, the colourful moorland surroundings of barrows, holed stones and chamber tombs will more than hold your attention. The B3218 crosses the path now but the ancient route carries on, skirting Woon Gumpus Common towards **Chun Quoit** and **Chun Castle**. The latter is the remains of an exceptionally large and strongly built Iron Age fortress with 12 feet (3.6m) thick walls, which until about 100 years ago, were still 12 feet (3.6m) high.

Before reaching Bosullow Common note that the map shows the site of a settlement. This was, in fact, the Iron Age village of Bosullow Trehyllys where its inhabitants were comparatively secure with Chun Castle in the vicinity. Beyond this, a modern road again crosses the trackway that rises to Watch Croft, Penwith's highest hill (827ft/252m). From here it is possible to make a slight detour and wander to look at Men Scryfa and the famous Men-an-Tol. Many people are sceptical about the tales told of cures at the latter site but they are said to still happen today. The ruined engine house of **Ding-Dong Mine** is easily visible from here. Tradition says that the famous tin mine was worked in Roman times. It re-started in 1814 but finally closed in 1928.

It is peaceful and lovely along here where the track runs high and almost parallel to the coast road to Zennor and St Ives, crossing the minor road from Treen to New Mill. Try Valley is marked on the map but not Try Round, said by tradition to have been a corral for mules. Further on, near Lady Downs a branch track goes off along the hill above Chysauster, passes the Castle-an-Dinas hill fort and eventually reaches Mount's Bay. Historians believe this to be the route referred to by Pytheas, the Greek geographer, who wrote that the people of West Penwith took their melted tin in wagons to export it from Iktis (St Michael's Mount).

For a short distance a metalled road now overlays the ancient track at Embla and Almaveor, names which go far back in history. They only occur elsewhere in Cornwall, north of Wadebridge at Chapel Amble. As with so many Cornish place names, these have been distorted over the centuries but their origins can still be recognised. *Amal* is Cornish for slope, boundary or ledge, and its plural *emlow* is Embla today and walkers who reach this area will be well able to confirm the existence of numerous slopes in the proximity.

After Coldharbour Moor, the track passes that now lonely church of Towednack, which was mentioned earlier. Its closeness to the Tinners' Way probably indicates that it is a place where the Celtic holy man or 'saint' who lived there would welcome weary travellers with rest and refreshment.

Road and pathway now run together down Rosewall Hill with the ivy-clad ruin of an engine-house reminding the world of the presence of tin. The ancient route ends at St Ives, through the part called Stennack (*sten* is Cornish for tin).

Lanyon Quoit, situated just off the Tinners' Way, with Ding-Dong Mine on the horizon

Places to Visit

PENZANCE

Chapel Street
Walk the street with the *Historic Chapel Street* leaflet from the Tourist Information Centre. Many of the buildings have tales to tell.

Penlee House Art Gallery and Museum
Morrab Road
Entirely local display reflecting the history and environment of Penzance Unrivalled collection of work by the Victorian Newlyn School of Painting.
☎ (01736) 363625
www.penleehouse.org.uk
Open: 10am-4.30pm Monday to Saturday all year, till 5pm May to September.

National Lighthouse Centre
Wharf Road, Penzance
Hands-on museum of the world's finest collection of lighthouse equipment. Audio-visual display. Reconstructed living quarters of a lighthouse keeper.
☎ (01736) 360077
Open: 10.30am-4.30pm Easter to end of October daily.

Trengwainton Gardens
A3071 (National Trust)
Unique garden with many exotic shrubs and trees. Wonderful views of Mount's Bay and the Lizard. Tea room, shop and plant sales.
☎ (01736) 362297
Open: 10am-5pm Sunday to Thursday, mid-February to October; till 5.30pm April to September.

Trip to the Isles of Scilly
Three modes of travel are available for day trips to the Isles of Scilly: helicopter, plane or boat. Helicopters depart from just outside Penzance on Mount's Bay for the 20 minute flight. Shuttle bus available from Penzance. ☎ (01736) 363871 for details. Flights operate from Land's End with a shuttle bus available from Penzance. Boats sail from Penzance quay. ☎ (0845) 7105555 for details of both these services.

AROUND PENZANCE

Marazion Town Museum
Town Hall, Marazion
Exhibition about historic Marazion including reconstructed jail cell.
Open: every day during the summer season.

St Michael's Mount
(National Trust)
When the approach causeway is covered there is a ferry service from Marazion. Owing to the quick tidal movement visitors will probably walk back so return tickets should not be taken. The small chapel is unusual in size and location. It is open on Sundays from June to September at 10.30 for Divine Service which begins at 11.00. Café and National Trust shop. Please note there are no facilities for dogs on the island. Paths are unsuitable for wheelchairs, prams and pushchairs. Sensible shoes are advisable.
☎ (01736) 710507 or 710265
www.stmichaelsmount.co.uk
Open: 10.30am-5.30pm Monday to Friday, April to October. The Castle and Grounds are open most weekends during the high summer

Above & below: Land's End

Right: Detail on the front of The National Trust's Egyptian House

Places to Visit

season. From November to March Castle will be open for guided tours Monday, Wednesday and Friday subject to weather and tides. Please telephone first to check.

Newlyn Orion Art Gallery
Newlyn Green, New Road
Donated to artists and the community in 1895 by Passmore Edwards.
☎ (01736) 363715
www.newlynartgallery.com
Open: 10am-5pm, Monday to Saturday.

The Pilchard Works
Newlyn
Factory with heritage museum, local history displays, examples of Newlyn copperware.
☎ (01736) 332112
www.pilchardworks.co.uk
Open: 10am-6pm Monday to Friday from Easter to October.

Mousehole Bird Hospital
Raginnis Hill
Opened as a bird sanctuary by the Yglesias sisters (1928) when they cared for an injured jackdaw found in a drainpipe.
☎ (01736) 731386
Open: daily, admission free.

NORTH PENWITH COAST

Geevor Mine
Pendeen
Ruins of famous tin and copper mine. Underground tours and museum
☎ (01736) 788662 www.geevor.com
Open: 10am-5pm April to October

daily except Saturday, 10am-4pm, Monday to Friday, November to March.

Pendeen Watch Lighthouse
Built by Trinity House in 1900. Its light gives four white flashes every second while the fog signal blasts 7 seconds every minute.
☎ (01209) 210900
Open: 11am-5pm; Sunday to Thursday, Spring Bank Holiday week, June and July; Sunday to Friday in August. Operational requirements permitting.

Wayside Museum
Zennor
On the St Ives to Land's End coastal road the exhibits include tools and implements connected with the mining, agricultural, quarrying and domestic life of Zennor. Bridge House gift shop.
☎ (01736) 796945
Open: 10.30am-5.30pm Sunday to Friday May to September, 11am-5pm Sunday to Friday, Easter and October.

Levant Steam Engine (National Trust and Trevithick Society)
Trewellard
Engine steaming days: April to October when open.
☎ (01736) 786156
Open: 11am-5pm Easter, May and Spring Bank Holidays plus Fridays; June, Wednesday, Thursday, Friday and Sunday; July to end September daily except Saturday. Winter, 11am-4pm Friday only (not in steam). Closed November and December.

LAND'S END PENINSULA

Land's End Holiday Complex

Range of family attractions and exhibitions at the Visitor Centre. Family restaurants and bar.
☎ (0870) 4580044
www.landsend-landmark.co.uk
Open: 10am daily except Christmas Eve and Christmas Day.

Porchcurno Secret Wartime Telegraph Museum

Porthcurno
Cornwall's secret wartime underground communications centre.
☎ (01736) 810966
www.porthcurno.org.uk
Open: 10am-5pm Sunday to Friday, April to October. Also Sundays in July and August. 10am-5pm Sundays and Mondays only, November to March.

Minack Open-air Theatre

Porthcurno
A unique open-air theatre fashioned from natural rock amphitheatre and the Rowena Cade Exhibition Centre with photographs, models and audio-visual displays. Coffee shop. Theatre performances are held from end of May to the middle of September.
☎ (01736) 810471
www.minack.com
Open: 9.30am-5.30pm daily from April to October; 10am-4pm daily October to March. Auditorium closed from noon to 4.30pm when there is a matinée.

What to do if it rains

Penzance
- National Lighthouse Centre
- Penlee House Museum and Art Gallery

Porthcurno
- Minack Theatre
- Rowena Cade Exhibition Centre
- Secret Wartime Telegraph Museum

Land's End
- Family entertainment complex

Pendeen
- Geevor Tin Mine
- Levant Steam Engine
- Pendeen Lighthouse

Zennor
- Wayside Museum

Newlyn
- The Pilchard Works
- Newlyn Orion Art Gallery

Marazion
- Town Hall Museum

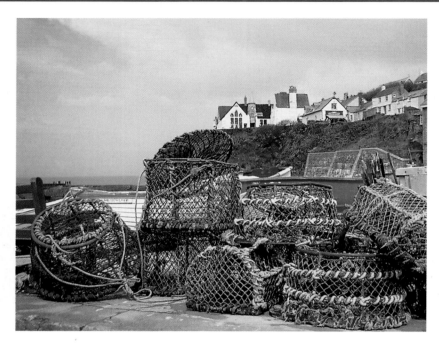

Legends cannot be avoided when telling the story of Cornwall, but the one particularly associated with St Ives is usually shrugged off in disbelief, for it is said that the holy St Ia, who was the first to come to this part of the coast, sailed across the water on a leaf!

The idea is very picturesque but seems extreme to be at all possible – that is, until one remembers the comparatively recent cross-Atlantic voyage that successfully re-enacted the journey undertaken by St Brendan many centuries ago. A replica of the saint's small craft was made, a mere wooden framework covered with hide and surely as close as could be to the 'leaf' of St Ia.

ST IVES

Apparently St Ia eventually established a settlement here and it later became the attractive fishing port of **St Ives**, but as miraculous leaves are in short supply today, people who want to see the town in comfort should leave their cars at Lelant Saltings if they are only staying a few hours. This avoids parking problems and adds another

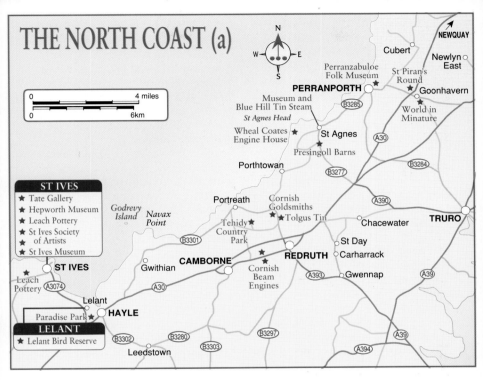

THE NORTH COAST (a)

NEWQUAY

Cubert

Newlyn East

Perranzabuloe Folk Museum
St Piran's Round

PERRANPORTH

Goonhavern

Museum and Blue Hill Tin Steam
B3285

World in Minature

St Agnes Head

Wheal Coates Engine House
St Agnes

A30

Presingoll Barns

Porthtowan

B3277

B3284

0   4 miles

0   6km

Portreath

Cornish Goldsmiths

A390

ST IVES
- ★ Tate Gallery
- ★ Hepworth Museum
- ★ Leach Pottery
- ★ St Ives Society of Artists
- ★ St Ives Museum

Godrevy Island
Navax Point

Tehidy Country Park

Tolgus Tin

Chacewater

TRURO

B3301

St Day

ST IVES

Gwithian

CAMBORNE

REDRUTH

Carharrack

Leach Pottery
A3074

A30

Cornish Beam Engines

A393

Gwennap

A39

Lelant

Paradise Park ★

HAYLE

LELANT
- ★ Lelant Bird Reserve

B3302

B3280

B3297

A39

Leedstown

B3303

A394

---

pleasure for, if the weather is fine, there can be few railway journeys more delightful than the small local train, which runs from St Erth to St Ives and collects passengers on the way. There is ample parking space at Lelant and the ride takes a little over 10 minutes, which most people say is all too short.

From the Saltings, with its interesting estuary scenery, the friendly train takes its passengers along the cliffside to give a clear view of the famous 5 mile (8km) stretch of the golden sands which edge the coast from St Ives to Godrevy Point. Vehicular access to the town is restricted during the season, though buses are available from Trenwith car park on the outskirts, so it is both wiser and more pleasant to arrive on the local train. The steep, winding cobbled streets of this 'picturesque seaside town par excellence', as it has been called, do much to retain its Cornishness. Looking over the water at Westcott's Quay where the Warren turns into Pednolva Walk, it is easy to understand why the St Ives Art Club decided to hold meetings in that wharfside fishing cellar – the view from there is so characteristic of the whole place.

Turner was probably the first artist to come here and paint scenes of the town. That was in 1811, but it was Whistler and Sickert who, in 1884, actually established the art colony there. Today the **St Ives Society of Artists** exhibit their work in their gallery at Norway Square.

In the first half of the twentieth century people like Sir Alfred Munnings, Lamorna Birch, Barbara Hepworth and Bernard Leach were active in St Ives. Leach, a potter, designed the tiled stone round the grave of Alfred Wallis, the self-taught primitive painter who is buried in Barnoon cemetery beside the car park. In 1920, Leach established a workshop at **Higher Stennack** on the B3306; it is still there and examples of his work are always on display. Stennack comes from *sten* (Cornish for tin) and the whole valley was once a profitable mining area. The most notable of the workings was probably Wheal Trenwith as it produced not only tin but also copper, pitchblende and the radium used by Madame Curie in her experiments.

Barbara Hepworth lived and worked near the harbour just behind the parish church. Many of her sculptures and paintings are on exhibition permanently since the Tate Gallery bought her studio and garden and now administers the **Barbara Hepworth Museum and Sculpture Garden**.

Since World War II other artists went to St Ives and produced work that greatly influenced the development of painting in Britain. As a result a new museum, **The Tate Gallery St Ives**, has opened. Managed by the Tate Gallery it displays local artist's work.

Earlier times can be recalled in a visit to the nearby **St Ives Museum**, a building with a history that is interesting on its own account. This site was originally Wheal Dream copper mine but it was unsuccessful like many others, so it was used as

Fishing traditions

On the island beside St Nicholas' chapel in St Ives, a huer's hut looks down on the harbour and Smeaton's Pier. In former days, the look-out posted there would watch for pilchards and then cry 'Hevva!' to the waiting fishermen. After a good catch the toast in the town would be to 'Fish, Tin and Copper'. Today, Cornish cooks remember the hey-day of Cornwall's fishing industry when they make their 'heavy cake'. When the men were on the beach waiting anxiously for the shout that would send them out to their nets, their wives stood beside them. Then when the welcome call announced the approach of a shoal, the women ran home to bake something good for their husbands to eat after toiling with their heavy nets. And it was the 'heavy' – or 'hevva' cake that took just the right time to prepare and cook, being ready, with its criss-cross net pattern on the top, to eat with a piping hot 'dish o' tay' when the weary fisherman returned home.

a store to cure and pack pilchards for exporting to Italy in the mid-nineteenth century. Afterwards the Bible Christian sect took it over, then it became a laundry and later a cinema. The first floor, however, continued to have a maritime connection when a British Sailors Society Mission used it to house shipwrecked mariners who were waiting to be repatriated.

It is strange to see animal traps on show but one could trap three mice inside at once and this is a strong clue to the reason for the local preference for cats. St Ives is known for two types of cat. One is short-backed and stubby-legged, the other a large, contented animal resembling Alice in Wonderland's Cheshire cat. It was no doubt the local interest in cats that probably accounted for the nursery rhyme that helps many youngsters learn to count, 'As I was going to St Ives'.

Between 1925 and 1941 there was a silk factory, on 'The Island', just behind the museum. A unique form of hand block printing on silk was practised here, known as Cryséde, and good examples of this can be found in the museum.

Five splendid sandy beaches, which can accommodate many people, form a golden crescent round the town. On one of them – or perhaps all – Virginia Woolf played when she was on holiday at Talland House and later brought these early memories of Godrevy into *To The Lighthouse*. Today St Ives, with its cliff walks, wind-surfing, fishing and sailing, still welcomes visitors to the essential Cornish atmosphere which people so enjoy.

The train returns from a small station above Porthminster Beach and as it moves away, Tregenna Castle Hotel, one of Cornwall's finest, with its castellated turrets, may be glimpsed high above on the cliff top. The next stop is Carbis Bay, which has such fine, smooth sands that it is perhaps the most popular of all the local beaches. This is in sharp contrast to the appearance it had in the last century when it was used as a dump for mining waste.

John Knill

A Large part of the main room of St Ives Museum is devoted to exhibits connected with John Knill (1733-1811), perhaps the most memorable of all St Ives' citizens. Customs officer, mayor, lawyer and lovable wealthy eccentric, Knill was at one time private secretary to the Earl of Buckingham and a trustee of his estate. Rumour has it that he was also a privateer, and he did have plenty of opportunity for this. On his instructions John Smeaton built the harbour pier which provided such necessary shelter for shipping and Knill built the Steeple monument just outside the town. He intended this to be his final resting place but he was buried in London. In his will he laid down that every 5 years there was to be a ceremony held on 25 July when ten girls and two widows should dance round the Steeple. A strange request but one that has kept his memory alive.

Above: Tate, St Ives

*Left top & bottom:
Life boat, St Ives*

THE HAYLE ESTUARY

Lelant is an unexpected place with a quiet individuality that has to be searched for. This probably stems from the knowledge that it was a thriving seaport in the Middle Ages, long before St Ives achieved popularity.

The church lies behind the Saltings in a village of old-world charm. It is dedicated to St Uny and was the parish church for St Ives as well until 1826. Inside are interesting memorials to members of the Praed family from Trevethoe, the mansion at the foot of Trencrom. William Praed (1620) and his family are remembered in a slate carving, with kneeling figures, flowers, sand-glass and skull. His famous descendants are Mackworth (whose portrait is in the St Ives Museum) and William. The former was the eminent engineer who planned England's canal system, the latter, the banker after whom London's Praed Street is named. Another building of the past is the abbey in Lower Lelant, a long, low sixteenth-century construction, and L-shaped as befits the period. Neither Trevethoe nor the abbey are open to the public.

The St Ives branch line ends at **St Erth,** which is another example of a once proud and busy place. The Star Inn was there in the seventeenth century when the Trewinnards startled everyone by introducing the first private coach to Cornwall. Truro Museum now has that same vehicle in its safe keeping.

Most drivers hurry through **Hayle,** glad when they are beyond it, but its present dullness does, in fact, hide one of Cornwall's oldest ports. This particular estuary has been important since Bronze Age times when copper and gold were sent from Ireland to Brittany via St Michael's Mount.

Centuries later, when the Industrial Revolution demanded the best in engineering, this part of the world provided it. The old wharves, still visible near the railway bridge, were once part of the great foundry and engineering business belonging to Harvey's – known throughout the world simply as 'Harvey's of Hayle'. They provided the world's largest diameter steam engine (12 feet/ 3.5m) to Holland for draining the Harlem Meer, where Schipol Airport is now situated. Known as the De Cruquius Engine it survives near Vijfhuizen on the N201.

Beside the B3302, which leads out of the square and up Foundry Hill, are some remains of this once extensive complex – the hammer mill and the old mill pond can still be found. Those who designed the town's modern purpose-built library were (fortunately) determined that Hayle's great past should not entirely be forgotten and now for all to see on its gable are three original wood patterns for gear wheels for mining machines made in Harvey's foundry in the late 1880s.

Today that secondary road makes its way to a more modern concept – **Paradise Park.** Here is a fine collection of the world's rarest and most beautiful birds, including flamingoes, toucans and free-flying parrots. Within the grounds there is also the Cornish otter sanctuary, an ambitious conservation scheme to help restore the otter to the local countryside.

Another project, probably even closer to Cornish hearts, is 'Operation Chough', a study into the possibility of re-establishing the chough in selected locations on the coast. This rare bird which, with its red beak and legs, was once a familiar sight on Cornwall's rugged cliffs, is associated with King Arthur and so synonymous with Cornwall that it appears on the County Council's coat of arms.

Detailed research has been done in other Celtic parts of Britain and results already show that the chough's decline is closely linked to the disappearance of the Large Blue butterfly. However in 2001, before any birds were released into the wild, three wild choughs appeared on the coast. Two of them bred successfully in 2002 and 2003

so later in 2003 some of the captive-bred birds were released in the hope that they will mate with the wild ones and form the basis of a colony for the future. All sightings of choughs in Cornwall should be reported to Paradise Park.

Copperhouse, now an extension of Hayle, has only the Copperhouse Inn sign and, by the old quay, walls built of dark green copper slag blocks, to serve as a reminder of its former importance as a copper smelting site. Across the Hayle Canal, the romantically named church at **Phillack** (St Felicitas) overlooks the water and nearby is Riviere House where Compton Mackenzie and his sister, the actress, Fay Compton, spent many happy childhood holidays.

The huge stretch of towans (sand dunes) which forms part of St Ives Bay is ideal for holidaymakers to walk, swim, or laze, although all lifeguard's warnings must be observed. **Connor Downs** is a

---

Elizabeth Arden

It would be wrong to leave Hayle without remembering a person who was born in the town and whose name is as internationally famous today as Harvey's was in the last century. She was **Florence Nightingale Graham**, born in 1884, one of the three children of a chemist who encouraged her experiments with cosmetics. The Graham family anticipated the collapse of Cornish mining and in 1908 emigrated to Canada. Young Florence soon moved to New York, became a partner in a beauty salon business but before long, opened her own beauty parlour on Fifth Avenue. She took the name of Elizabeth Arden from the novels, *Elizabeth and her German Garden* and *Enoch Arden*. In 1915 she introduced mascara and eye-shadow and eventually extended her business to thirty-five countries. She also achieved another first when she opened her health farms. In 1966 she died but the company she founded continues to thrive.

Selected Car Drives

A circuit around Newquay

Leave Newquay on the A3075 to Goonhavern. Turn right on to the B3285 and drive slowly for just over 1 mile (1.5km) so that you do not miss the entrance on the right to Piran Round, Cornwall's largest open-air theatre during medieval times – used for 3-day cycles of miracle plays. Follow the road to a junction and leaving the B3285 turn right above the sand dunes to Gear and Cubert. Watch for a T-junction with a right to Newlyn East. This little village is delightful and narrow lanes will take you to Trerice and the Lappa Valley Railway, not adjacent but close. Kestle Mill is on the A3058, follow the road to Quintrell Downs and there wander along the A392 but take a left hand turn towards St Columb Major. You will not get lost. More lanes from there, when you have left the handsome church, will take you to Castle-an-Dinas – a magnificent Iron Age fort. Sir Arthur Quiller-Couch wrote an intriguing novel involving this fort and Fowey. He called it Castle D'or. It is fascinating detective work in history. You are about 4 miles (6.4km) from Tregonetha on the B3274, a road which will take you to a T-junction at the A39. Between 1 and 2 miles (1.5-3km) along there in the St Columb Major direction take the first right for St Mawgan and the delights of the Lanherne Valley. Follow the Trenance direction and you will come to Mawgan Porth and the B3276 which will take you back to Newquay.

Wadebridge to Padstow and back to Wadebridge via the coast

Leave Wadebridge on the B389 road to Padstow and enjoy the villages of St Issey and Little Petherick – especially the churches. Into and out of Padstow on the B3276, where after the village of Treator the second right will take you to Harlyn Bay and semi-circle out to the B3276 again. Drive along it to Porthcothan, small but delightful. About 2 miles (3km) along here you will find Bedruthan Steps, an impressive National Trust section of the coast. Return towards Porthcothan and the first lane on the right will, if you watch the signs, take you to the almost hidden church of St Ervan. Turn right through nearby Rumford and you are on the B3274. Cross the A39 at Winnard's Perch and head for St Breock Downs and narrow lanes which will lead you down to St Breock on the edge of Wadebridge.

sprawling development beside the A30 above Gwithian and many historians think it possible that the ancient city of Connor (Irish for 'haven') lies there beneath the dunes.

THE COAST AROUND ST AGNES

Gwithian itself is a small village with a low-towered fifteenth-century church. The unusual sight of thatch here makes it an artist's delight: animal lovers, however, take pleasure in watching the seals which are sometimes seen at Navax Point (belonging to the National Trust) beyond Godrevy Lighthouse. The cliffs all round here are turfy and good for walking but bathers will find that the water is often stained by the Red River, which collects tin waste on its way to the sea.

In July and early August, the cliffs of **Reskajeage Down** between the B3301 and the sea, are brilliant with gorse and heather. Once past the fearful Hell's Mouth, however, the coastal footpath is easier and safer. The views along the coast towards St Agnes Head and St Agnes Beacon are really spectacular on a bright day; the colours sometimes appear almost too brilliant to be real.

Most of the land between Carvannel Downs and the A30 was once the vast Tehidy estate and belonged to the **Basset** family until about 1921. In 1983 the local council bought the estate's 250 acres (101 hectares) of woodland and restoration work has been in hand ever since. The whole area has been used to encourage the public in matters of environmental conservation as well as offering them a variety of recreational facilities. An events programme is published each year and includes bird watches, bird survey opportunities, etc. The **Country Park** was officially opened in 1987. Quite near the western end of the Park is Magor Farm and it was here that remains of a Roman villa were discovered, something very unusual in Cornwall.

Royalist shipwreck

In 1649, **Godrevy Island** was the scene of a notable shipwreck. After the execution of King Charles I, many loyal subjects tried to save some of his lace-trimmed garments and other possessions and sent them abroad for safe keeping. Unfortunately the ship carrying them was wrecked and only a few of the royal clothes were washed ashore – together with the only survivors, a man, a boy and a dog.

From these roads, and for some distance around, can be seen the Carn Brea monument at Carnkie, Redruth, which was erected to the memory of **Francis Basset de Dunstanville**, a great local benefactor. His main concern was to improve the lot of the numerous poor, especially those who risked their lives gathering the succulent herb that grew in dangerous places on Samphire Island. He built **Portreath Harbour** in 1760 and this not only afforded protection to the ships, but also facilitated the loading and unloading of copper ore. Before that, the ships had to be loaded from the beach, a very irksome task. By 1840, when mining was at its peak, the population of this area was about 30,000 with people at work in mining as well as all the ancillary industries connected with it.

Inland, pleasant minor roads afford a quiet drive towards either Portreath or St Agnes while the section of the north coast path between Portreath and St Agnes has been described as the finest walk in Cornwall. **Porth Towan** and **Chapel Porth** have fine sandy beaches, but the undertow of currents and lifeguards' warnings must always be heeded. All round the National Trust's land at Chapel Porth and inland for some way, there are derelict mine buildings in profusion. The heathery slopes of the cliffs still only partly cover the great heaps of arsenic waste that have been there for so long. In the mid- and late nineteenth century, **St Agnes** parish was one of Cornwall's most active mining areas and those who worked here boasted that *Sten Sen Agnes an gwella yn Kernow* ('St Agnes' tin is the best in Cornwall'.) All these little porths or landing places have been used since very early times and foundations of the chapel trad-itionally dedicated to St Agnes can still be seen in the cliffs at Chapel Porth.

Driving along the B3277 notice the **Presingoll Barns** complex on the right-hand side. Entrance is free and there is plenty of parking space for vehicles while visitors wander round to see potters at work and candles being made. For a small charge they can try their hands at the potter's wheel and candle

Wheal Coates, west of St Agnes on the coastal path

Walks

St Piran

4 miles (6.4km) approx • easy • 2 hours

Map: OS 1:25,000 Explorer Series 104: Redruth and St Agnes

Park your car beside the minor road that leads north-east from the B road about 1 mile (1.5km) east of Perranporth. The path you need starts opposite the lane from Rose. Go through the gate and follow the well-walked path marked with white stones. Bear slightly right following the acorn marker posts of the Coastal Path and aim for the stone cross on the skyline. Placed there about AD900 this Celtic cross marks the site of the Norman church built as a successor to St Piran's Oratory. Then downhill towards the sea and on through the dunes until you reach the mound covering St Piran's Oratory topped with a rough granite block marked 'St Piran'. Your way continues towards the sea, well below with extensive views right and left. Follow the left path, cross a concrete road and continue on the cliffs. Perranporth is soon within view and the way is gently sloping to the beach. Cross the sands keeping left to meet the river and follow the track beside it out to the road. Left here then left again at a waymarker, up steep steps. Stay to the left of the clubhouse and cross the road to a stile. Continue diagonally up a field towards a goal post then another stile takes you over the road to an enclosed path leading to a lane and after a right turn you will find your car.

Part of the Saints' Way

7 miles (11.2km) • quite strenuous • 3-4 hours approx

Map: OS 1:25,000 Explorer Series 106: Newquay and Padstow

At the start of the Saints' Way leave the lych gate of Padstow's church and walk along wooded Hill Street. Then cross New Street, continue along Dennis Lane, past the boating lake and turn left at a footpath sign, then follow Saints' Way signs for about 3 miles (4.8km). After Little Petherick Church, the Saints' Way lies a few hundred yards along the main road before turning right up the valley to Mellingey. Leave the Saints' Way here, follow yellow arrows then after a stile, stepping stones and a footbridge, the path leads to St Issey Church which you leave by the north gate. Cross the main road, follow the yellow arrow to the right, go left after the stile then over a footbridge staying with the path through a right hand gate and keep the hedge on your right. At the road go right, then left and after about 400 yards (365m) take the right signed path. This continues over a grassy bridge up the left of a long field to a gate at another road. Carry on with this, signposted Old Town Creek, and you will reach the River Camel. Leave the

Halwyn car park, go up the steps to the old railway line – now the Camel Trail – and turn left into Padstow.

Crantock

4 miles (6.4km) approx
• easy • 2 hours

Map:
OS 1:25,000 Explorer Series 104: Redruth and St Agnes

Leave Newquay along Crantock Street, cross Tower Road, along Atlantic Road and descend Trethellan Hill signposted to the Gannel. Cross the plank bridge and at the field by Penpol Creek follow the path left to a gate into a wood. Through this is another gate into a sloping field and walk up to a gate on the left of Penpol House, finding a lane to Crantock. The village is very ancient and a lane below the church leads to Crantock Beach and sand dunes. To complete the circuit, leave the village by Beach Road, take the path indicated right through a gate and follow it through bushes and fields for it will take you to the steps down to the pedestrian bridge back to Newquay.

dipping. Delicious teas, fudges, jams and chutneys are available. Take a picnic there or enjoy the Bakehouse refreshments.

On the edge of St Agnes you will find the **Parish Museum**. The handsome **Miners' Mechanics' Institute** in the centre of the village is a different reminder of the past. Built in 1893, it was one of the first of many gifts from the Cornish philanthropist, Passmore Edwards, who was anxious to help the men educate themselves. It is now a club, but inside there are some interesting old mining records. The fine old church lies low beneath the road beyond the Institute. Carrying on down the hill go slowly and notice the picturesque miners' cottages at **Stippy Stappy** along the left side which overlook the area of Peterville.

The north coast route continues along the B3285 towards Perranporth but it is worthwhile making a detour down the first lane on the right after Barkla Shop. This is narrow and steep and motorists need to travel slowly so that they do not miss the thatched cottage called 'Harmony Cot', birthplace of the famous painter, John Opie, who is buried in St Paul's Cathedral. Beyond the ford over the Silver River, so named because of its trout, the lane climbs towards the B3284.

An alternative detour on the left hand side of the road goes to **Blue Hills Tin**. Here the Wills family has been producing tin for almost 30 years and the process can be followed on site. Custom designed giftware and jewellery can be purchased.

Watergate Bay

Leave the car here and walk the short distance along a narrow lane to Trevaunance Cove, which is possibly the real heart of St Agnes and once a busy port from which ships sailed with their cargoes of tin and copper. A glance at the cliffs would make anyone wonder how an important harbour could ever have been built in such a place, but success was only achieved after several efforts. The final attempt of 1793 resulted in completion in 1797 but then stagings had to be constructed on the cliffs so that cargoes could be transferred by means of a horse-whim – a satisfactory arrangement which made Trevaunance Cove the scene of a very lucrative trade.

On the coastal side of the B3285 are the headquarters of the Cornwall Gliding Club, just beyond Cligga Head, an ideal place for bird-watching. Views from these cliffs rival the Mediterranean in the varied colours of the sea, sand and rock formation.

Halfway along the short main street is a turning to the left. It can easily be missed but to do so would mean losing the opportunity of seeing the **Perranzabuloe Folk Museum.** Housed in a handsome Victorian building, this small but fascinating collection of exhibits includes material that depicts life in the parish from prehistoric times.

Beyond the village on the north side is a stretch of sand dunes, once visited by pilgrims from many lands. They came to pay homage to St Piran, patron saint of tinners whose chapel, as old as that of Iona, is now protected by concrete because inroads by the sea had despoiled most of the ancient building. The coast path at the extreme end of Perran Beach is in an area now used by the military so wait for the sentry to give the go ahead if the red flag is flying.

The B3285 climbs out of Perranporth, passing **St Piran's Round**, an impressive Iron Age fortification, adapted in the Middle Ages as a *plen-an-gwary* (playing place) where religious instruction was given in the form of miracle plays. This open-air theatre has an amphitheatre that is 50 yards (46m) across with circular terraces for the audience. In 1969 and 1973 productions of the Cornish medieval plays were performed here – the first time for many centuries.

Goonhavern village, at the crossing of the B3285 and the A3075, is where visitors can enter **World in Miniature.** The world's major landmarks are recreated in miniature among 12 acres of lovely gardens. Rides, young children's soft play and much more offer entertainment for the whole day here.

IN AND AROUND NEWQUAY

About 5 miles (8km) along the A3075 is **Newquay** – a lively town with something for everyone in all weathers and voted first among Cornwall's holiday resorts for its magnificent beaches. At low tide these become one bay but each has a different character when the tide comes in.

Newquay existed as a port in the mid-fifteenth century and the export of pilchards to the Mediterranean was extremely profitable during the seventeenth and eighteenth centuries when the huer's hut below the Atlantic Hotel came into its own. In 1838, **Joseph Treffry** of Fowey decided to use the shelter of this harbour for his china clay exports so he built a new quay. For 40 years cargoes came and went until Par was developed and usurped Newquay's usefulness.

The list of attractions here covers everything holidaymakers expect at a popular resort. Some surprise visitors – particularly the pleasantly situated **zoo and leisure park** set in 8 acres (3.2 hectares) of landscaped gardens, 5 minutes away from the town centre. One or two days could well be spent here during a Newquay holiday.

Today Newquay is renowned for surfing and offers great facilities for devotees of this exciting sport but there is much more besides for those who prefer safer pastimes. **Trenance Park** has gardens, a toboggan run, miniature golf and the indoor delights of **Water World** with its tropical fun pool and flumes. In the big, pink building on St Michael's Road is **Tunnels Through Time**, a mix of fact and fiction that brings alive the history and legends of Cornwall. Further on, at Towan Beach the **Blue Reef Aquarium** takes visitors on an undersea safari to see the life of the oceans.

Towan Head, which stretches out to sea past the huer's hut and the golf course, boasts a small castellated tower and private chapel belonging to the Molesworth family and from here

Cornwall offers another fine two-way expanse of distant coastline. **Pentire Point East** at the opposite arm of Fistral Bay has good views and the vantage point was also appreciated by prehistoric man: tumuli remains have been found to prove this.

There are numerous places of interest near Newquay, including Porth Reservoir off the A3059 to St Columb Major. Along the coast road there are prehistoric round barrows on Trevelgue Head, which lies beyond the bay of Porth on the B3276.

On high ground behind **Watergate Bay** lies **RAF St Mawgan**, formally affiliated to the parish of St Columb Major, the first local authority to be so linked. Come here in August for the International Air Day. The date varies but details can be found in local papers.

Further north, the smallness of **Mawgan Porth** is delightful with the tranquil Lanherne valley leading inland, little known though very lovely. Halfway up the valley and in the shelter of long-established trees **St Mawgan** village hides its charms. The church has Cornwall's best collection of brasses, mainly of the Arundells whose former home was Lanherne, the nearby manor house. It has been a Carmelite monastery since 1794 and the small chapel is open to the public.

The creeper-clad inn opposite seems to have an out-of-place name, The Falcon. Nevertheless it is particularly apt as, during the persecution of Roman Catholics in Reformation days priests celebrated Mass in secret and the signal

THE NORTH COAST (b)

to the faithful that it was about to begin would be the freeing of that particular bird.

The road climbs through leafy lanes to another village that has been important in the past – **St Columb Major**. Once considered a possible site for Cornwall's cathedral it is best known now perhaps for the Shrove Tuesday Hurling Contest when a ball of silver-coated applewood is used in the Town versus Country game. This custom was once a feature of most village feast days and is believed to have originated as a pagan festival in honour of spring.

The handsome church dominates the houses around and, proud of its fourteenth-century foundation, plays host to a popular annual music festival. The Ring o' Bells inn

Above: Tolcarne Beach, Newquay Below: Trerice Manor

across the road is a secular reminder of the fine tradition of bell-ringing associated with this church. And a mere few hundred yards (metres) away is the Red Lion, proud of a former landlord, James Polkinghorne, also Cornwall's most famous wrestler. An unusual memorial on the roadside wall depicts him in action. A short way along the A39 towards Wadebridge is the **Cornish Birds of Prey Centre** where flying displays take place twice a day and visitors also have the opportunity of coarse fishing or quiet walks.

Over the roundabout at the beginning of the bypass there is a sign to Castle-an-Dinas, about 2 miles (3km) along the road. There is only pedestrian access across private land but it is worth the climb for the panoramic view beyond Goss Moor to the china clay country. These remains of a massive Iron Age fort are some 700 feet (213m) above sea level and composed of three concentric rings, hedges and ditches. The single entrance emphasises the wisdom of prehistoric builders.

Black Cross and **White Cross**, which lie between Castle-an-Dinas and Quintrell Downs, could have been named as important stations for pilgrims to Holywell. Or perhaps they were depots for the black and white tin from the moorland. In either case **Summercourt September Fair**, one of Cornwall's oldest, would have been involved.

On the A3058 Summercourt to Newquay road, **Dairyland** offers an unusual look at country life. It is a working farm with 'space-age

milking on a merry-go-round' where 160 cows are milked to music in one of Europe's most up-to-date modern rotary parlours. The museum of rural exhibits in another part of the farm displays tools and instruments used on farms in the past.

At **Kestle Mill** hamlet on the same road in the Newquay direction, a narrow lane winds steeply up to the charming National Trust property of **Trerice Manor**. Protective trees stand round this popular Elizabethan house which is small enough to be a home, yet retains the quality and character of the Royalist Arundells who rebuilt it in 1571. This secluded manor house contains fine fireplaces and plaster ceilings, oak and walnut furniture, and tapestries; a small museum in the barn traces the

Wild West hero

The hamlet of **Ruthvoes** about 6 miles (9.5km) east of Newquay was the birthplace of a man little remembered here, Deadwood Dick, folk hero of many Wild West stories. Born in 1847, Richard Bullock started work in the clay industry then, emigrating to South Dakota became a bullion guard for the Homestake Mine owned by Senator Hearst. Richard's expert marksmanship earned him the nickname 'Deadwood Dick', but in spite of many hazardous journeys on duty, he died peaceably at the good age of seventy-three.

development of the lawn mower! A summer garden has some unusual plants and there is an orchard of Cornish fruit trees.

The **Lappa Valley Railway** at **Newlyn East** takes visitors in a miniature steam train along part of the original GWR Newquay to Chacewater track. At the end of the short ride to a leisure park with various attractions, the historic engine house and stack of the disused East Wheal Rose can be seen here. This was Cornwall's richest lead-producing works until a cloudburst brought disaster to the miners and closure to the mine. The handsome ruin is all that remains.

The road from Newlyn East to **Cubert** and **Holywell** is so straight that it probably follows an ancient pilgrim way. The well which gives the latter place its name is, in fact, not on the beach but about a quarter of a mile (400m) away at Trevornick Farm. This lies behind the extensive dunes set in a wide area of National Trust and Ministry of Defence land – footpaths are clearly defined. The Trust path leads to Kelsey Head and West Pentire on the Newquay side of Porth Joke and is strangely remote though so near to the busy holiday resort. Here the cliff flowers are especially delightful in spring and early summer while the little cove is ideal for families who want to avoid crowds. Porth Joke's unusual name comes from the fact that it was once the haunt of choughs – *chogha* being Cornish and the plural of jackdaw to which family the chough belongs.

It is pleasant to walk from **Crantock** to **Cubert Common**, one of the few enclosed commons in the country, now National Trust land. Another path to take follows the line of the Gannel to Trevemper and Newquay, and, though the beach of this inlet is good for children, it can be dangerous, as the

Legend of the travelling saints

Crantock, just outside Newquay, is an attractive village centred on the Round Garden, the little orchard in the middle belonging to the National Trust. Its ancient collegiate church is on a hill over-looking the Gannel, a sandy estuary. St Carantoc and St Cubert are thought to have been missionary 'saints' who, like others of their kind, travelled in pairs and then settled near each other. The former founded a monastery here and the monks prospered by controlling the estuary trade. It was famed for its learning and had a library long before the days of Caxton. A house in the village – Great Weston – was named after one of the prebendaries who taught here in the collegiate days. In the late sixteenth century it was recorded that Crantock had seven churchyards and seven other parishes to administer. Some historians, however, believe that Langarroc was its original name and a legend of a wicked city buried beneath the sands may perhaps have some foundation here.

river runs swiftly in under the cliffs of East Pentire. A short and different way back to Newquay at this point is by passenger ferry from West Pentire.

PADSTOW AND WADEBRIDGE

Padstow is the next holiday centre along this north coast and rests quietly on past memories. Buildings here date from the Middle Ages and are still relatively unspoiled, with slate-hung and stone cottages and their colourful sheltered gardens edging the one-way route to the harbour. Today, small coasters from the Continent berth next to gaily-rigged yachts. It all looks so peaceful – a very different kind of activity from the scenes of several hundred years ago when Sir Walter Raleigh, then Lord Warden of the Stanneries, presided in the sixteenth-century courthouse on south quay.

Overlooking the harbour is Rick Stein's famous **Seafood Restaurant**. Established in 1975, his television series twenty years later confirmed its status as one of Britain's leading fish restaurants. **The National Lobster Hatchery** can be found on the quay. Perhaps some of the young lobsters released from here into the wild return in catches for the restaurant.

The name of **Thomas Martyn** means little to most people but we

Padstow Harbour

should all be lost without the modern 1 inch maps he originated. Born in Gwennap in 1695, he came to Padstow to teach and pass on his scientific skills. After this he was employed to make surveys of large Cornish estates such as the manors of St Ewe and Tolverne and his work was so accurate that he was eventually prevailed upon to undertake a similar task for the whole of Cornwall. By 1748 he issued his 1 inch to 1 mile map which was not only accurate but beautiful and sold for three guineas each, long preceding any similar publication.

St Petroc, Cornwall's chief saint, settled here in the sixth century and the church dedicated to him is still mostly unrestored from the building which dates from the fifteenth century. Notice its unusual font of blue-black Catacleuse stone from the nearby quarries at Harlyn Bay. The name can also be spelt Cataclew's, as seen on the map at Cataclew Point. The rock here is Palaeozoic but variable in character – dark grey or blue and sometimes even yellowish.

Behind the church and screened from the road by a castellated wall is **Prideaux Place**, one of the few Cornish manor houses still occupied by the family for whose ancestors it was built. In 1987 it was opened to the public for the first time in 400 years and visitors can wander round the 20-acre (8 hectare) deer park and marvel at the great chamber inside the house, gazing up at the embossed plaster ceiling which depicts scenes from the Bible. That dates from about 1585.

The 'Saints' Way'

As you look across Padstow harbour you will be standing at the start of an ancient 26 miles (42km) track across Cornwall now known as the 'Saints' Way'. It was originally used by Bronze and Iron Age traders who preferred the land route to Fowey rather than the dangerous waters at Land's End when they travelled to Brittany from Ireland and Wales. Much later, Celtic Christians also travelled overland and followed the same way but they stopped to build churches, erect granite crosses and open up holy wells. It is in remembrance of them that this long walk has now been established as the 'Saints' Way'. This could well be the central point of an entire holiday because along the way there are so many different aspects of the Cornish scene to be enjoyed.

North of Padstow the public footpath leads to **St George's Well** and on to **Stepper Point** where the spectacular cliff scenery remains unspoilt. There are tracks all round past **Trevone Bay** to Trevose Head. Motorists have to shuttle to and from these coastal points as there is no connecting road. The fine farmstead at the entrance to the hamlet of **Treator** on the B3276 is the birthplace of Sir Goldsworthy Gurney, another great Cornish engineer.

After Trevone Bay, with its clean sand, where rock eddies can be

---

'Obby 'Oss festival

There is one special day – 1 May – when all the world seems to come to Prideaux Place at Padstow. That is when the 'Obby 'Oss festival takes place and the doors here are opened to the blue horse who dances in the staircase hall to the music of an old traditional tune.

Parking is not easy in Padstow during the season and on May Day it is impossible, especially with crowds lining the narrow streets waiting for the procession of this unique folk festival. It takes the form of a dance struggle between 'Oss and Teazer and is thought to represent the conflict between winter and summer or even good and evil, as seen in the story of St George and the dragon. A short distance from the town a spring dedicated to the saint is believed to have gushed forth from the rock immediately he set foot there. But whatever lies behind the old custom, the procession of horse, teazer, dancers, singers and musicians still makes its way annually between houses decked with flags and greenery.

---

dangerous, is **Harlyn**. It is interesting historically because of the gold lunulae and the many prehistoric remains discovered there early in the twentieth century when workmen, digging foundations for a house, uncovered a Neolithic cemetery. Some of the antiquities are to be seen in the museum at Truro.

The toll charged to drive to the point at **Trevose Head** is little enough to pay for some of Cornwall's wildest and roughest coastal views. Few golf courses can be as well sited as the links at Trevose. Open to the headland, with more than ten beaches and the ruins of the chapel where St Petroc converted Prince Constantine close by, they must be unique.

The coastal footpath is difficult to negotiate along these very exposed cliffs, and agile walkers who venture down the steep path to **Fox Cove** will find a delightful place of retreat even at the busiest times. The National Trust have saved the cliffs at **Porthcothan** and in 1966 also acquired 220 acres (89 hectares). That land stretches from **Porth Mear**, past several fine small coves, a fine rock arch and beyond Park Head to **Diggory's Island** at the north end of **Bedruthan Steps**. These rock stairs became eroded to danger point but have recently been restored. There is an information centre, shop, tea-room and car park near this justly famous beauty spot with its spectacular cliff scenery.

Arable fields are under cultivation right to the cliff edge and flocks of sheep are surprisingly numerous. Tamarisk hedges, which are unusual in Cornwall, are planted here not for their beauty but because they afford the most effective protection from salt spray blown off the sea during gales.

After the pleasures of Padstow and its nearby coast, visitors will find it strange to be directed to a disused aerodrome. But it is a pity to miss the church at **St Eval** (pronounced as in 'ever') standing lonely and surrounded by dreary concrete flats, once busy runways. The rather severe exterior of St Eval church belies its character. It is, in fact, one of the most friendly in Cornwall, with open doors for visitors.

In complete contrast, **St Ervan** church is hidden in the wooded seclusion of its churchtown at the end of a narrow lane between sections of the old aerodrome. It is built on a circular Celtic site high above a lush valley and a golden angel at the door – perhaps it is the saint himself – invites you to enter. Inside, there is the Lord's Prayer in Cornish, and some fine old slate headstones on the walls.

From here the lanes wind through Rumford and over the B3274 to the parish of **St Issey**. The rich brown and red-brown stone quarried nearby is used locally, its warm colours reflected from the walls of cottages whose bright gardens border on the road. Where the lane joins the A389 Padstow Road, there is another Ring o' Bells.

Little Petherick takes up a considerable amount of the A389 from here to Padstow, but it is such a delightful village that no one complains. Old slate-hung houses lean towards the mill stream as if sharing a secret. The church is small and very Anglo-Catholic since the beginning of the twentieth century. There is little left of the tiny church that was here 600 years before – only two bells, some bench ends, a font and the thirteenth-century marble slab to Sir Roger

Lemporu, unusually decorated with a human head and a foliated cross. Athelstan Riley became patron here in 1898 and restored building, furniture and vestments to former High Church traditions.

RAF connection

During World War II, squadrons of Coastal Command flew from St Eval station; their badge incorporated a likeness of the church. In March 1959, 205 Squadron presented their standard to this place of worship, where it still hangs. The handsome font cover is an additional remembrance of that occasion. Today, padre and vicar share services as the congregation is drawn from RAF St Mawgan and the civilian homes in this scattered parish.

Wadebridge is interesting for several reasons – its name, its position, its bridge and its own pleasant character. Historians believe that 'Wade' indicates that it had probably been used by the Romans, who crossed the River Camel at that point because of the *vadum* or ford there. In the Middle Ages, before the bridge was built, there was so much traffic at this fording point that chapels were erected to greet travellers and pilgrims. **St Michael's** at the **St Breock** end was licensed as early as 1382 and about 1468 a bridge was built between it and the **King's Chapel** at the eastern end. They were both sold for secular purposes by Queen Elizabeth I in 1591.

So many tales exist about the construction of what Carew called 'the longest, strongest and fairest bridge that the Shire can muster' that more needs to be said about it. In 1538, Leland gave the following interesting account:

Wadebridge wher ther was a fery 80 yeres syns and menne sumtyme passing over by horse stoode often in great jeopardie, then one Lovebone, Vicar of Wadebridge,

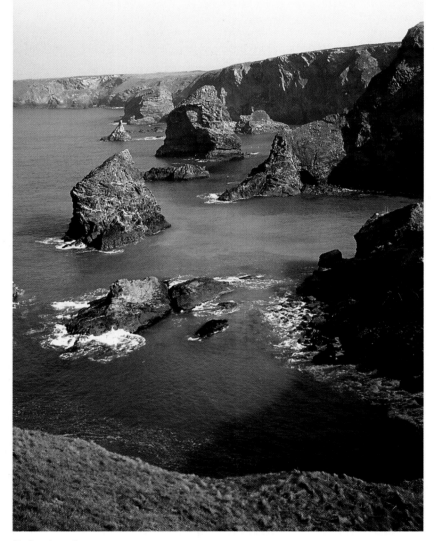

Bedruthan Steps

moved with pitie began the bridge and with great paine and studie, good people putting their help thereto finished it with xvii fair and great uniforme arches of stone. One told me that the foundation of certein of th' arches was first sette on so quick sandy ground that Lovebone almost despaired to performe the bridge untyl such tyme as he layed pakkes of wolle for fundation.

Porthcotham Bay

The Bridge on Wool inn sign agrees with this report and so do those who appreciate that wool solidifies when wet and compressed. Others believe that money to build the bridge came from wealthy sheep farmers in the area, especially those from Bodmin Moor. More recently the bridge has been widened on several occasions to cope with modern traffic, the latest in 1994.

Today those who stand by the river and gaze at the 13 arches of the old bridge looking down stream will see it overarched by the modern bridge over the bypass. This too is a feat of engineering and quite elegant but will it stand the test of time? While by the river look for the little egrets that can be seen there, an unusual bird in the British Isles.

The area around the bridge is depicted in a mosaic by Emma Spring (she also worked with the children on the mosaics at Saltash). It stands by the entrance to the Co-op car park and was presented to Wadebridge by the North Cornwall Visual Arts Project. The slate quays and stone wharves which can still be seen in places beside the river are, however, little more than ghostly reminders of the great trading days of the town, situated where the old pilgrims' way to the Mount crosses the trade route from Ireland to Europe.

Eventually, railways brought a different kind of traffic – holidaymakers and goods to Wadebridge and Padstow, but the line beside the Camel estuary is now only for pedestrians. It provides quiet walking or cycling on the **Camel Trail** – the raised swan nesting mounds are of special interest. The station buildings remain and part of them house the **John Betjemen Centre** with its memorabilia of the poet.

To the south of Wadebridge, an extensive showground lies on high ground beside the A39 from St Columb. **The Royal Cornwall Show** is held here in June when Cornish talents compete in every field. Vintage car rallies and all the many other events taking place here are well advertised. The St

Breock standing stone is also on these, the St Breock Downs. Wadebridge's **Parish Church of St Breock** lies in a tree-encircled valley a little out of the town. It rests peacefully away from the traffic.

NORTH OF THE CAMEL ESTUARY

To explore the area north of Wadebridge, begin at **Egloshayle** (estuary church) on the A389 Bodmin road. The church itself lies on the corner of a lane but is impressive with its 80 foot- (24m) high tower. Inside there is a door, which commemorates the fact that Vicar Loveybond (Elizabethan variant of Lovebone) gave both the tower and a grand east window of five lights. The dedication is thought to be to St Conan, which is unusual in Cornwall.

The lane climbs and twists away to Above Town, turns left, then right at the next junction where it meets unexpected country. The bridge over the River Allen is scarcely a car's width, which indicates the narrowness of the way ahead to **St Mabyn**, a village of many footpaths – all worth exploring.

Three miles (5km) beyond lies well kept **St Tudy**, where there is much of interest. Born and buried here was Richard Lower, the first to perform an operation of blood transfusion direct from one animal into the vein of another and then from man to man. He became the most noted physician in London and was in attendance on Charles II. Unfortunately his interest in politics was ill-timed and the Titus Oates affair caused him to lose everything – his position, his practice, his credit and his Fellowship of The Royal Society. He died at the age of sixty in 1691. There is a monument to Charles Bligh, a member of this St Tudy family, on the wall of St Tudy church, and **Captain W Bligh** of *Bounty* fame was born here.

North from here along the B3266 the village of **Michaelstow** shelters in a valley where the blue and white of wild bluebells and garlic make the churchyard a lovely sight in early summer. High above this protected community the Iron Age earthwork is named on the map as **Helsbury Castle**. Within it is the ruin of a chapel and not far away is Helsbury Farm and Helstone, recalling the possibility of an original cult that worshipped the sun (*howl* in Cornish). When Christianity came to the area, a chapel was built to exorcise the pagan associations and was dedicated to St Michael, whose name was also given to the place where people had settled in the valley below.

It does not matter which of the narrow lanes you take from here to cross the A39 and reach **St Teath**. This is another village that has long since lost its former importance. The church, which is in the centre, was built within a circular Celtic site and so follows the worshipping tradition of centuries but there is now no trace of the collegiate institution once established here.

The countryside picture changes now with open land much more in evidence as the byways join the

B3314 and climb to Tregeare Rounds where the lane before Pendoggett turns sharply towards the sea. As the road nears the coast, the number of footpaths increases – all leading down the valleys and along the cliffs towards Port Gaverne, Port Isaac and Port Quin.

Each of these places has a different history, and has been important in its own way since before Tudor times. **Port Gaverne** used to support a thriving pilchard industry that brought prosperity to the small community even as late as the nineteenth century. The National Trust now owns the beach and two groups of cellars where fishermen used to make and store their pots, nets, sails and gear as well as process their catch.

The name of **Port Isaac** often puzzles those unfamiliar with the Cornish language. It means simply the 'corn port' (*porthysow*) – although it once had additional trade in pilchards and supported a good trade in slate. Now its narrow, twisting streets tumble down to the postage-stamp beach where visitors pay to park their cars in season – at low tide of course. It is a place popular with artists, lovers of small buildings like doll's houses and those who like walking. On the west side of the tiny bay is **Port Isaac Pottery** in what was the United Methodist Free Church. The interior of the church remains intact with gallery and pulpit both of which are used to great effect to display paintings. Hand thrown and individually painted pottery is produced here.

From here the coastal foot-path keeps faithfully to the cliffs but motorists have to run inland through **St Endellion**. The church is another of the various collegiate establishments in Cornwall and has both an interesting history and especially fine bench ends. The ringers' rhyme in the tower is noteworthy as it was written by Nicholas Roscarrock, a recusant whose manor, Tresungers, still retains its former Tudor grandeur and is considered by some to be Cornwall's finest seventeenth-century building.

Witch hunt

Ann Jefferies who was born at St Teath in the early seventeenth century when witch hunts were beginning is still remembered. She entered the service of Moses Pitt, a man unexpectedly well educated for those times. From him she learnt about the healing powers of herbs and helped many with her knowledge. Unfortunately, one of the harsh Tregeagles was jealous of her popularity and had her committed to Bodmin Gaol as a witch. But, though she was deprived of food, she survived her ordeal and was eventually released. Then she married a Padstow man and carried on with her work of healing until she died.

Port Quin is a sad, beautiful place – a place of tragedy. It now belongs to the National Trust, which has adapted the fishermen's

This page: Port Isaac

Opposite page: Sea urchins for sale at Port Isaac

cottages, and the tiny cove, once again, has a cared-for look. In the last century this hamlet was home to fishermen and others employed at the Doyden antimony mine. But eventually it failed and the miners emigrated to Canada. At a later date all the remaining men of the little port sailed out together to fish, were caught in a storm and none survived. Small wonder that Port Quin is known as the village that died, for that is exactly what it did do and is only slowly coming to life again now.

Doyden Castle which looks down from the cliffs edging the cove was built as a gambling retreat in 1839 by a colourful character called Samuel Symons whose home was near Wadebridge. The National Trust bought it and so it is kept in good order. Approaching Polzeath look for the **Porteath Bee Centre**, a living exhibition of bees with a shop full of products from the bee.

Just below lies **Polzeath Beach**, fine for surfing and consequently very popular. Beginners will find tuition at **Surf's Up Surf School** and may be lucky enough to spot the seals and dolphins who swim here regularly. Visitors can learn more about the marine life of the area at the **Polzeath Voluntary Marine Wildlife Area Visitor Centre** adjacent to the pitch and putt course. A series of events takes place over the summer to promote greater awareness of this fragile environment.

The Doom Bar opposite Daymer Bay is composed of sand which makes a good fertiliser and has its own legend. The story goes that a mermaid had once guarded the port of Padstow, but after being mortally wounded by a young man who was tired of her advances, she cursed the place, withdrew her protection and caused the sand to pile up and hinder shipping. It still does, but has now become a blessing as its benefits to farmers are a partial compensation for the loss of shipping revenue.

Rock has wide and beautiful sands and is an estuary beloved by both artists and yachtsmen because of its rare combination of colour and sheltered freedom. It is also a place for sportsmen who tire of the sea –**St Enodoc** has a golf course nearby. The little chapel at St Enodoc was buried in the sands but dug out and restored in 1863. It is mainly Norman but both tower and spire are unusual in Cornwall – the latter dating from the thirteenth century. **Sir John Betjeman**, the Poet Laureate who died in 1983, chose to be buried here because he loved Cornwall dearly and the area of the Camel estuary best of all.

The road back to Wadebridge lies through **St Minver**, another village famous for its bellringers. Like St Endellion, the church has a painted ringers' rhyme and, like Lostwithiel, a broached spire.

Trewarnon Bridge which takes the traffic over the River Amble is of particular interest as it is perhaps the only one built after the Reformation that is worth looking at. It has all the appearance of a medieval design with similar pointed arches, but it is, in fact, little more than a century old and was built by the Georgian squires who found riches under the ground and controlled the destinies of Cornwall through their wealth.

Poet's memorial

The National Trust owns 700 acres (283 hectares) of the land from Trevan Point to **The Rumps** and Polzeath Beach. Saved from bungalow development by popular appeal in 1935, this fine historic promontory might be considered a poet's memorial. Lawrence Binyon sat on this headland and found inspiration for his famous poem *For The Fallen*, with the words that are quoted on Remembrance Day throughout Britain:

'They shall grow not old, as we that are left grow old;
Age shall not weary them, nor the years condemn.
At the going down of the sun and in the morning
We will remember them.'

May is the best time to come here for the flowers are specially lovely then and this is one of the few places where pillow-lava – a volcanic rock which looks like pumice-stone – reaches the surface. Still quite visible are the ruins of an Iron Age cliff castle.

What to do if it rains

St Ives
- St Ives Museum
- Tate St Ives
- St Ives Society of Artists
- Barbara Hepworth Museum

Hayle
- Paradise Park

St Agnes
- Presingoll Barns
- Parish Museum
- Blue Hills Tin

Perranporth
- Perranzabuloe Folk Museum

Newquay
- Waterworld

- Blue Reef Aquarium
- Tunnels Through Time
- Dairyland
- Trerice Manor (National Trust)

Portreath
- Cornish Goldsmiths
- Tolgus Tin

Padstow
- Prideaux Place
- Padstow Museum
- Lobster Hatchery

Wadebridge
- Betjeman Centre

Polzeath
- Porteath Bee Centre

Places to Visit

ST IVES & THE HAYLE ESTUARY

Leach Pottery
Higher Stennack
Established by Bernard Leach in
1920. Still used as a pottery.
His work is also on display.
☎ (01736) 796398
Open: 10am-5pm, Monday to
Saturday, all year.

Barbara Hepworth Museum and Sculpture Garden
Barnoon Hill
Administered by the Tate Gallery,
all in the sculptor's former home.
☎ (01736) 796226
website and hours as Tate St Ives.

St Ives Society of Artists
Old Mariner's Church, Norway
Square
Gallery overlooking the harbour,
committed to support of work with a
bias towards the 'open air' principle
of its founders.
☎ (01736) 795582
Open: 10am-4.30pm Monday to
Saturday and Bank Holiday Sundays,
March to end of October.

Lelant Bird Reserve
Quay House
Overlooking the Hayle estuary an
open hide is available in the grounds
of Quay House.

Tate St Ives
☎ (01736) 796226
Open: 10am-5.30pm daily, March to
October. 10am-4.30pm, Tuesday to
Sunday, November to February.
www.tate.org.uk

St Ives Museum
Wheal Dream
Unique collection of artefacts
covering all aspects of local life.
☎ (01736) 796005
Open: 10am-5pm Monday to Friday,
10am-4pm Saturday, Monday before
Easter to October.

Paradise Park
Hayle
Collection of the world's rarest birds,
otter sanctuary, birds of prey.
☎ (01736) 757407
www.paradisepark.org.uk
Open: 10am-5pm May to September
daily, 10am-4pm spring and autumn,
10am-3pm November to February.

AROUND ST AGNES

St Agnes Parish Museum
Well displayed collection of exhibits
connected with local history.
☎ (01872) 552181
Open: 10.30am-5pm daily Easter to
end of September.

Tehidy Country Park
Best approached from B3301 at
North Cliffs/Reskajeage Downs.
Free access. Visitor Centre on South
Drive. Open: all day and every day
for walks.

Presingoll Barns
St Agnes on B3277
☎ (01872) 553007.
Open: 9am-5pm daily all year,
9.30am-4.30pm during low season.

Perranzabuloe Folk Museum
Ponsmere Road, Perranporth
☎ (01872) 572121
Open: 10.30am-1pm and 2-4.30pm

Places to Visit

Monday to Saturday, Easter, then May to mid-October.

Blue Hills Tin Streams
Trevellas, near St Agnes
Discover the skills of the ancient tinner on the fascinating journey from rock to metal on a tour of the works.
☎ (01872) 553341
Open: 10.30am-5pm Monday to Saturday, all year.

Portreath

Cornish Goldsmiths
All you ever wanted to know about gold. See jewellers at work and pan for gold.
☎ (01209) 218198
www.cornishgoldsmiths.com
Open: 9.30am-5.30pm Monday

to Saturday, 10.30am-4.30pm Sunday all year.

Tolgus Tin
Located with the Cornish Goldsmiths' complex
The last large tin stream works in Cornwall currently being restored to working condition.
☎ (01209) 218198
Open: 9.30am-5.30pm (dusk in winter) Monday to Saturday, 10.30am-4.30pm Sunday.

World in Miniature
On B3285 at Goonhavern
Models of the 'wonders of the world' set amidst delightful gardens. Jurassic Adventure World. Fairground rides.
☎ (0870) 4584433
Open: from 10am daily, Easter to end of October.

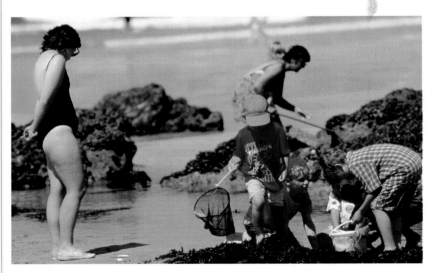

Above: On the beach at Newquay
Opposite page: Sloop Inn, St Ives

IN & AROUND NEWQUAY

Newquay Zoo and Leisure Park

Trenance

Wide variety of animals both large and small, animal encounter sessions, feeding times and keepers' talks. Assault course, and Dragon Maze.

☎ (01637) 873342

www.newquayzoo.co.uk

Open: 9.30am-6pm daily Easter to October, 10am-dusk daily November to Easter.

Places to Visit

Waterworld
Trenance Leisure Park
Fun pool, 25m pool, gym,
sauna and solarium.
☎ (01637) 853828
Call to check opening times.

Blue Reef Aquarium
Towan Promenade
Underwater viewing and hands on
exhibits, Kingdom of the Seahorse,
demonstrations, talks and special
presentations.
☎ (01637) 878134
www.bluereefaquarium.co.uk
Open: 10am daily.

Tunnels Through Time
St Michael's Road
Life size characters bring to life
stories of bygone days in a mix
of fact and fiction.
☎ (01637) 873379
Open: 10am Sunday to Friday,
Easter to October. Also Saturdays
during school holidays and bank
holiday weekends.

Holywell Bay Fun Park
3 miles (4.8km) south of Newquay
Go-karting, fairground rides, play
area and pitch and putt.
☎ (01637) 830095
Open: 11am (earlier in high season)
daily April to September, Sunday,
Tuesday, Wednesday and Thursday in
October, daily for the last week of
October.

Dairyland
On A3058 Summercourt-Newquay
road
Working farm and museum with
farmpark and playground, nature
trail and heritage centre.

☎ (01872) 510349
www.dairylandfarmworld.com
Open: 10am-5pm Easter to
October daily.

Trerice Manor
SE of Newquay
A very attractive National Trust
property – this small manor house
was rebuilt in 1571. It has
contemporary fireplaces and plaster
ceilings. ☎ (01637) 875404
Open: 11am-5.30pm daily except
Tuesday and Saturday, April to
October (closes 5pm in October).
Open Tuesdays also during summer
school holidays.

Lappa Valley Railway
St Newlyn East, near Newquay
Steam train carries visitors along part
of GWR Newquay-Chacewater line.
Leisure park and East Wheal Rose
(engine house and tall chimney
stack) at end of journey.
☎ (01872) 510317
www.lappavalley.co.uk
Open: 10am-5pm daily Easter
to September, plus some days
in October.

Screech Owl Sanctuary
Nr Indian Queens, Goss Moor,
St Columb
Large collection of owl species,
pets' corner, play area.
☎ (01726) 860182
www.owlsanct.freeserve.co.uk
Open: from 10am daily, all year.

Cornish Birds of Prey Centre
On A39 at Winnards Perch,
nr St Columb Major
Sanctuary for birds of prey, flying
displays, coarse fishing lakes.

☎ (01637) 880544
www.cornishbirdsofprey.co.uk
www.meadowsidefisheries.co.uk
Open: 10am–5pm daily, all year.

PADSTOW & WADEBRIDGE

Prideaux Place
Padstow
An Elizabethan house (and deer park) with a magnificent embossed ceiling.
☎ (01841) 532411
Open: 1.30-5pm Sundays to Thursdays, Easter, mid-May to mid-October.

Padstow Museum
Market Place
☎ (01841) 532574
Open: 10am-12noon and 2pm-5pm Monday to Friday, 10am-12.30pm Saturday.

Carnewas, nr Bedruthan
(National Trust)
Bedruthan Steps with beautiful coastal views, information room, shop and tea room.
☎ Shop (01673) 860563
☎ Tea room (01637) 860701
Open: shop, 10.30am-5.30pm daily, April to October. Tea room, 10am–5.30pm daily, April to October; 11am–4pm weekends only November to February.

The National Lobster Hatchery
South Quay Padstow
Aims to enhance lobster stocks around the coast. Visitor centre.
☎ (01841) 533877
www.nationallobsterhatchery.com
Open: 10am-6pm daily May to mid-September; 10am-4pm Monday to Saturday mid-September to April.

Shires Family Adventure Park
A39 near St Columb, 6 miles (9.7km) south of Padstow
Indoor and outdoor attractions for children, shire horses and other farmyard animals.
☎ (01841) 541215
Open: 10am-5pm daily Good Friday to October.

Betjeman Centre
Wadebridge
Former station houses memorabilia of John Betjemen.
☎ (01208) 812392
Open: 10am-4.30pm Monday to Friday, all year.

NORTH OF THE CAMEL ESTUARY

Polzeath Marine Visitor Centre
Adjacent to pitch and putt course
Visitor Centre established to show in a graphic and original fashion most of the life on the seashore.
☎ (01208) 863181
Open: 10am-5pm most days, May to September.

Porteath Bee Centre
Nr Polzeath
Learn about bees and enjoy the bee products.
☎ (01208) 863718
Open: Exhibition, Daily Easter to October. Shop and Pooh Corner, open all year.

Port Isaac Pottery
Working pottery and gallery of ceramics and paintings.
☎ (01208) 880625
Open: 1–4pm in winter; 9.30am to late in summer.

7. Bodmin & The Moor

The town of Bodmin, Cornwall's geographical centre, stands on the Moor beside the River Camel where the twentieth-century A30 (bypassed in 1976) crosses the ancient trade route from Ireland to Europe. Its name means 'abode of monks' for the town grew up around the priory which had been built by St Petroc's followers who settled here in the fifth century.

BODMIN

In 1086, Bodmin was Cornwall's only town and has since been a coinage centre, a meeting place for the Assize Courts (which have now been moved to Truro) and the home of Cornwall's Infantry Regiment. But when Truro became the cathedral city, Bodmin's im-portance rapidly declined and an air of regret for what might have been still seems to linger in the town.

There are, however, a number of interesting places to visit both in and around Bodmin. **St Petroc's** is an imposing building and the largest parish church in Cornwall. Under lock and key in an ivory

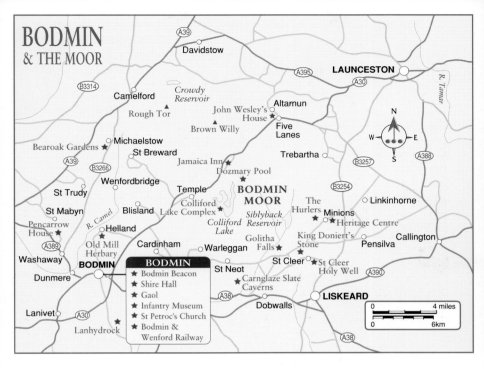

BODMIN & THE MOOR

Davidstow

LAUNCESTON

Camelford

Crowdy Reservoir

Rough Tor

John Wesley's House

Altarnun

Brown Willy

Five Lanes

Bearoak Gardens ★

Michaelstow

St Breward

Trebartha

Jamaica Inn ★

Dozmary Pool ★

St Trudy

Wenfordbridge

Temple

BODMIN MOOR

Linkinhorne

St Mabyn

Blisland

Colliford Lake Complex ★

Siblyback Reservoir

The Hurlers ★

Minions ○★ Heritage Centre

Pencarrow House ★

Helland

Colliford Lake

Golitha Falls ★

King Doniert's Stone

Pensilva

Callington

Washaway

Old Mill Herbary

Cardinham

Warleggan ○

St Cleer ★ St Cleer Holy Well

BODMIN

BODMIN
- ★ Bodmin Beacon
- ★ Shire Hall
- ★ Gaol
- ★ Infantry Museum
- ★ St Petroc's Church
- ★ Bodmin & Wenford Railway

Dunmere

St Neot ★ Carnglaze Slate Caverns

LISKEARD

Lanivet ○

Lanhydrock ★

Dobwalls

0 — 4 miles
0 — 6km

casket, the relics of the saint are preserved – so precious that when a jeweller was asked to value them he said he could not because they were beyond all price. In 1177 these same relics were stolen by an Augustinian monk but were later recovered by Prior Roger of Bodmin after some brilliant religious detective work. Each year, at the annual mayoral elections, the treasures are taken out of the church and carried in procession through the town. At the lower end of the churchyard, down Priory Road, is **St Guron's Well** set in the wall at the roundabout. This is believed to be named after a little-known Celtic saint who came here even before Petroc.

A few hundred metres up Turf Street is Mount Folly, probably the old friary garden, as Folly is a corruption of a Cornish word with that meaning. The **Shire Hall** was the Assize Court until 1988 and it has now been restored to reveal its architectural features of an extraordinary interior cantilevered staircase and the imposing solid granite front façade. The Tourist Information Centre is housed there now along with **The Courtroom Experience.** Visitors can watch a courtroom drama played out and sit as members of the jury.

In the nearby **Guildhall** are two relics from the past. One is a bell, the other a stone corn measure inscribed 'However ye sell – BF 1563 – your measure fyll'; perhaps a warning that the local Weights and Measures official was keeping watch for cheats. Close by is the Turret Clock, a reminder of what happened after the 1549 Prayer Book Rebellion. It was here that the mayor of Bodmin, Nicholas Boyer, was hanged for his part in the uprising.

Bodmin's famous sons

Today the names of Belling and Quiller-Couch are probably better remembered than that of Boyer. John Belling (1680-1761) was a burgess and clockmaker in the town. Today his descendants manufacture electrical equipment used throughout the world. Sir Arthur Quiller-Couch (1863-1944), known as 'Q' was the internationally accepted author who was born in Bodmin. Opposite St Guron's Well, on the wall of the *Cornish Guardian* offices, a memorial plaque marks 'Q's birthplace.

The right fork at the top of Turf Street leads to the 160-foot (49m) Beacon, a pleasant picnic area with fine views. The 144-foot (44m) obelisk at its summit commemorates General Walter Raleigh Gilbert who was given a baronetcy by Queen Victoria for his distinguished service in India.

At the top of St Nicholas Street are the War Memorial and The Keep where the **Duke of Cornwall's Light Infantry Regimental Museum** is housed. There is no charge for admission and even for those with little interest in military matters there is much to catch the eye among the collection of guns, standards, medals and regimental memorabilia which covers 250 years.

From here, Halgavor Road leads down to moorland where a Mock Mayor's Court was held in medieval times. The name, translated from the Cornish, means 'fine for tin streaming and keeping goats' (therefore Goats' Moor). The latest OS map retains the old name in the area south of Bodmin and is marked 'Halgavor Moor' (SX 072652).

Beyond Halgavor Plantation lies **Lanhydrock** – over 2 miles (3km) south-east of Bodmin. Here is everything that most visitors could wish for to enjoy a day of varied pleasure in and around the estate. It is a seventeenth-century house largely rebuilt after a fire in 1881, superbly sited above the Fowey valley and Respryn Bridge. There are fifty rooms open to view in the house alone and a splendid garden.

Respryn Bridge, east of the house, was one of the most important in Cornwall during the Civil War and was held for King Charles when Royalists were encircling the Parliamentarian troops at Lostwithiel in 1644. Four years later, however, although Cromwell's victory was not generally celebrated in Cornwall, Lord Robartes, who owned the estate and had made his fortune from tin, wool and banking, planted an avenue of trees at Lanhydrock and so proclaimed his allegiance to the Roundhead cause.

The Long Gallery was untouched by the fire and in this 116-foot (35m) room the magnificent plaster ceiling depicting scenes from the Old Testament is still in perfect condition. The many acres of garden and woodland given to the National Trust – the latest as recently as 1970 by the 8th Viscount Clifden – are particularly beautiful with fine shrubs, formal gardens and woodland walks. They include Brownqueen Wood, which was the monks' deer park when Lanhydrock belonged to St Petroc's Priory before the Dissolution. The gatehouse (1651) and church are also interesting. There are open-air theatre and other events in summer and a music festival in November.

Take the Fletcher's Bridge turning at the first junction beyond Carminow Cross to find **Castle Canyke** (GR 087658), one of the chain of Celtic Iron Age settlements serving prehistoric tinstreamers and later used on the Ireland to Brittany trade route across mid-Cornwall.

The area south-west of Bodmin along the A389 is equally fascinating. **Lanivet**'s Panda Inn sign puzzles most people who see it for the first time. But the explanation is simple – the bamboos which thrive in this valley went to London Zoo to feed Chi-Chi, the famous panda. A chapel tower rising mysteriously behind a charming slate-hung house is another of this village's curiosities. It is, in fact, the

remains of **St Benet's Abbey**, a leper hospital in 1411 and a Courtenay mansion in the sixteenth century.

The lane opposite the Panda Inn leads to the old Bodmin-Truro coach road – a straight up-and-over way with fine views at the top. Just beyond the farmstead of Mount Pleasant, as this road joins the A30, a lane on the right leads off into a mass of narrow byways of peace and quiet. Through Lower Woodley and Ruthernbridge, with its ancient packhorse bridge, the lane climbs past peaceful farms, numerous little unnamed bridges and on to the old granite cottages clustering round **Withiel** church. In June a festival of flowers and music tempts visitors to linger in this remote village with its many footpaths branching away from the church.

A short distance on the right along the Roche road is another byway – this one leads to the tiny village of **St Wenn**.

Solemn warning

The church at St Wenn is another high and lonely place but is of special interest because of its sundial warning over the porch. Even on a bright day in summer, this place remains solemn. 'Ye Know Not When' say the letters on the face of the old time-keeper.

The country all round here is green and uncluttered and the lanes meander across the valley past

Walks

Roughtor

6-7 miles (9.5-11km) • easy climbing • about 4 hours

Map: OS 1:25,000 Explorer Series 109: Bodmin Moor

After exploring St Breward, the granite village and one of Cornwall's highest, drive down to Tuckingmill, then right at the junction following the mainly unfenced way to a No Through Road sign, passing another saying 'Roughtor 43rd Wessex Division War Memorial' and on into open woodland. The road is bordered by fir on the right till the sign of 'Private Access – No Admittance, Fern Acre Farm' on a huge block of granite shows the place to park the car. The walk begins gently up Alex Tor towards Stannon Clay Works. Leaving the farm track on the right make for Roughtor (Rowtor); in a direct route across the springy turf you arrive at Louden Hill with its Logan Rock (a rocking stone). On to the top with the bronze memorial tablet where once was a chapel dedicated to St Michael. Along this summit are remains of Bronze Age stone enclosures to be noted before descending to a little bridge at the south-easterly valley bottom. This crosses the De Lank River and a well-defined, zigzagging and steep path leads to the summit of Brown Willy with superb views. Follow the path back down to the bridge and head across the moor, keeping the farm track to your right.

Siblyback Lake to Golitha Falls

7-8 miles (11-13km) • easy • 4 hours

Map: OS 1:25,000 Explorer Series 109: Bodmin Moor

Park the car on the east side of Siblyback Lake, north of St Cleer. A lakeside path running south leads to the dam, passing many small sandy beaches on the way. Follow the path to Trekeivesteps, which winds through bracken and gorse before reaching a minor metalled road and a left turn. A pleasant downhill walk leads to Draynes Bridge, built for packhorses in the fifteenth century to cross the River Fowey. The walk downstream is beautiful at any time of the year and made interesting by the need to negotiate occasional stepping stones and footbridges. The sound of water pouring over rocks grows louder as the Golitha Falls are approached. (Note the pronunciation as Goleetha). Walk into the sheltered glade of the falls, a series of small waterfalls and gorges with grassy banks suitable for peaceful picnics and enjoy the beauty before returning to Draynes Bridge. Turn right towards the Doublebois to Minions road and there turn left in a roughly easterly direction. About 800 yards (730m) along this road is King Doniert's Stone erected by the local Old Cornwall Society to remember the ninth-century king of East Cornwall who drowned just 800 yards (730m) away. Follow the road eastwards to a way on your left that leads back to the car park.

Lanhydrock

Distance and time to suit walkers • easy

Map: OS 1:25,000 Explorer Series 107: St Austell and Liskeard

The Lanhydrock Estate consists of nearly 1,000 acres (405 hectares) and the variety of walks through the park and woods offers all visitors a wide, personal choice. Look out for those that connect with the Camel Trail and the Bodmin-Wenford railway – three delights in one day.

Pencarrow Mansion

Rosenannon to St Breock Downs and the prehistoric long-stone or, in the brilliance of furze and heather, to Nanstallon, Dunmere and Bodmin.

Along the road (A389 to Wade-bridge) to **Washaway** is a sign to **Pencarrow**, one of the few fine mansions open to the public and still lived in by the owners. It stands in a perfect setting of 50 acres (20 hectares) of formal and woodland gardens cared for by the owners, the Molesworth-St Aubyns. The house is at the end of a mile (1.6km) long drive (which was cut through an ancient British en-campment) past fine rhododen-drons, camellias and hydrangeas – all under the shelter of towering beech trees. It was probably built about 1771, but the estate has actually been in the family since the reign of Elizabeth I. The owners are often about the grounds and always have a welcome for visitors, which is something that should put it at the top of anyone's itinerary.

An ancient custom

Bodmin is where one of Cornwall's ancient customs used to be celebrated and has now been revived. This was the Bodmin Riding, a horseback procession in July, when guildsmen rode to the priory, received garlands and, after a church service proceeded to take part in various sporting events. The revival has been extended to include mock battles, re-enactments and pageants and is called **Bodmin Riding and Heritage Day**.

Bodmin Jail on Cardell Road is an award-winning museum where models of inmates 'stare' at you from narrow windows. There is also a restaurant and shop. The prison is almost 200 years old and was built because Launceston Jail,

175

apart from being too small and dilapidated, was not central enough. Former days are made very real now by the skilful use of models and properties from the Royal Shakespeare Company while clever lighting and sound effects have been incorporated to recreate startling scenes. At strategic points round the prison complex large information boards not only explain the numerous tableaux but also give background details about life in the gaol at the relevant periods.

Since its closure, Bodmin Jail has been used for purposes varying from manufacturing engineering products to a nightclub. Now its present use as a museum is probably better suited to its structure, although the château-like main gates are so handsome that they seem almost a misrepresentation of the tragic events once enacted within the walls.

The mystery of Bodmin Jail

One intriguing story, still shrouded in secrecy, tells that the Crown Jewels and the Domesday Book were stored here for safety during World War I. The idea was that if an invasion were to take place the treasures could easily be taken to Falmouth and shipped to the secure haven of America. No-one knows just how true the story is but in spite of all doubt, local people accept it as a fact.

BODMIN MOOR, WESTERN SIDE

It is easy enough to reach the centre of Bodmin Moor by driving straight along the A30. Much more interesting is the route through lush valleys making the Moor itself seem even starker by comparison when it is reached at last. Opposite the Hole in the Wall public house on the A30 ring road, Pool Lane leaves the town through Berry Lane and quickly away from the general hustle and bustle. The high land here gives views over the River Camel as does the village of **Helland**. This small place has a church with one of Cornwall's oldest memorials and an old mill house with a delightful herb garden, **The Old Mill Herbary**. Here about 5 acres (2 hectares) of semi-wild terraced gardens and a mini arboretum are home to a large variety of herbs, unusual and rare species of wildflowers, shrubs, trees and climbers.

Deep in the valley below is an early fifteenth-century bridge in fine condition (probably because it is away from main roads). For centuries, every donkey in Cornwall was known as the miner's friend but there are few to be seen here today. Memories of former days are still alive at Helland Bridge – nearby there is a place where these gentle animals were once kept. It is called Donkeys' Pool.

Not far from the Longstone crossroads on the B3266 is **Colesent**. Although this is a dead end it is worth the short detour to see the woods below. There are views from here over the Camel but motorists will have to make other choices. One way is through the tiny hamlet of **Merry Meeting** – a place to visit just for the name, though it is quiet and charming. Up-river lies **Wenford Bridge**, so small that many pass it by, but for many years, until his death in 1983, it was home and workshop to the internationally-famous potter Michael Cardew. Still active in his eighties he had enough energy to create works of art envied by many and right up till his death his enthusiasm and fascination for the craft of pottery remained undiminished.

Moorland travel consists very much of criss-crossing rivers or avoiding them altogether. From Wenford Bridge it is a question of taking the short route south on the east of the Camel and passing china clay works, then crossing the De Lank River to **Blisland**. Much has been written about this village because it looks so different from every other one in Cornwall. Granite cottages, the Manor House and the old inn are set round what is almost a village green. The dedication of the church to St Protus and St Hyacinth is rare. So is the building's beautiful interior with its breathtaking rood screen, restored in 1896 in pre-Reformation style and one of the finest in Britain.

Away from the village, on Pendrift Common, is **Jubilee Rock**. It is 700 feet (213m) above sea level and so the views from here are excellent. In 1809 a Lieutenant Rogers made a place for himself in history by carving this great boulder with coats of arms of royalty and noble families as well as various symbols of agriculture and industry.

From Blisland, beside the Manor House, two other roads twist to the north and climb higher to moorland. Here visitors can find a place to picnic and get a different view of the Camel before taking the Bradford road to **Kerrow Downs**, a wild area, but not like Stevenson's 'naked moor' because the boulders and heathers provide a low landscape that is so characteristic of Cornwall's moorland regions. There is an old clapper bridge at **Bradford** and it is tempting to sit beside it and think of the days when it was busy with sheep, shepherds and wool merchants with their packhorses laden for market.

There is another clapper bridge at **Dulphy** which carries the narrow road over boulder-strewn moorland to **St Breward** which, at 720 feet (219m) above sea level, is Cornwall's highest village. This whole area was more thickly populated by prehistoric man than anywhere else in the region. Hut circles, stripple stones, stone circles and the unexcavated King Arthur's Hall are all within walking distance. There is plenty of scenery here to fire the imagination. Like Luxulyan, this is another granite village, solidly built against all weather. The stone for the houses and cottages came from nearby De Lank quarries which also sent granite to London's Blackfriar's Bridge, the Wolf Rock Lighthouse, Eddystone and Beachy Head Lighthouses, as well as harbours and other buildings in distant parts of the world.

There are various ways from here to Roughtor including several moorland paths. The quickest for motorists is to drive down the steep hill into the woods at **Tuckingmill** and turn either left or right. The latter route, which passes eventually through **Watergate**, is for those prepared to brave some very narrow but lovely lanes. The more straightforward road over the Gam Bridge goes right along the B3266 near to Michaelstow, but at **Valley Truckle** just before Helstone, turns to Watergate and the moor again. Truckle is a misformation of Tucking with its wool trade associations.

Roughtor, sometimes spelt Rowtor, is understandably popular and in the season the small car park is rarely empty. Here Forestry Commission woods are pleasing to the eye in this barren treeless locality. Near the stream is a monument marking the spot where the unfortunate eighteen-year old Charlotte Dymond was murdered in 1844 by her lover who was hanged at Bodmin for his crime. The National Trust own 174 acres (71 hectares) of the land about Roughtor which, rising to 1,300 feet (400m), is the second highest

Above: Horses on Bodmin Moor
Opposite page: A Celtic wayside cross on Bodmin Moor

point in Cornwall. It was a Bronze Age settlement and remains include hut circles and enclosed fields with signs of lynchet cultivation. This tor was given to the Trust in 1951 by Sir Richard Onslow, as the 43rd (Wessex) Division memorial to its men who died in World War II. The bronze tablet is set within foundations of the ruined chapel of St Michael.

The signpost at the crossroads along Jubilee road past Roughtor Farm points to Davidstow. About 1 mile (1.5km) along is **Crowdy Reservoir** which shines a deep aquamarine on bright summer days. There are opportunities here for wind-surfing, and birdwatching from a special hide, but permission must first be obtained from the South-West Water Authority.

THE CENTRAL MOORLAND

The sudden flatness of the road through Davidstow Woods is a strange contrast to much of the countryside. Crossing a deserted airfield it skirts the northern edge of Bodmin Moor along softer lanes leading to **Altarnun**. Here the old Launceston to Bodmin road used to carry coaches over the picturesque fifteenth-century bridge in the centre of this tiny village, the heart of Cornwall's largest parish. Beside it is the Cathedral of the Moor, a handsome building dedicated to St Non, mother of the Welsh St David. The church is as fine inside as out, with 79 Tudor bench ends and massive piers, each pillar made from a single piece of moorstone. Northey Burnard's slate carvings in the churchyard are said to equal the best in Europe.

The highest place in Cornwall, **Brown Willy** (1,375ft/420m), lies behind **Jamaica Inn**, an eighteenth-century coaching stage made famous by Daphne du Maurier's novel of the same name, in the tiny hamlet of **Bolventor**. The hill is reached only by footpaths, as the nearest road stops at Codda, about 1 mile (1.5km) in from the A30. The source of the River Fowey is between nearby Maiden Tor and Buttern Hill. Opposite Jamaica Inn there is a road that leads to one of Cornwall's mysteries – **Dozmary Pool**. In the midst of nowhere it seems, this area of water is reminiscent of lines by R L Stevenson about 'a naked moor, and a shivering pool.'

In 1533 Dozmary was reported to be fourteen fathoms deep but no one knows how it exists as no stream flows into it and it drains no part of the moor. One legend says that there is an underground connection with the sea, possibly because the name means 'drop of sea'. It has a strange unearthly beauty and an exhilarating brilliance that attracts people whether they want to solve its riddles or not. Two legends remain very firmly associated with this interesting place. One about King Arthur and Excalibur, another how the villain Tregeagle lost mansion and parklands beneath these waters and was condemned to empty Dozmary using only a limpet shell with a hole in it.

A short distance away at **Colliford** beside a new reservoir is the **Colliford Lake Park Complex** where many endangered species of animals can be seen in the 60-acre (24 hectare) conservation area. Of different interest is the twelfth-century Cornish Long House, a

---

John Wesley

At Five Lanes, near Altarnun lies Trewint and **Isbell Cottage**, famed for its associations with John Wesley. A Burnard carving of Wesley's head should be noticed on the façade of the Methodist chapel at Altarnun. This cottage lies in a lane which runs parallel to the A30 and it was here that Wesley stayed six times with the hospitable Elizabeth and Digory Isbell, conducting services from the stone porch and on one occasion baptising one of their babies.

He journeyed to Cornwall in an endeavour to bring people back to the Anglican Church, which he begged them never to forsake. But events took quite a different turn, resulting in the establishment of the Methodist movement, causing the great eighteenth-century schism in the Church of England. After some time the Trewint rooms fell into decay but in 1948–50 they were restored to their eighteenth-century style. Now a special service is held here annually on Wesley Day, 24 May – others on Sunday afternoons during July and August.

Selected Car Drives

Bodmin to Pencarrow and return
Take a lane off the A389 in central Bodmin towards Berry Tower, passing the cemetery on the left, making for Helland. At Helland Church, take the left turn where the junction road falls down to Helland Bridge. It rises on the other side, crossing the B3266 to St Mabyn then down across the River Allen. Immediately left follow a very minor road over a railway line to Castle Killibury, an ancient earthwork seen on both sides of the lane which meets the A39. Take the left road towards Croanford and Pencarrow where the 1 mile (1.5km) long drive flanked by huge rhododendrons, specimen conifers and blue hydrangeas, leads to the Georgian house. The Washaway road (A389) takes you back to Bodmin.

Bodmin to Jamaica Inn, the Eastern Moor
About 12 miles (20km) eastwards from Bodmin along the A30 lies Jamaica Inn and Daphne du Maurier country. At Bolventor the road is signed to Dozmary Pool with its alleged connections with King Arthur. On the road leading to St Neot the moorland views are very fine. Colliford Lake Country Park lies to the right. The stained glass windows at St Neot should be seen before driving across the river to Pantersbridge and Warleggan then round the lanes to Cardinham. Join the A38 in the lovely Glynn Valley where a right turn leads back to Bodmin.

single-storey dwelling with a thatched roof and cob walls typical of the period – a rare sight in the region.

Walkers can cross the moor to **Temple**, but motorists have to return to the A30 and drive towards Bodmin, turning left on to the old coach road to this hamlet. From the china clay works at **Hawk's Tor** there is a track which leads through Temple. It was the old way for tinners who, having won their ore from that great granite outcrop, guided laden packhorses down the Warleggan Valley to the harbour of **Lostwithiel**. The simple church stands on the site of a house built by the Knights Templar as a hospice for pilgrims on their way to the Mount. It was that foundation which eventually put it outside episcopal jurisdiction to become Cornwall's Gretna Green with an unsavoury reputation. That extra-legal status continued till about 1744.

THE MOORLANDS EAST OF THE RIVER FOWEY

To explore the southern area it is advisable to start from Bodmin where the A38 dips into the Glynn valley woods; there has been a considerable amount of road widening here recently but it is still delightful, especially in spring and autumn. The road runs close to the

River Fowey and provides easy access for fishermen.

At the far end of this valley, from Doublebois, narrow, bouldery lanes, colourful in spring, climb to the quiet grey village of **St Cleer**. It has several interesting features, its handsome church tower, and the roadside holy well carefully restored by Captain Rogers in 1864 as a memorial to his grandfather, the Reverend John Jope, vicar of St Cleer, 1776–1844.

From St Cleer, the road leads to **Trethevy Quoit**, an ancient monument standing in a field at the back of some cottages – seeming to guard them. It is a megalithic chamber, 7 feet (2.1m) long and about 9 feet (2.7m) high. The shape is that of a capstone supported by five uprights. It is believed to have been constructed some 4,000 years ago by Bronze Age people for use as a burial chamber for their tribesmen. These huge granite slabs were probably taken from the moor but it is not yet known what method was used to place such great weights into position.

Beyond the Crow's Nest hamlet more narrow lanes climb up to open moorland below Caradon Hill. In this landscape of deserted mines, **Pensilva** seems to be at the top of its own quiet world. Yet in the mid-nineteenth century it and the surrounding villages were so crowded that they looked more like the mining camps of Colorado and the far West. Today the moors are for sheep and those who enjoy walks away from roads. It is a pleasant, easy path up to Caradon where, as well as views to Brown Willy, Plymouth and Dartmoor,

there are blueberries to pick in summer.

North of Pensilva are **Caradon Town** and **Linkinhorne**, once both busy mining centres, but the former is now only a handful of houses. Linkinhorne church, set in its frame of trees, has an unusually handsome granite tower and fine wall paintings rediscovered as recently as 1891 and representing the Seven Works of Mercy and the Seven Deadly Sins.

Beyond Coad's Green on the B3257, a narrow lane on the left leads downhill to Trebartha and East Moor. From Trebartha Barton, a lane ends in lonely moorland high among prehistoric hut circles. There are paths everywhere and numerous places to explore **Smallacombe Downs** being particularly exciting with its views over King Arthur's Bed and the River Fowey on the far side.

Memorial to a mathematician

Daniel Gumb's memorial can be found at Linkinhorne. He was a unique Cornishman who lived with his wife and children in a house built under a granite slab near the Cheesewring on the moor. But he was no idler. He taught himself mathematics and the works of Euclid in order to study astronomy, working out the more complicated geometric problems on rocks. His carvings can still be seen by those with really keen eyes.

Above: Altarnun Church

Below: Jamaica Inn

Twelve Men's Moor is here, too, an ancient tin-streaming area known for seven centuries by that name. History records that in 1284 the prior of Launceston granted a lease there to 12 hard-working tinners. Among them were men with names that deserve to be recorded, such as Boglawoda, Cada, Foth, Trewortha and Broda. The road from Beriowbridge to Henwood, so busy in the past, is wooded and delightful, climbing up again to moorland. It is so peaceful yet so full of memories, with old engine houses and mine chimneys.

At **Minions**, parts of an old mineral railway track can still be seen and in numerous places nearby there are Neolithic and Bronze Age monuments. Paths from this hamlet lead to the **Cheesewring** where, until the 1950s, quantities of silver-grey granite were quarried and sent to Liskeard and Looe to be exported. The main fascination of this place for most people is the strange stone formation called the Cheesewring. It is the remains of a cairn where large thick oval slabs balance precariously. The rocks, about 22 feet (6.7m) high and 17 feet (5.2m) in diameter have been formed by nature and weathered over the years to the fantastic shape that remains.

Beside Minions is **Caradon** – its modern television mast at the top of the 1,210-foot (369m) hill. On the right, past the houses is a notice to **The Hurlers Stone Circles**. These strangely-shaped stones have, not unnaturally, given rise to local legends. Whatever the legend says, the facts are that these shapes suit their environment and add to the feeling of Cornwall's past that lingers still on Bodmin Moor. Archaeologists tell us that these ancient megaliths are excellent examples of three Neolithic or very early Bronze Age circles. Excavation at the nearby Rillaton Barrow revealed a gold cup which is now in the British Museum.

At Common Moor, a lane on the right leads to **Siblyback Lake**, one of the best recreational reservoirs in Cornwall. Those who want to fish or sail need permission from the South-West Water Authority but otherwise there are walks and picnic areas for the general public.

THE MOORLAND WEST OF THE RIVER FOWEY

Redgate lies at the crossroads where there is a signpost to the hamlet of **Draynes** (originally Drayness) – its bridge probably the first over the Fowey. It was recorded in 1362 and carries a very ancient track from Caradon to Bodmin. Here a car park is close to the footpath which leads through dense beech woods to the **Golitha Falls**. The water cascades for over 800 yards (800m) of twisting cataracts and the Fowey is seen in majestic splendour. The pronunciation is 'Goleetha' which means obstruction.

The Draynes to **St Neot** road is undulating, sloping steeply to this remote village. High beside the road stands the church dedicated to a kindly dwarf. The interior is famous for its well preserved fifteenth-century and early six-

King Doniert Stone

There is another English Heritage site, **King Doniert Stone**, at the road-side just beyond Common Moor. Here, however, are actual historical records carved on two granite monoliths. One is inscribed with the Latin words *Doniert Rogavit Pro Anima* – 'Doniert prayed for his soul'. Doniert is thought to have been Durngarth, King of Cornwall in the latter half of the ninth century.

teenth-century stained glass conveying the impressive beauty of pre-Reformation windows. They tell the story of the Christian religion from the Creation but the windows of St Neot and St George were later additions. Look for the five historic crosses in the churchyard.

Although there is little now to indicate a busy industrial past, St Neot and the Loveny Valley were much involved with the wool trade as well as silver, copper, tin and slate. A short distance down the wooded valley are the **Carnglaze Slate Caverns**, known to have been worked from ancient times. Visitors taken round on guided tours can see another aspect of the Cornishman's skill when confronted with the need to 'win' any substance from under the surface. One of the surprises is the great lake, a sight as dramatic as the Blue Grotto on Capri.

During World War II the Royal Navy used the first cavern at Carnglaze as a rum store. It has recently been converted to a 400-seat auditorium called the **Rum Store** and during the summer a variety of performances are held here. The shape of the cavern ensures that the acoustics are outstanding.

The road back to the moor leaves St Neot and climbs to Goonzion Downs and Pantersbridge – a name with a double meaning, appropriate for a double bridge. A charter of 1241 mentions a place on the high road to Bodmin called Pontiesu, named by the Knights Templar as 'Jesus Bridge' or Pont-jesus and later corrupted to Pantersbridge. It has charm in its own right, and the second roadway, which eventually took the increasing traffic from Liskeard to Bodmin, is something that adds to its character.

Due north is a farm track to **Warleggan** – one of the names Winston Graham used in his *Poldark* books. The village is today a desolate, ghostly place, almost deserted, perhaps because the last resident vicar, disapproving of the congregation, locked them out of the church and afterwards preached to cardboard figures.

The way back to Bodmin passes through **Mount** and **Cardinham**. Here, two ruined castles and echoes of the ancient nobility still remain.

Places to Visit

IN & AROUND BODMIN

St Petroc's Church
Largest parish church in Cornwall.
☎ (01208) 73867
Open: 2-4pm daily Easter to end of September. Other times by arrangement with the clergy and church warden.

Duke of Cornwall's Light Infantry Regimental Museum
The Keep
Cornwall's premier military museum. Military exhibits.
☎ (01208) 72810
Open: 9am-5pm Monday to Friday all year.

Bodmin Jail
Berrycombe Road
A chilling exhibition of prison life with pillory, stocks, dungeon and execution block, well presented and maintained. Shop and restaurant.
☎ (01208) 76292
Open: 10am-6pm daily, Easter to mid-October (11am on Saturday). Telephone for winter opening times.

Shire Hall
Mounty Folly
Fine building that houses A Courtroom Experience, a Tourist Information Centre and a Town and Countryside exhibition.
☎ (01208) 76616
Open: 10am–5pm, Monday to Saturday.

Lanhydrock
(National Trust)
$2^1/_2$ miles (4km) SE Bodmin
A seventeenth-century house, largely rebuilt after fire in 1881. The gatehouse (1651) and north wing are unaltered. Good restaurant facilities.
☎ (01208) 73320
Open: 11am-5.30pm late March to October daily except Mondays (closes 5pm in October). House open Bank Holiday Mondays at same time. Garden open throughout the year 10am–6pm.

Bodmin and Wenford Railway
Bodmin
From Bodmin Parkway to Boscarne Junction. Many special events.
☎ (0845) 125 9678
www.bodminandwenfordrailway.co.uk
Open: March to 1 January. Trains every day during high season and school holidays, less often at other times. Timetable varies with season, telephone or check website for details.

Pencarrow
Off the A389 and B3266 at Washaway
Historic Georgian mansion owned and occupied by the Molesworth-St Aubyns. Refreshments.
☎ (01208) 841369
www.chycor.co.uk//pencarrow
Open: 1.30-5pm Easter to mid-October, Sunday to Thursday. June to mid-September and bank holiday Mondays open 11am. Gardens open daily during the season.

Above: Golitha Falls

Below: Bodmin Moor

Places to Visit

THE MOORLAND EAST OF THE RIVER FOWEY

Trethevy Quoit
Near St Cleer
A handsome prehistoric burial chamber of five standing stones and a capstone. There is free access at all times.

Minions Heritage Centre
Former mine engine house that describes 4,000 years of history on nearby Bodmin Moor.
☎ (01579) 362350
Open: All year round, 10am-5pm (often late in summer) admission free.

Siblyback Lake
1 mile (0.6km) through Common Moor
An extensive recreational area with space for walks and relaxation.
☎ (01579) 346522

THE MOORLAND WEST OF THE RIVER FOWEY

Golitha Falls
3 miles (4.8km) N Dobwalls
Here the River Fowey cascades through deep woodland over shelves of smooth rock once obstructing its path. Parking facilities by the road at the entrance to the Falls. The path starts across the road and entrance is free. Toilet facilities.

Carnglaze Slate Caverns and Rum Store concerts
Near St Neot
Underground slate caverns of unknown extent though work has been done here for over 200 years.

Guided tours to the famous subterranean lake with its blue-green water. Jumper and sensible shoes advisable. Music performances of all kinds in the Rum Store.
☎ (01579) 320251
www.carnglaze.com
Open: 10am-5pm daily except Sunday, all year.

BODMIN MOOR WESTERN SIDE

Crowdy Reservoir
Off A39 Camelford-Bude road
Walks all round but for other pursuits permits are needed.

Helland Bridge
Old Mill Herbary
Camomile lawn and named unusual culinary, medicinal and aromatic herbs.
☎ (01208) 841206
Open: 10am-5pm daily except Wednesday, April to September.

CENTRAL MOORLAND

Isbell Cottage
Trewint, off A30
A place of pilgrimage for Methodists. On 24 May open-air services are held here. This cottage is not a museum but has many treasures.
☎ (01566) 86158
www.wesleycottage.org.uk
Open: 9am-dusk every day except Christmas Day.

Jamaica Inn
Bolventor
Now popular restaurant. Buildings genuinely Georgian but spoilt inside with simulated Tudor. Still retains

some old-world charm. Daphne du Maurier room.
☎ (01566) 86250
www.jamaicainn.co.uk

Daphne du Maurier's Smugglers Museum
Jamaica Inn
The Jamaica Inn story told in tableaux, sound and light. Collection of smugglers' relics.
☎ (01566) 86250
Open: February, March, November, December 11am-4pm; April, May, June, September 10am-5pm; July and August 10am-7pm.

Colliford Lake Park Complex
A30 Bodmin to Launceston follow signs to right
A delightfully sited area of 60 acres (24 hectares) with rare breeds of birds, cattle, poultry, sheep and twelfth-century Cornish Long House. Lakeside walks, pets corner, picnic areas, indoor play areas. Refreshments.
☎ (01208) 821469
www.collifordlakepark.com
Open: 10.30am-5pm daily Easter to October.

What to do if it rains

Bodmin
- Duke of Cornwall's Light Infantry Museum
- Lanhydrock (National Trust)
- Bodmin Jail
- Shire Hall

Washaway
- Pencarrow

Wenford
- Bodmin and Wenford Railway

Trewint
- Isbell Cottage

Bolventor
- Jamaica Inn and Museum

St Neot
- Carnglaze Slate Caverns

8. North Cornwall

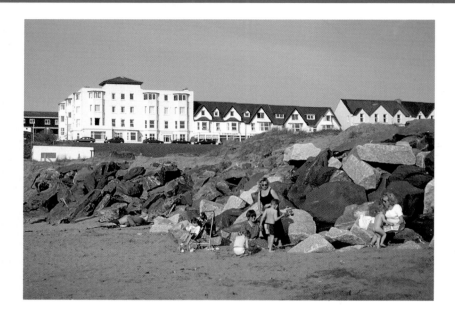

Robert of Mortain established Launceston as Cornwall's northern gateway and ancient capital when he built his strategic keep in about 1067 at the top of precipitous slopes overlooking the Tamar. He probably built Polston Bridge at the same time, thus re-routing the ancient pilgrim way from Kilkhampton. The first charter of Launceston's Borough Archives proudly calls the new road *Via Regalis Cornubiensis* – The 'Royal Cornish Way'.

Ownership of land was still a feudal matter in Norman times, especially in the case of Polston Bridge. Estates in Cardinham were only given conditionally – the condition being that when the Earl of Cornwall crossed the Tamar at this point, the Lord of Cardinham would meet him and, bearing his riding cloak, stay with him for 40 days or as long as he was in Cornwall. This ancient feudal custom still holds good, though today's dues are different. Prince Charles, who is Duke of Cornwall, went to Launceston in 1973 and received his rights from the Lord-Lieutenant. They were a brace of greyhounds called Whisky and Soda.

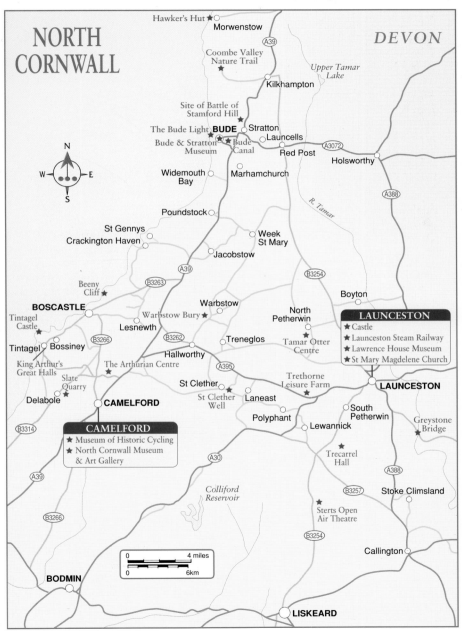

NORTH CORNWALL

DEVON

Hawker's Hut ★
Morwenstow
A39

Coombe Valley
Nature Trail ★

*Upper Tamar
Lake*

Kilkhampton

Site of Battle of
Stamford Hill ★
The Bude Light ○ **BUDE** ○ Stratton
Bude & Stratton ★ Bude ○ Launcells
Museum ○ Canal
Red Post
A3072
Holsworthy

N
W ● E
S

Widemouth ○
Bay
○ Marhamchurch

A388

R. Tamar

Poundstock ○

○ Week
St Mary

St Gennys ○
Crackington Haven ○
○ Jacobstow

Beeny
Cliff ★
B3263
A39
B3254
Boyton

BOSCASTLE ○
Warbstow ○
North
Petherwin
Tintagel
Castle ★
Warbstow Bury ★
Lesnewth ○
B3266
B3262
Trethorne
Tintagel ○ Bossiney ○
Hallworthy ○
Treneglos ○
Tamar Otter
Centre ★

King Arthur's
Great Halls
Slate
Quarry
The Arthurian Centre ★
A395

Delabole ○
○ **CAMELFORD**
St Clether ○
St Clether
Well ★
Laneast ○
Trethorne
Leisure Farm ★
LAUNCESTON
★ Castle
★ Launceston Steam Railway
★ Lawrence House Museum
★ St Mary Magdelene Church

LAUNCESTON

B3314
Polyphant ○
Lewannick ○
South
Petherwin ○
Greystone
Bridge ★

CAMELFORD
★ Museum of Historic Cycling
★ North Cornwall Museum
& Art Gallery

A39

A30

Trecarrel
Hall ★

A388

*Colliford
Reservoir*

B3266

B3257
Stoke Climsland ○

Sterts Open
Air Theatre ★

0   4 miles
0   6km

B3254

Callington ○

BODMIN ○

LISKEARD ○

LAUNCESTON

English Heritage is responsible for the upkeep of **Launceston Castle** which is a fine monument overlooking the town and the surrounding countryside. A cylindrical keep and ruined curtain walls are all that remain, but it is still worth a visit if only to understand its importance as a strategic site.

Immediately below, in Castle Street, is **Lawrence House Museum**, a handsome period house full of exhibits relating to the history of the town and neighbouring places. It is one of Cornwall's best museums – its moulded plaster ceilings are particularly fine. A steep road – with one-way traffic down – leads to the parish church.

A stroll around the town through its narrow streets reveals examples of architecture from Tudor times to the modern day. Look upwards to see the town clock and old signs such as the boot above a former shoe shop. Streets in Launceston are short and, although **Southgate** is two roads away, it is, in fact, reached in a minute. This handsome Norman arch, all that remains of the walled town defences, has been widened to accommodate increasing traffic. Above the arch and up a flight of extremely steep steps are rooms with a history, as they were originally for soldiers on guard duty and later housed the town's criminals.

Visitors who see Launceston on market day will be very much aware of the **White Hart Hotel** with its sturdy door. Historians believe that not only the door but the entire doorway, complete with columns, may have been rescued from the chapel of the castle, possibly when the stronghold fell to Cromwell in 1646.

AROUND LAUNCESTON

This pleasant town is a good holiday centre for studying the old packhorse bridges crossing the Tamar, Kensey and Inney Rivers and the neighbouring picturesque valleys where quiet corners of

Memorial church

The church of **St Mary Magdalene** in Launceston was built under tragic circumstances by Sir Henry Trecarrel who owned an estate a few miles south of the town. While engaged on building his manor house there, he lost both his wife and little son and, grief-stricken, gave up all thought of completing his home and devoted his life to building the church and all matters concerning it. Particularly notable is the superbly carved granite exterior with not an inch of this hard stone undecorated. The motifs vary from prayers and angels to roses, pomegranates and coats of arms – those of Trecarrel and Kelway are on the upper storey of the south porch. The church was probably completed by Kelway who, it is believed, married one of Trecarrel's daughters.

countryside are still to be found. The Tavistock B3362 road from Launceston leads immediately to leafy lanes, some unusually narrow for motorists used to motorways. This way lies **Greystone Bridge** (1439) described by Cornwall's historian, Charles Henderson, as 'the fairest bridge in the two shires which it links together... for beauty of situation and perfection it has no superior in the Western Counties'. Today, it is frightening to watch juggernauts roll across but in spite of everything the structure stands firm. This proves the skill of medieval builders who were paid with indulgences – the conscience money of sinners who repented, hoping to buy their way to Paradise.

The sharp slate hedges of this area are screened by ferns and the lanes meander peacefully by re-mote places like **Lawley Bridge** and **Beale's Mill**, to **Tutwell** and **Horsebridge**. After **Greystone**, the Tamar winds through some of the finest inland scenery in Cornwall, mainly woods once belonging to the great Benedictine house of Tavistock. The name Horse-bridge has no animal origin but is a corruption of Hautes Brigge, then Hawte Brig. The flat wide meadows on either side are a great contrast to the wooded valleys of the upper and lower Tamar.

Since 1337, **Stoke Climsland** and much of the surrounding land has been Duchy of Cornwall property, including the church patronage. The first duke, the Black Prince, was a good landlord, much concerned with the responsibilities of

his estates and in 1354 he gave six oaks from this deer park (now a farm) towards the construction of **Stoke church**. This old building stands central to the village, which is high above rolling pasturelands and rural countryside and there is a quiet contentment about the lane running between it and the village shop opposite.

Stoke Climsland Post Office

Low beams and small cool windows are part of the charm of this cottage, also one of the oldest post offices in the country. Little can have changed here since it held the important position as an early Penny Post receiving house in 1839. Formerly, it had been a dwelling for workers attending to church repairs.

A footpath opposite the church leads to Duchy Home Farmland where many prize-winning cattle are now bred. At the left of the road towards Kelly Bray is **Shutta**, which many miss because it is set a good way back. This is a privately owned sixteenth-century farmhouse which incorporates some interesting features of local history such as a huge granite bowl used for cider making and doors from White-ford, one of Cornwall's oldest manors. Seven entrances, 52 doors and 365 windows were built into Whiteford. Nothing remains of it apart from the name of a nearby

Launceston Castle

farm, the doors here, others on Duchy property and some Adam chimney pieces in Buckingham Palace.

About a mile north of Bray Shop (B3257) a lane leads to the quiet countryside of **Trebullet**. Trebullet comprises two hamlets – Lower Trebullet is near Trecarrel Bridge, from which a steep lane leads to the other group of houses not named on the map. A left turn at the crossroads in their midst goes to **Trecarrel Hall**. Charles I stayed at the hall on his way to do battle at Liskeard. The bridge is not one he crossed – that was swept away by flood-waters in 1847.

Visitors may see Sir Henry's great banqueting hall at Trecarrel. He built it to last – the great beams on its cradle roof are as strong as when they were first lifted there. This might have been another Cotehele but for the deaths of his wife and child that changed everything. The chapel is also here, with its gallery where the lord of the manor and his lady attended Mass. Perhaps the saddest sight is the pile of great stones lying by the farm gate where they were left almost 500 years ago.

The B3254 runs back to Launceston through the broad open fields of **South Petherwin**. Before completing the return turn south to see the **Sterts Theatre**. Established in 1982, this spectacular, covered openair theatre is open all year and houses a gallery and runs a full programme of workshops. Performances are held throughout the summer months. Returning to Launceston visitors will pass Botathan farm-house which witnessed scenes of ghosts and exorcism in the seventeenth century.

The hilltop church at **Lewannick** is built of a stone which is not seen in many other parts of Cornwall. It is dark green and was quarried at **Polyphant** village across the A30. The almost circular churchyard indicates a very early Christian site, possibly fifth century AD. Here are two 'gravestones' with inscriptions in Latin and Ogham (an ancient British alphabet which consists of only twenty letters). Today people go blackberrying among the neglected stone outcrops. A visit to this place is worthwhile.

Not many visitors go along the lanes to **Laneast**, though Sir John Betjeman called the church an unspoiled version of Altarnun. A Norman foundation, it was reconsecrated in the fifteenth century when the 38 pew ends were carved. Today it is very much loved and cared for, with fresh flowers to scent the building. John Couch Adams was born in the parish of St Sidwell's Laneast in 1819 and a black tablet on the wall names him the greatest astronomer since Newton. It also recalls his discovery of the planet Neptune. Truro cathedral also has a memorial to him and in Launceston Museum there is a bust by the sculptor Northey Burnard.

There are walks from here to **St Clether**, but for the motorist the road runs along a ridge, dropping a little to the church, its holy well, a small hall and one house. This well building is the oldest in Cornwall with its own chapel and stone altar. There is a serenity, too,

Walks

Week St Mary

5 miles (8km) • some hills • 2¹/₂ hours

Map: OS 1:25,000 Explorer Series 111: Bude, Boscastle and Tintagel

At Week St Mary's village square walk from the post office then right to Bude. After 800 yards (730m) take the footpath through the gate at left of hotel. Follow it to Ashbury Farm, through the yard, out at the far gate, along the track to your left then down to the woods. Ashbury Iron Age fort is on your right as the path drops to a stile by a stream. Over the bridge turn right, follow the hedge and stream to a stile leading to remains of Burycourt medieval manor. Leave by the gate to a forest track which comes to a road where you turn left up the hill, and past the house at the top go through a gate on the right. Go on by the hedge to a track above forestry and walk to a gate into a lane. A sunken lane lies to the right – the old road to Week St Mary and a mill – not a public right of way but the owner allows walking. At the bottom go left across a stream into a field and through a right-hand gap to follow the hedge up into a lane and past a farm to the road. Turn left and beyond the road junction go over a stile on the left to the return path to the village.

Bude Canal

5 miles (8km) • moderate • 2¹/₂ hours

Map: OS 1:25,000 Explorer Series 111: Bude, Boscastle and Tintagel

From Bude Visitor Centre go along the canal towpath inland until Whalesborough Wood where the route crosses the main A39. In front is Hele Bridge: turn left here and over it to the path, following it beside the canal and up the inclined plane to Marhamchurch. At the pumping station leave the towpath and go down the lane to the left, following it downhill and across the river where ahead of you, after turning right, is Hele Mill. Before the mill turn left, join the path up the steps where a gate on the right at the top of the field leads to the old road. Turn left past the farmhouse to a gateway with a fine view of the Bude valley then retrace your steps past the houses and turn left into a lane. Cross the A39, go down to the Bude sewage works as this track leads to the old railway. Go for a short way then turn left down embankment steps to a fenced path beside a ditch. By the railway bridge turn left at the minor road, crossing the field on the right, respecting any stock in there. The road leads to Rodd's Bridge and so to Bude.

which draws people to this remote place. The Lord's Prayer in Cornish is to be found in the church, and there is a stained glass window of the saint.

As you drive along the A395, stop at **Trethorne Leisure Farm** near Piper's Pool. Youngsters enjoy it here with pony rides (shire horses for the adults to ride), animals to feed, indoor and outdoor play areas, falconry displays and ten-pin bowling.

Sheep are very much part of the landscape round Launceston, especially north of this road at **Treneglos** hamlet, where the old Cornish 'trev' is no more than a triangular green beside a church and two or three houses. It is almost as high as nearby **Wilsey Downs** where there are walks to prehistoric tumuli. Celtic tribes were forced to seek safety and live above the wooded valleys – Warbstow Bury, north from Wilsey and Treneglos is a good example of this and ranks with Castle-an-Dinas and Chun Castle as one of Cornwall's largest ancient sites. Choose this place for a picnic and walks on a sunny day.

From this expanse of fields and farms, the lane plunges deeply down between hedgerows not despoiled by harsh council machines to **Tuckingmill** near Canworthy Water on the River Ottery. Fleeces from farms on the high ground once kept the local woollen mills busy and villagers in full employment. Now the cottages are quiet, those beside the river reflecting on their changed position in life.

The road from **South Wheatley** to **North Petherwin** is narrow and undulating but wooded and pleasant. After much study, St Paternus came to this place in the sixth century and the small church-town remains apart from the main group of houses at Petherwin Gate in a typically Cornish manner. There is a poignant memorial here to three sisters – Susanna, Margaret and Ann who died young about 350 years ago.

Selected Car Drives

Tintagel to Widemouth Bay

From Tintagel the B3263 to Boscastle is very pleasant but for a different view do not take the left turn downhill to the village but carry on for about a mile (1.5km) then take the first left – a secondary road which will carry you up and down steeply to Lesnewth. About a mile (1.5km) past the church a sign to Tresparrett is the one to follow then on to Tresparrett Posts. There the minor road crosses the B3263 to Higher Crackington, Middle Crackington and for drivers with good brakes on to Crackington Haven. Steep and narrow are the lanes into and out of this cove between Cambeak and Pencarrow Point where fierce cliffs have wrecked many a ship. After St Gennys Church, a place of peace in its own grassy square, pass left for Coxford and Millook. Here the views are magnificent: the road is narrow and steep but rising out of it the undulations of Penhale Cliff lead to the ease of a road by the sands of Widemouth Bay. Follow that cliff road and Bude awaits you. Then the A39 will offer a wide safe way to your holiday centre.

The **Tamar Otter Sanctuary** is nearby and in the 23 acres (9.3 hectares) of this, the first branch of the Otter Trust, there are British and Asian otters. Deer run wild and there are peacocks, wallabies and numerous waterfowl.

Boyton, once a thriving town, has now shrunk to a hamlet. It stands on high ground overlooking the wide and lush valley of the river Tamar. The parish is proud of Agnes Prest of Northcott, a Protestant martyr, burned at Southernhay in Exeter in 1557 for refusing to accept the doctrine of transubstantiation. She shares a memorial with Thomas Benet outside Maynard School in that city. There are numerous walks here, some on high ground and others down in the valley. Either way, it's a tranquil area for rambling.

Motorists returning to Launceston pick up the B3254 road at **Ladycross,** probably once associated with Tavistock Abbey, and return to Launceston over the Yeolmbridge. This is Cornwall's oldest and most perfectly finished bridge, the only one with a ribbed vault and pointed arches, similar to that of the north gate of Launceston Castle.

On the hill north of the River Kensey and level with Launceston Castle is St Stephen's, once a collegiate establishment and consecrated in 1259 which makes it the mother church of Launceston. The original borough of St Stephen's grew up around the monastery below the present church and from it Launceston's old name originated – Lanson or Dunheved. There are arguments for both but the former is more Celtic as it comes from Lan Stephen's ton, *lan* being Cornish

---

Around Bude to the north

From Bude follow the A39 a very short distance south but watch for a left turn to Marhamchurch. Stop and see the church if it is open. Drive straight through Hobbacott to the Buttsbear Cross T-junction and there turn left along the B3254, cross the A3072 at Red Post to Launcells Cross. Here your way is left and first left to Launcells Church. Return up out of that valley and turn sharp left into Stratton and the site of the Battle of Stamford Hill. About a mile (1.5km) on the A39 in the Kilkhampton direction, turn left for Poughill. The return road to the village will be signposted Stibb and Coombe. Continue on to Crosstown and Morwenstow – a cluster of houses centred on the Bush Inn and Hawker's Church. Leave Morwenstow through Gooseham towards Woolley but turn right in the village towards the A39 junction where a left turn will take you into Devon. Your way is to the right for Kilkhampton. Make for Thurdon, Dexbeer and Broomhill Rider and take the right turn at the village junction after a steep road up from the Tamar Valley. It will take you through Rhude Cross and along the river valley to Bush and the A39, Stratton and Bude.

for holy ground.

Today, this area of the Kensey Valley keeps a little of its past – a packhorse bridge, slate-hung cottages overlooking the mill complex and a toll house, where Launceston's wealth once lay. The building of St Thomas was formerly the chapel of St Stephen and stands as the lone reminder of Launceston's pre-Conquest religious past.

In the Kensey Valley, the **Launceston Steam Railway** will take you back into history as Victorian locomotives pull their coaches through one and a half miles (2.4km) of beautiful scenery along the track-bed of the old North Cornwall Railway. Among the museum's many exhibits is a restored 1905 Robey horizontal steam engine and tours of the workshops are on offer.

CAMELFORD

The rest of north Cornwall can be divided into two sections, each with a character of its own. **Camelford**, about 16 miles (26km) north-west of Launceston along the A395, can be a base for seeing King Arthur country. Motorists driving north from Wadebridge on the A39, approach this quiet market town through the lovely Allen valley, a route starred with primroses and bluebells in spring. A peaceful place now, Camelford was once a lively pocket borough, busy with wool and cloth-making as indicated by the nearby hamlet of Valley Truckle (Cornish for tucking-mill).

Well signposted from the A39

and worth a visit, is the **North Cornwall Museum and Art Gallery**. This exhibition opened in 1973 in an old coach house to display a collection of items reflecting rural life in north Cornwall. A section of the building has been constructed to resemble a typical moorland cottage interior and in addition, changing craft and painting exhibitions are held throughout the season. Those who have seen it are not surprised to learn that it has been featured on both television and radio as well as being given the Pilgrim Trust Award for the best small museum in Britain.

A couple of miles north west of Camelford is an example of modern technology, **GAIA Energy Centre**. Based at Delabole wind farm, GAIA invites visitors to explore the world of renewable energy by means of an entertaining, interactive exhibition. (At the time of writing GAIA is subject to a takeover bid and its future is uncertain. Please check before visiting.)

The westward coast roads from Camelford all pick up the B3314 where **Delabole**, about two and a half miles (4km) away, is well signposted. The village is clean and attractive but the focal point is the slate quarry which has been producing fine slate for many centuries. Look out for the millennium clock beside the road in the village, made entirely in slate.

Northwards along the B3266, the road crosses the high plateau of Waterpit Down, pleasant with extensive views and the ubiquitous sheep. A roadside cross here is a

Delabole Slate Quarry

Pack saddle donkeys were first used to remove the rock: horses were next and now lorries provide the transport. The great quarry is 500 feet (152m) deep and over one and a half miles (2.4km) round. Richard Carew included it in his 1602 Survey of Cornwall, John Wesley wrote about it in the eighteenth century and Eden Phillpotts made it the subject of his novel *Old Delabole* (1914). The skills they all admired are still practised today and masons produce items such as church altars and fine flooring, memorial stones and plant holders. The name of the local inn has strong links with the quarry, being known as the Bettle and Chisel. After learning about the names of various slate tiles – Ladies, Countesses, Duchesses, Queens, Rags and Imperials – it is interesting to see them on the old cottages and walls for many miles round about.

tenth-century stone carved with interlaced ornamentation. It has weathered considerably since it was set up as a pilgrims' way-marker. A maze of narrow lanes leads eventually to **Lesnewth**, very remote but once an important place where Cornish kings and chieftains held court (*Lis* means court/palace and *Noweth/Newith*, new). The church of St Michael is securely built into the hillside opposite a farm and easily missed as the roof is at road level.

BOSCASTLE AND TINTAGEL

Walkers will find that several paths lead away from this unusual church-town into the lovely **Valency Valley** but motorists have to cross the latter for the B3263 Boscastle road at the head of the valley, partly owned by the National Trust. The drop down to **St Juliot's church** is steep but typical of roads in this area.

At **Boscastle**, the original inner harbour was built by Sir Richard Grenville in 1584; with 61 acres (25 hectares) of adjoining cliffs, it is National Trust property. There is a NT information centre open in the summer in the Old Smithy. It is hard to believe that it was once Launceston's port for shipping slate, corn and tanning bark. Cargoes of food and coal were imported here. Today, few would care to negotiate even a small motor yacht between the sharp, twisting rocks of this narrow inlet, but local boatmen who know the dangers, take visitors out to see a different view of the cliffs, especially the one some call King Arthur's Head. Pause at the **Museum of Witchcraft** before leaving Boscastle to learn about the ancient rites.

Steep, heather and gorse-clad cliffs and a narrow strip of water make Boscastle. Little enough, but it is very popular and no doubt the Valency Valley adds to its appeal. It runs inland for 5 miles (8km) and in spring it is a delight – in autumn,

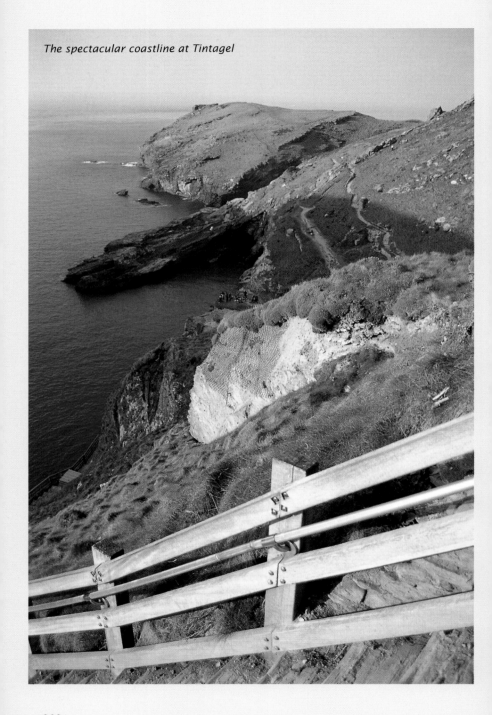

The spectacular coastline at Tintagel

Above: Boscastle Youth Hostel

Left: Tintagel Castle

Below left: Boscastle

Below right: Tintagel

unbelievably beautiful. About 132 acres (54 hectares) of it are National Trust property and this includes **Sentry Ground**, the ancient sanctuary ground of Minster church. Nearby Forrabury Common is a unique survival of Celtic land tenure in long rectangular plots known as 'stitches'.

Motorists climb out of Boscastle to pass Trevalga and arrive at **Trethevy** (the head of Rocky valley) along the B3263. Walk down the valley to the cliffs and look for the maze: two rare labyrinth pattern carvings.

Glorious cliff walks

The cliff walks from here to Tintagel are nothing less than splendid, especially on a fine spring day when there is a profusion of wild flowers and a mass of sea birds. In June, puffins can be seen on Long Island but not, alas, without binoculars. **Rocky Valley**, the walk from these cliffs to **Trevalga**, is one of exceptional beauty. In fact a day spent here would not be wasted.

Bossiney village is now a quiet hamlet but in 1584 it was the centre of a 'rotten' borough whose MP was Sir Francis Drake. Long before that, Bossiney Court was mentioned in the Domesday Book. It stands on ground once owned by the first Duke of Cornwall, the Black Prince.

It is difficult to know where Bossiney ends and **Tintagel** begins because of recent buildings. Many suggest that Tintagel should be avoided as commercialism spoils the memory of King Arthur. Perhaps there are too many gift shops here but there is also much to enjoy. **King Arthur's Great Halls** tells the story of King Arthur and his Round Table in a modern, electronic show while also on display are examples of the art of stained glass and the craft of the local stonemasons.

In the centre is the **Old Post Office**, one of the National Trust's most picturesque properties. This small fourteenth-century stone house with an ancient slate roof of fairy-tale curves was built on the plan of a medieval manor with a large hall. It is called the Old Post Office because it was the letter-receiving office for the district, opened by the GPO in 1844.

A dusty, easy slope (a Land Rover is also available for those who prefer it) takes visitors to the foot of **Tintagel Head**, which is Duchy of Cornwall property. On this magnificent promontory are the well preserved remains of a Celtic monastery as well as the ruins of one of the Black Prince's castles.

English Heritage has charge of another castle – on the land overlooking the narrow division between cliff and headland. This is the remains of a medieval stronghold built by Earl Reginald of Cornwall. On the other side of the valley is **King Arthur's Castle Hotel**, an outstanding place built to accommodate holidaymakers flocking here as a result of Alfred Tennyson's Arthurian poetry. Even in 1897, this building was thought to detract from the spirit of the area and the 14-acre (6 hectare) headland was eventually bought for the National Trust as a memorial to the Poet Laureate. Away from the village is the **Church of St Materiana**. It is a fine Norman building and should be visited when walking along Glebe Cliff, which has a viewpoint with wheelchair access.

After leaving Tintagel by the B3263, there is a lane to the left beyond Penpethy Farm which is worth exploring. For archaeologists, the lonely mound of **Condolden Barrow** is an intriguing monument, as some people believe Queen Iseult to be buried there.

Across the B3266 at **Slaughterbridge** is Worthyvale Manor, an ancient and beautiful place on an estate crowded with history. Worthyvale Manor was recorded in the Domesday Book of 1086, but was important even before that, when in 823, a decisive battle took place in Worthyvale fields. The Saxon leader Egbert was victorious and later became the first king of all England.

Slaughterbridge is now the site of the **Arthurian Centre** for it was here that King Arthur is said to have led his Celtic forces into battle against Mordred, where the lane crosses the River Camel. Both were killed and a large stone inscribed in Latin still lies on the riverbank, giving the name Slaughterbridge an irrevocable link with the past even though historians consider it to be merely legendary. There are walks to the stone and to the battlefield and the Land of Arthur Exhibition is nearby.

BUDE

Those who live in **Bude** do not consider their pleasant town to be at all remote or forgotten, but in the far north of Cornwall, it is an area with its own special character and quite different from any other part of the Duchy, a friendly, attractive place offering a warm-hearted welcome to visitors.

In the 1830s, Sir Goldworthy Gurney built the toy-like castle beside the beach. Today it houses the offices of the town council who maintain the building, keep the gardens colourful and have transformed the former gardener's shed into a café and information area. Gurney invented the Bude light to illuminate the castle. He created a bright light by injecting a stream of oxygen into an oil flame and then reflected this single light throughout the castle by means of mirrors. He went on the improve the lighting in the House of Commons by means of three Bude Lights, a system used for 60 years until the coming of electricity.

To celebrate the Millennium and Gurney's invention the **Bude Light** was erected in front of the castle. Using coloured concrete and fibre optic lighting the sculptors crafted a slender cone, some 29 ft (9m) high, set in a paved area and small amphitheatre. At night the cone lights up to show the patterns of the constellations in the sky above.

Nearby, the old forge beside the canal has become the town's **Historical and Folk Museum** displaying a wide variety of exhibits. The museum is appropriately sited on the lower wharf facing the Bude Canal, which was built in 1826 by Sir Thomas Acland.

Bude, however, did not become a canal port, it developed into a quality holiday resort, probably best known for some of Cornwall's finest surfing beaches. Visitors fish the canal because it is regarded as one of the finest coarse-fishing waters in the West. A 2-mile (3km) stretch of quiet level walking along the tow path is not only pleasant but of special interest for lovers of wildlife. About half a mile along, a bird hide has been erected.

Bude Canal

This canal was almost unique in Britain, as it was not primarily built to carry goods to the coast, but to transport huge quantities of shell sand inland to sweeten the acid soil and so improve large areas of otherwise unproductive land. The original 30-mile (48km) stretch from Bude to Launceston carried barges fitted with wheels and these were hauled up inclines by stationary steam engines.

Ebbingford Manor, the town's oldest house, dating from the twelfth century, is off Vicarage Road which runs beside the canal. This small but charming building was at one time home of the Arundells, who were related to Henry VIII and Lord Baltimore, the founder of Maryland. It is not open to the public.

It is hard to believe that wrecks were a terrifying commonplace in the early days of the nineteenth century, for the pleasures of Bude, which include golf and twelve tennis courts for visitors, are only for relaxation. There is safe salt-water swimming in the pool, while beyond the castle are sands and surf comparable to those of South Africa and Australia!

Marhamchurch lies south of Bude and across the A39 through high banked hedges and narrow climbing lanes. It is an unusual rectangular village set on a ridge and seems to be keeping watch over the surrounding farmland. Its wide central road leads to the Norman church, low and square near the war memorial. The solid fifteenth-century oak door is always open and is one of its interesting features, as is the encased sanctuary knocker. A former rector, Brother Peter, came from the Girondist House of the Holy Cross at Bordeaux and was the incumbent of Marhamchurch in 1458. His service here was so happy that after his death his ghost returned to the old rectory, where he has apparently often been seen, even in this century.

Village celebrations are the same here as at all other churches with Celtic origins – their feast day usually follows the church festival. The tradition at Marhamchurch is a rare one. On **Revel Day** – after 12 August – Father Neptune crowns a local schoolgirl who then rides through the village on a white horse.

The narrow lanes to the south are undulating and delightful, with the high views showing the agricultural nature of the region. Take your time and enjoy a slow, relaxing drive south, through Week Orchard, Week St Mary, Treforda and into Jacobstow. Here the church, embraced by trees in a roadside dell, is easily missed and the unspoiled hamlet is charming because of its very solitude. Nearer the coast the wooded lanes are lost in high open fields again.

Wainhouse Corner is a junction on the A39 where the way leads to the fearful cliffs of **Crackington Haven** and for a considerable distance, north and south, the coastal footpath crosses National Trust land. This tiny cove was a harbour for colliers in the eighteenth and nineteenth centuries and their captains must have been intrepid sailors to navigate here. **Cambeak** promontory on the southern arm of Crackington Haven stretches into the sea like a great lizard and gated paths lead to **Trevigue**, a sheltered farm. Cars may be left here for a further walk to **High Cliff**. This is Cornwall's highest coastal point and the views are typical of this northern area.

Bude Canal

The Thomas Hardy Connection

In 1870, at the age of 30, Thomas Hardy was sent to North Cornwall to draw up plans for the restoration of St. Juliot's Church. At that time he was working as an architect, specialising in church architecture. The building was in a ruinous condition when he arrived to inspect it but following renovation work, which he organised, it was re-opened two years later.

St Juliot's Church, an isolated building dedicated to St Julitta still stands at the head of Valency valley. The brass and ruby oil lamps Hardy installed in the church during restoration are now to be seen in Wellington Hotel, Boscastle. St Juliot Rectory remains, a reminder of when Hardy stayed there to continue the work on the church and court his Emma. Lovers of Hardy's works will know how the famous man returned again and again to court the rector's sister-in-law, Emma Gifford and how she persuaded him to leave architecture for literature and later married him in 1874.

Although he is better known for incorporating the Dorset landscape into his works, these early visits to North Cornwall also had an influence. Beeny Cliff, Buckator, Penally and Pentargon are among the places he loved and incorporated in his second novel, *A Pair of Blue Eyes*. Beeny Cliff at Boscastle was loved by Hardy and Emma – she sketched it and he wrote from there. Hardy's poem *Moments of Vision* describes the cliff outline of Penally Point, the northern arm of the Boscastle harbour – resembling the neck, head and beak of a bird of prey. Many years later he wrote a poetic drama *The Famous Tragedy of the Queen of Cornwall* in which Condolden Barrow featured.

Today this area offers much to enjoy and the features that Hardy and Emma visited are still there. There is a nature walk, mostly alongside the little river, from the church of St Juliot down to the harbour and the Valency Valley, some 5 miles (8km) long and partly owned by the National Trust, remains lovely and unspoilt.

Northwards, on the cliff out of the Haven stands **St Gennys Church**. It is almost alone in its fold of green fern on the cliffside and ornamental cherry trees give it a fairy-tale lookin spring. One of the treasures here is the altar tabernacle, a splendid piece of church furniture. Handsomely embroidered kneelers also add to the glory of this Celtic church where prayers have been said since St Gennys established his humble cell on these cliffs.

The road to **Millook** is narrow, steep and badly cambered in places but it can be negotiated with good brakes and the use of bottom gear. Once safely out of the valley, the wide road past the Common falls away to a startling panorama across Widemouth Bay and north to Morwenstow. The spectacular sands of **Widemouth Bay** stretch away almost endlessly. Once they were dreaded by sailors but now visitors can enjoy adventure holidays here and learn canoeing, and wind-surfing.

NORTH OF BUDE

Cornwall has not revealed all its treasures yet – there is much to see between Bude and Morwenstow. Some say that this area is the best of all. The A3072 road goes to **Stratton,** which, though it has fallen below Bude in status, was important in Roman times. Its character, however, is quite different.

Poundstock church

Dedicated to the dwarf hermit, St Neot, this building is beautifully sited in a dell away from the main road. Murals and exceptionally handsome bench ends are among the interesting features. Beside the churchyard the Gildhouse of stormy history is used for parochial church meetings.

It seems gentle enough now but it was not so in the fourteenth century. Then local villains were commissioned as Collectors of Subsidies and lawbreakers wielded more power than good citizens. Affairs reached a climax in 1357, however, when armed men swarmed into the church as a priest was celebrating Mass, killed him at the altar and desecrated the vestments and sacred vessels. It was not long before the killers were caught and punished and **Poundstock** returned to peace again. It still retains much of its medieval beauty. The Gildhouse served many purposes: poorhouse, school, and substitute church. The windows are original and worth studying.

Stratton is rightly proud of Anthony Payne, the Cornish giant who was born at The Tree Inn, and died there too. This huge man weighed 532lb (240kg). His portrait by Kneller is in Truro Museum. He devoted his life to the service of his master, Sir Bevil Grenville, whose troops defeated the Roundheads at the Battle of Stamford Hill in 1643. A plaque on the wall at Stamford Hill marks the site.

Away from the main road, but worth seeing, is **Poughill** (pronounced 'Puffle') **Church,** dedicated to St Olaf, a Dane. There are two large wall representations of St Christopher, repainted by Frank Salisbury and a Tazza Cup and Paten, beautifully shaped and richly decorated. The clock in the tower has a memorial tablet which is rarely seen but worth mentioning. It says of Sir Goldsworthy Gurney: 'His inventions and discoveries in Steam and Electricity made communication by land and sea so rapid that it became necessary for all Britain to keep uniform clock time.'

Those following the coastal walk will have increasingly fine views especially near Stowe Barton where the road dips into the Coombe valley. This handsome farm was built on the site of Sir Richard Grenville's home, unfortunately pulled down in 1739: today only the stables remain.

The bridge at **Coombe** carries a tablet – now very weathered – which commemorated King William IV's contribution to its building. In the early days of the nineteenth century, the ford here was a danger to the lives of men and animals so the Reverend R S Hawker of Morwenstow appealed to the king for financial help and eventually a bridge was built. Duckpool is a good place to swim and the National Trust cliff, **Steeple Point**, affords an ideal vantage point for walkers. The nearby Coombe Valley is also Trust land. The cottage at the entrance to this valley is of special interest though people rarely notice the cross-shaped window above the door. Here Hawker spent his honeymoon and began writing *Trelawney*, the poem which is now considered to be Cornwall's anthem.

As the road climbs out of this valley, it continues north past the dish aerials of the Government's Composite Signals Organisation Station – an imposing sight. Beyond is **Morwenstow**, which is almost the end of Cornwall but is full of history and known as Hawker country. For 40 years, till 1875, this famous parson-poet was vicar here. Wrongly styled an eccentric, he startled his fellow churchmen by righting many wrongs and frequently risking his life to rescue shipwrecked sailors and give Christian burial to the bodies of the drowned. In the churchyard is what might be a memorial to his brave dedication – the figurehead of the *Caledonia*, wrecked on the rocks below in 1842, leaving only one man alive. Petitioner for his parishioners' cause at a time of dire poverty, and restorer of the harvest festival, Robert Stephen Hawker's achievements will long be remembered. He wrote fine poetry in a hut on the cliff top, now National Trust, and his unique vicarage chimneys modelled on church towers, can just be glimpsed in the woods below the church.

The Bush Inn, a few hundred yards away from the churchtown, is unusual in retaining the traditional sign, the sign of a bush, once given to all taverns to signify where drinks were sold. It is an old inn where the Morwenstow Union Friendly Society probably met in the late eighteenth century. It had a thatched roof until a few years ago, but now that has gone and some of its charm has disappeared as well.

The end of Cornwall is reached where Marsland Mouth lies below Marsland Cliff – the scene of many shipwrecks in days of sail – but the lane turns inland to **Woolley**, where there is not an end but a beginning. For among the marshes at Woolley Barrows, Cornwall's River Tamar, which marks the boundary with Devon, has its source. The A39 road south, which was the pilgrim highway to St Michael's Mount, goes to **Kilkhampton**. The church here is worth a visit because it has a splendid lychgate, good pew ends and numerous Grenville monuments.

From the B3254, the road leads to the **Tamar lakes** with fly-fishing on the Upper, coarse on the Lower and walks, picnics and much else to enjoy in beautiful surroundings. The first of these reservoirs, Lower Lake, was created in 1820. From here the river flows south to join the sea at Saltash where this journey around Cornwall began.

Places to Visit

IN & AROUND LAUNCESTON

Launceston Castle
A fine ruin overlooking the town. It was the chief seat of Robert of Mortain, brother of William I. Views are impressive.
☎ (01566) 772365
Open: 10am-6pm (5pm in October) daily April to October. 10am-4pm Friday to Sunday, November to March.

Launceston Steam Railway and Museum
Below the castle
Five miles (8km) round trip through the Kensey valley on the trackbed of the old North Cornwall Railway, Victorian locomotives pull coaches which allow passengers to enjoy the scenery. Museum of Vintage Transport.
☎ (01566) 775665
Open: From 10am. Late May bank holiday and June, Sunday to Wednesday. July, August and September Sunday to Friday. Also Easter holiday, and October half-term Sunday to Friday.

Lawrence House Museum
Castle Street
A Georgian town house given to the National Trust in 1964 to preserve the character of the street. The moulded plaster of the ceilings is exceptional. It is let to the local Borough Council as a museum.
☎ (01566) 773277
Open: 10.30am-4.30pm Monday to Friday from Easter to mid-October. Other times by appointment.

The Arthurian Centre
Slaughterbridge
Land of Arthur Exhibition on the site of Arthur's last battle. Walks, play area, shop and refreshments.
☎ (01840) 212450
www.arthur-online.com
Open: 10am–5pm.

Warbstow Bury
3 miles (4.8km) N A395 Launceston-Camelford road (SX 201909)
An impressive prehistoric defensive earthwork: fortress, double-walled and two gateways protecting barrows. King Arthur is said to be buried there.

Trethorne Leisure Farm
Piper's Pool A395
Ideal for young children with animals to see and ponies to ride. Four lane ten-pin bowling alley.
☎ (01566) 86324
Open: 9am-11pm, Monday to Saturday all year.

Sterts Theatre
Upton Cross, Bodmin Moor
Covered open air theatre, studio and gallery.
☎ (01579) 362962/362382
Open: All year, theatre performances in summer only.

Tamar Otter Sanctuary
North Petherwin
Enjoy a sight of British and Asian otters, golden pheasants, wallabies and water deer roaming free. Tearoom and shop. Come at feeding times (noon and 3.30pm).
☎ (01566) 785646
www.ottertrust.org.uk/earsham

Places to Visit

Open: 10.30am-6pm 1 April (Good Friday if earlier) to 31 October daily.

AROUND CAMELFORD

Camelford Museum of Historic Cycling
From 1818 to present day machines on exhibit.
☎ (01840) 212811
Open: 10am-5pm Sunday to Thursday all year.

North Cornwall Museum and Art Gallery
The Clease, Camelford
☎ (01840) 212954
Open: 10am-5pm Monday to Saturday April to September.

Delabole Slate Quarry
Follow AA signs from Camelford
☎ (01840) 212242
www.delaboleslate.com
Open: Tours Monday to Friday at 2pm, May through to September. All other times by appointment.

GAIA Energy Centre
Delabole
☎ (01840) 213321
www.gaiaenergy.co.uk
Open: 10am-6pm daily
NB At the time of writing Gaia was the subject of a takeover bid. Please check before visiting.

IN & AROUND BOSCASTLE & TINTAGEL

National Trust shop and information centre
The Old Forge, Boscastle
☎ (01840) 250353

Open: 10.30am-5pm daily April to October.

Tintagel Old Post Office
(National Trust)
A small fourteenth-century stone house built as a medieval manor, charming garden.
☎ (01840) 770024
Open: 11am-5.30pm (4pm in October) April to October daily.

Tintagel Castle
(English Heritage)
Cliff-side remains of a medieval castle built on prominent site in mid-twelfth century by Reginald, Earl of Cornwall.
☎ (01840) 770328
Open: 10am-6pm daily April to September, 5pm in October, 4pm November to March and 7pm mid July to the end of August.

King Arthur's Great Halls
Fore Street, Tintagel
Tells the story of King Arthur and also displays local craftsmanship. Shop.
☎ (01840) 770526
Open: Daily, all year.

BUDE

Bude and Stratton Town Museum
Old Forge, Lower Wharf
There is considerable emphasis on shipwrecks and lifeboats in this excellent maritime and industrial museum.
☎ (01288) 353576
Open: 11am-5pm daily Easter to September.

Bude Canal

A remarkable piece of engineering in being the longest tub boat canal in Britain – and with inclined planes – but it was a project devised before engineers had power and the materials to make it successful. Today, Sir Thomas Acland's brilliant scheme is a place of recreation for visitors, especially anglers and walkers.

The Bude Light

Bude Castle
Spectacular sight at night especially when the sky is clear.

NORTH OF BUDE

Hawker's Hut

(National Trust)
Vicarage Cliff, Morwenstow
Perched on the edge of the cliff overlooking the fearful rocks where so many ships foundered and whose men he saved, Parson Hawker built his shelter. Access by footpath from churchyard gate.

Upper Tamar Lake

Off A39 near Kilkhampton
80 acres (32 hectares) for watersports and trout fishing. Hire of dinghies, canoes, kayaks and wetsuits.
☎ (01288) 321262

What to do if it rains

Launceston
- Lawrence House Museum
- Steam railway and museum
- St Mary Magdalene Church

Camelford
- North Cornwall Museum and Art Gallery
- Museum of Historic Cycling

Boscastle
- Visitor Centre by the harbour

Tintagel
- Old Post Office (National Trust)
- King Arthur's Great Halls

Slaughterbridge
- The Arthurian Centre

Bude
- Museum

Morwenstow
- Church

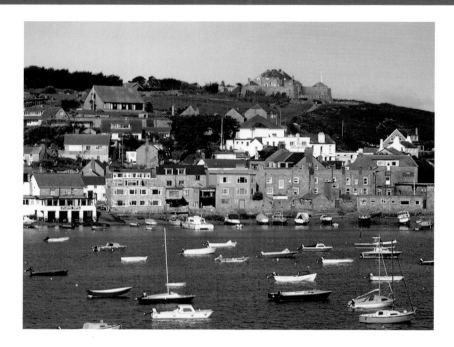

The Scillies consist of more than 300 islands but only six are inhabited. These are St Mary's, Tresco, St Martin's, St Agnes, Bryher and Gugh and they have a total area of only 4,400 acres (1,780 hectares). St Agnes, though almost the smallest, has the special distinction of being the most southerly inhabited point in Great Britain. Situated about 26 miles (42km) west of Land's End, this interesting geographical grouping is unique in its relationship to the mainland.

Though associated with Cornwall, the people are not part of it, as any true Scillonian will stoutly maintain. Nor do they belong to the rest of England, in spite of the imposition of taxes that would make it appear so.

GETTING THERE

For a considerable saving of time, most visitors prefer to travel from the mainland by air, from Newquay, Penzance or perhaps St Just, while, although the crossing

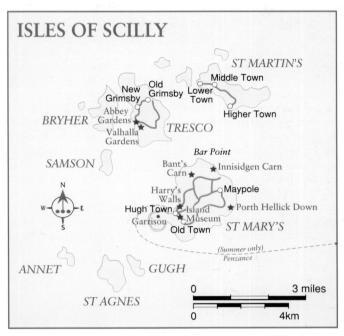

ISLES OF SCILLY

ST MARTIN'S
Middle Town
New Grimsby · Old Grimsby · Lower Town
Abbey Gardens
BRYHER · Valhalla Gardens · TRESCO
Higher Town

SAMSON

Bar Point
Bant's Carn · Innisidgen Carn
Harry's Walls · Maypole
Hugh Town · Island Museum · Porth Hellick Down
Garrison · Old Town · ST MARY'S

(Summer only) Penzance

ANNET · GUGH
ST AGNES

0 — 3 miles
0 — 4km

can be extremely rough, even in summer, others enjoy the sea journey.

'ISLES OF TRANQUILITY'

The first sight of the islands seems to contradict the various names given to them over the centuries – Isles of the Blest, Paradise Islands and the Lotus Isles. The immediate impression is of rocky outcrops with scarcely any vegetation in sight, but soon the unusual peace and quiet, which is part of Scilly's charm, takes over and the almost complete absence of vehicles makes itself felt. As a result, it is easy to relax and enjoy the startling blue of the sea, silver sands on empty beaches with birds and flowers that are so different, not to mention the stone 'library' of prehistory which consists of more than 150 Bronze Age relics. The fact that all the inhabited islands have maintained their reputation as a lifeline to tranquility is largely the result of extremely careful administration by their owners, the Duchy of Cornwall and their tenants, the Island Council, who have prevented any development that might spoil the unique beauty of the Scillies.

WHEN TO GO

Unlike anywhere else in the British Isles, Scilly, with its exceptionally soft climate, is the ideal place for open-air holidaymakers to visit in late February or early March. This is the time when the flower harvest is at its height and the fields of floral 'sunshine' rival even the brilliance of the sun. The atmosphere is different from that of the summer season and visitors enjoy being part of the concentration on flower exporting which pervades the islands in early spring. The flower show, which takes place in March is, of course, connected with the seasonal business but it is no ordinary one and claims to be the oldest in the country, because Scillonian growers were among the first to promote the growing of flowers as an industry.

The flower growing industry began here in a somewhat strange manner when one William Trevillick, who farmed on Rocky Hill, St Mary's, packed a few blooms in his Aunt Ellen's hatbox and, as an experiment, sent them to Covent Garden. The date of that inspired idea is thought to be as early as 1867, but it makes little difference. What is important is that it came at a time when the islanders were desperate for a new source of income.

Old industries had gone – kelp-making, which ended with the introduction of synthetic iodine in 1835, was superseded by boat-building. But this, in its turn, ended in about 1870 when sail gave way to steam; so the flower industry which resulted from Trevillick's brain child was greeted with considerable enthusiasm.

It was was further encouraged by Augustus Smith of Herefordshire who leased the islands between 1835 and 1872 and became, in fact, a self-appointed lord of the Isles and benevolent landlord, using all his resources for the good of the community. Not only did he help the incipient flower industry, but fostered the potato trade and brought Guernsey cattle over to improve the quality of the milk. He is also acknowledged to be the one who pioneered compulsory education here long before it appeared on the mainland – altogether a remarkable man whose enthusiasm and foresight undoubtedly saved the Isles of Scilly from the fate suffered by some Scottish islands where inhabitants were forced to leave their homes for lack of employment. But the flower growing industry, too, is unfortunately in decline, although many of the fields are still golden in the spring. Today's industry is tourism.

ST MARY'S

St Mary's is the main island. **Hugh Town** – that rather grand name for such a small 'capital' – is built on the isthmus which separates the Garrison area from the main part. It is here that many visitors stay after their arrival at the air terminal near Old Town or at the harbour of Hugh Town. In this small capital there are numerous shops, two banks, the main post office and three churches, each of a different denomination. The Town Hall serves a dual purpose as it shares its officialdom with performances of concerts and plays during the season. **The Isles of Scilly Museum** has a variety of interesting displays which cover the archaeology, wildlife and history of Scilly. Its central feature is a fully-rigged pilot gig (a Scillonian speciality) and there are also an appropriate number of wreck relics.

The fast, slim gigs also had other uses. The *Klondike* for example, which is now in the museum at St Mary's, usually went out on coastguard duty and was the vessel involved in the changeover of crewmen on the Bishop Rock

Walks on St Mary's

Porth Hellick

3 miles (5km) approx • easy • 1$\frac{1}{2}$ hours

Map: OS 1:25,000 Explorer Series 101: Isles of Scilly

Take the road past the lifeboat slip, then turn to the right past Parting Carn. By turning right again at the second turning arrive at Salaker and on to Porth Hellick beach. Follow the coastal footpath from here, past a deep point curving to Pelistry Bay. Here you return to Hugh Town by way of Holy Vale.

The Telegraph Walk

5 miles (8km) • easy • 2 hours

Map: OS 1:25,000 Explorer Series 101: Isles of Scilly

Start again on the road past the lifeboat slip, then join the footpath along the shore by Porthmellon. This skirts the uncompleted sixteenth-century fortifications known as Harry's Walls, soon joining the Porthloo road up to the golf course beyond which is Telegraph Tower, the island's highest point. North of this tower a lane leads near Bant's Carn Burial Chamber (about 1800BC) and the excavations of a village (about 200BC-AD300) on Halangy Down. Follow eastwards to Bar Point and on to two Bronze Age burial chambers at Innisidgen. Continue to Watermill Cove and Pelistry so that you can make your way back to Hugh Town via Holy Vale.

The Peninnis Walk

2 miles (3.5km) approx • easy • 1$\frac{1}{2}$ hours

Map: OS 1:25,000 Explorer Series 101: Isles of Scilly

Follow the road up the hill from the Church of St Mary the Virgin and turn sharp right just before reaching the top. A fork to the right 50 yards (46m) along this road leads to the hospital and beyond it, Buzza Tower, an old windmill adapted to commemorate King Edward VII's visit in 1902. The left fork is King Edward's Road which leads to Peninnis with its lighthouse, a gate and a Cornish stile giving access to the headland. Here rock formations such as Pulpit Rock, Tuskless Elephant and the Walrus are subjects for artists and photographers: all will follow the coastal path to Porthcressa and back to Hugh Town.

St Mary's

The origin of gig-racing

Naturally there is a considerable amount of boating and fishing here, and from St Mary's Quay, the popular sport of gig-racing can be watched and enjoyed every week during the summer. The history of these unique craft apparently began in 1790 when 'a gentleman in holy orders' placed an order for one to be built at the Peters boatyard of St Mawes. He specified a six-oared boat that could be used for saving life on the treacherous north coast of Cornwall. Tradition has it that this vessel was the first Padstow lifeboat and members of the old shipbuilding fraternity there say that a six-oared gig would certainly fill the role.

With their capacity for greater speed than most vessels, it is only to be expected that when smuggling was part of life, these gigs should have been used for illegal purposes. And this was indeed the case, for records show that trips involving contraband goods were made regularly from Scilly to the port of Roscoff in Brittany.

But this specially designed island craft also suited local pilots who were more interested in legitimate business and they would race their boats out into the Channel, each hoping to gain the fee by being the first to reach any sailing ship needing guidance through the dangerous coastal waters. And from that, the idea of racing for fun evolved, especially when the prize was more golden guineas than the crew could earn in a week as pilots. Sometimes the men would row many miles, even after work, to take part in one of the many regattas which were held all round the Cornish coast in the last century. These lapsed after World War I, however, and no more gigs were built. It was not till the 1950s that gigs were seen again: a Newquay man decided to encourage the revival of building these special vessels and eventually there were four gigs from Scilly fully restored. In the early 1960s, races began on the island and are now a familiar part of the summer scene. It is good to know, too, that the knowledge of gig-building has not disappeared and that the skills are being passed on at Cornwall College in Falmouth.

Lighthouse. Another one, however, had a much more romantic task – to transport wedding parties – and this pleasant work carried on till 1929 when the last bride to travel to her wedding by gig went to Tresco from her home on Bryher.

There are numerous dramatic accounts, too, of gig crews, employed in work on salvage operations, who returned with unusual cargoes. On one particular occasion, goods listed after a wreck were stated as 'lard, frozen geese, turkeys and two hundred fat bullocks'. Not the romantic kind of underwater treasure that most people envisage in these circumstances but nevertheless there must have been a profit for someone.

INTER-ISLAND TRIPS

St Mary's Quay is also the point of departure for inter-island boat trips. These are particularly delightful in the spring when the seabird sanctuaries can be seen at close quarters (the Island of Annet is closed to all visitors from mid-April to late August so that nesting birds may be protected.) Atlantic grey seals can also be seen easily from these inter-island launches. It is easy to understand why some visitors consider these particular boat trips to be the highlight of their holiday on Scilly.

BEACHES

Perhaps one of the greatest attractions of the Isles of Scilly is the seclusion of its sandy beaches. They are all safe for bathing and even in high summer remain uncrowded. There are, however, two danger spots. The sand bars connecting St Mary's with Toll's Island and St Agnes with Gugh are unsafe when the water flows over the two bars, but that is only at high tide. The clear waters attract skin-divers particularly, on account of the marine life and the numerous wrecks. The authorities, who know the swell conditions and tidal streams, recommend divers to operate in groups under super-vision, particularly as the nearest decompression chamber is at Plymouth, some 120 miles (190km) away.

GARRISON WALLS & GATE

If the weather is right, visitors usually take a short circular walk around the Garrison walls on their first evening as the fine sunsets over Samson are not to be missed. This is when they begin to appreciate the wisdom of the local council ruling: '**Caravans, motorised caravans and similar vehicles may not be brought to the islands. Private cars are most unwelcome and are quite unnecessary for the enjoyment of a holiday in the islands** (there are approximately 9 miles (15km) of road on St Mary's).' Taxis and bus services cater for all necessary transport.

Garrison Gate was not built till 1742 although Star Castle (an hotel since 1933) was constructed in 1593 at the top of the hill as a defence against possible Spanish attack. The population then moved from Old Town to greater safety near the castle.

There is a coast path here as elsewhere on the island, but another leads straight down to Woolpack Point where two rusty old cannons still point seawards as if awaiting the enemy. From here, if the weather is good, there is a fine view across St Mary's Sound to the islands of St Agnes and Gugh, but it is a place to be avoided during a north-westerly gale.

EXPLORING THE REST OF ST MARY'S

Returning to Hugh Town, the road passes the Duchy of Cornwall's Land Steward's impressive granite offices. They overlook Porth Cressa, St Mary's central and most popular beach.

The exploration of the main part of the island begins at **Peninnis Head.** The shorter way leads to the church, begun by King William IV and finished in 1837 by Augustus Smith. Past the vicarage is the island power station, skilfully built in an old quarry, and at the top of the hill is Buzza Tower. This was constructed in 1821 as an old Spanish-style windmill to grind corn; after which it was converted into a tower to commemorate King Edward VII's visit in 1902. It now has an even more useful role as a landmark for shipping. A bumpy track along a granite-walled lane leads eventually to Peninnis Head, a magnificent, rugged promontory at this southern extremity of St Mary's. Here, even the granite has been smoothed and weathered by storms; the resulting shapes deserving names such as the Tuskless Elephant, the Toastrack and the Kettle and Pans (where shrimps are plentiful).

OLD TOWN

The path to Old Town and its bay passes the medieval church, now only fragmentary remains of a once large cruciform building. The churchyard is full of memorials to Scillonians and other seamen wrecked off this coast. Some of the men were from Sir Cloudesley Shovel's ill-fated fleet, notably Henry Trelawny, son of the famous bishop from Pelynt, near Looe, captain of one of the ships. Here, too, the victims of the *HMS Schiller* disaster (1851) are buried. A memorial for those who died in both World Wars and a monument to Augustus Smith are also to be found in the cemetery.

From Hugh Town the road goes past the lifeboat slips and turns right at Parting Carn for Porth Hellick. The coast path also reaches this point too. Here is the quartz monument to Sir Cloudesley Shovel whose flagship *Association* was wrecked in 1707, and the most valuable underwater treasure ever located round the British Isles, which belonged to it, was discovered in 1967. Since then the *Romney*, *Eagle* and *Firebrand* have been found, the last-named as recently as 1981. The admiral's personal plate alone would be worth a small fortune today, but the hazardous diving conditions have clearly hindered rescue operations, although divers still persevere.

On these downs is a group of five chambered tombs, all very close together. Most of these 4,000-year-old passage graves are crumbling, the best preserved is maintained by English Heritage.

PELISTRY BAY

The coastal path carries on to Pelistry Bay where the sand is especially beautiful (felspar and quartz) and the sea views hard to beat. This is where swimmers need to avoid bathing when the sea covers the bar. Inland is Holy Vale, believed to have been the site of either a convent or a monastic cell and the path continues to picturesque **Watermill Bay**, past coastal indentations, before returning to Hugh Town.

PORTH HARRY

Telegraph Walk, in Hugh Town, as it is called, starts at the lifeboat slips and leads to Porthmellon and Porth Harry. Here are the uncompleted sixteenth-century fortifications –

Harry's Walls. Visitors can enjoy the facilities of the golf course beyond Porthloo Beach, but coastguards at Telegraph Tower are always on watch and also send meteorological readings to the London Air Ministry for weather forecasting. On the rough cliff slopes near Bant's Carn, is another English Heritage property. This encompasses a pre-historic burial chamber and village of the Roman period.

BAR POINT

At the pine-fringed northern tip of St Mary's lies Bar Point where there is some of the best bathing. Here are two more English Heritage monuments, the Innisidgen pre-historic burial chambers.

Before leaving St Mary's, Scilly's main island, there is an interesting point to consider about the west-ern lighthouses. Eight of them can be seen from here on a clear night. Bishop Rock, Peninnis Head, Sevenstones and Round Island are in the locality. Further away are Wolf Rock and Long-ships off Land's End, while on Cornwall's mainland, Pendeen and the Lizard are also visible.

TRESCO

The 750 acres of **Tresco** might well be considered a complete nature reserve, the population living mainly in a line of hamlets across the central neck of the area. It differs from the other islands as it is leased privately from the Duchy. There are no cars, caravans or motor cycles, nor is camping allowed. The beauty of this place,

and probably the conservation of the entire group, is due to the vision of Augustus Smith.

Augustus Smith

In 1834 he lived first on Tresco and built a huge Victorian house there before emigrating to St Mary's. This extraordinary man with the very ordinary name was a far-sighted visionary from Hereford who gave the islands new life simply by rooting out the cause of their deterioration – an ancient system of land tenure.

These old ways had resulted in serious unemployment caused by a surplus population so he put the men to work building roads and the wall boundaries which were the beginning of the famous **Tresco Abbey Botanical Gardens**. Smith created them on the site of a tenth-century Benedictine abbey and in the equable climate and natural shelter of Tresco, made the barren island blossom with sub-tropical plants sheltered by Californian and Monterey pines.

South from Timothy's Corner at **New Grimsby**, the path leads past the Bulb Farm (picking starts here before Christmas) and skirts **Appletree Bay**. At low water it is possible to walk across the flats to Samson though speed is essential to avoid being cut off. Here, above the road, stands a granite monument to Augustus Smith and his

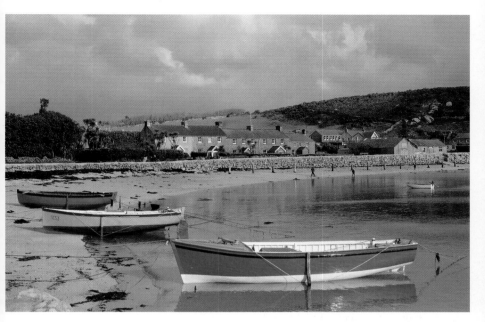

New Grimsby, Tresco

successors. He designed it, intending it to stand beside his grave at St Buryan in West Penwith, but there was insufficient space so it remains here.

Inland lies the **Great Pool** which, with the smaller Abbey Pool, occupies about 46 acres (19 hectares). A great concentration of bird life on these waters attracts bird lovers, who come especially to see the rare migrants that breed here. About fifty species nest in the island and probably more are seen here than anywhere else in Europe.

The northern part of Tresco has cliff walks on heather, ling and short springy grass which lead to Cromwell's Castle. This substantially built round tower with its 12 foot- (3.6m) thick walls was erected

in 1651 as a defence against the Dutch. There is King Charles' Castle, too; a long, low oblong fort but so badly sited that the guns could not operate. **Castle Downs** has early tin-workings, and on the headland at **Piper's Hole** there is evidence of three more. Intrepid and agile visitors may scramble down this gully and find a large freshwater lake. Candlelight turns this unexpected discovery into a miniature fairyland, but it is only for experienced climbers. Old Blockhouse, an old artillery battery, is nearby.

TRESCO'S GARDENS
Through the beauty of Abbey Wood there is a way to the **Abbey Gardens** themselves. It is im-

223

possible to describe such a place briefly for it is unique. But there are more than 5,000 species of plants from a hundred countries and from every climatic region in the world – many brought by Scillonian seamen returning home from their voyages.

Yet within this paradise is another – the **Valhalla Gardens**. It is an appropriate name for the collection of figureheads and other relics washed ashore from over seventy ships wrecked in the area. This place is strange and eerie but it should not be overlooked.

THE OTHER ISLES

Samson consists only of two hills joined by an isthmus. It has become famous as the setting Sir Walter

---

Places to Visit

ST MARY'S

The Garrison and Star Castle
Garrison Gate was built in 1742 as part of the garrison wall extending round the promontory. Today there are batteries, a park and promenade. Star Castle was a fortress erected by Elizabeth I and has walls projecting at eight salient angles. The inner building had two upper storeys and a bellcote. 18ft-thick ramparts and a dry moat surround it. Since 1933 it has been an hotel.
☎ (01720) 422317
Open: 9am-12noon Monday to Friday.

Underwater Island Safaris
'Nowhere', Old Town
Diving and snorkeling safaris. Novice dives. Wreck and reef diving for qualified divers. Assortment of organized underwater explorations for the totally inexperienced diver.
☎ (01720) 422732.

Isles of Scilly Museum
Church Street, Hugh Town
Built in 1967, it displays all facets of past and present life on the islands.
☎ (01720) 422337
Open: Monday to Saturday 10am-12noon, 1.30pm-4.30pm and 7.30pm-9pm throughout the summer season. Wednesday afternoons only in winter.

Isles of Scilly Pottery
The Garrison
☎ (01720) 422741
Open: 9am-12noon Monday to Friday.

Phoenix Stained Glass Studio
Porthmellon
See stained glass artifacts being made or join an afternoon workshop.
☎ (01720) 422900
Open: 10.30am–12.30pm and 1.30-4.30pm, Monday to Friday, 10.30–12.30 on Saturdays.

Harry's Walls
Begun about 50 years before Star Castle. Originally square with four bastions.

Bant's Carn
This burial chamber was probably built about 2000BC.
It remained in use for 500 years.

Besant used in his novel *Armorel of Lyonesse*. There is also a kistvaen or burial chamber here.

Bryher has been called 'the pearl of Scilly', but it is wild and un- tamed with lovely views but little else. People visit the outer islands for bird-watching – **St Agnes, Gugh** and **Annet,** which is a bird sanctuary.

With so much of nature at peace it is small wonder that these rocky outcrops have been called the **Lotus Isles.**

Innisidgen Carn
There are two monuments, upper and lower. The former a mound about 26ft (8m) in diameter.

TRESCO

Abbey Pool
A 12-acre (5 hectare) area populated with geese and ducks. It is popular with bird lovers.

Great Pool
A similar place to the above.

Tresco Gardens
Sub-tropical shrubs, palms and vegetation.
Open: 10am-4pm all year. Shop shut in winter.

Valhalla Gardens
A museum for the preservation of carved, wooden figureheads from over seventy ships wrecked in Scilly. It is housed in a building especially constructed by Augustus Smith about 1860.

Cromwell's Castle
Built in 1651 by Admiral Blake of the Republican forces, a 60-foot (18m) circular tower and granite platform commands the channel between Bryher and Tresco. Well preserved and finely situated. Entrance high up and reached by ladders. On the roof are six gun ports. Free access.

King Charles' Castle
This earthwork is of similar design to others in the period. A pentagonal fort was added in the Civil War. Free access.

The Old Blockhouse
This was built at the end of the sixteenth century as an artillery battery. It is above Old Grimsby.

Fact File

GETTING THERE

By Air

Brymon Airways, a wholly-owned subsidiary of British Airways, operates four flights a day between London Gatwick and Newquay airport. Flights are available from Dublin and Cork to Plymouth and from Belfast, Dublin, Guernsey and Jersey to Exeter (☎ 0845 7733377). Car hire is available at the airports.

By Road

The M4, M5 and M6 motorways have made travel to Cornwall simple and straightforward, while within Cornwall itself, the two major holiday routes, the A30 and A38 continue to improve, with fast dual carriage-ways as far as Bodmin and most of the way to Penzance. If you enter Cornwall via North Devon, then there is the Atlantic Highway, the A39, which you can join via the A361 from junction 27 on the M5.

By Coach

National Express offers direct services from London, the South-East, the North-East, the Midlands and from Yorkshire. The service from London Victoria and Heathrow Airport runs up to five times a day. For tickets and credit card bookings ☎ (08705) 808080 www.gobycoach.com

By Rail

There are regular intercity services from London (Paddington), the Midlands, Northern England and Scotland, stopping at Plymouth, Bodmin, Liskeard, Truro and Penzance. For bus links to other places in Cornwall
☎ (01209) 719988
    National Rail Enquiries – train times and fares information
☎ (08457) 484950 www.nationalrail.co.uk

ACCOMMODATION

A wide range of all types of accommodation, from camping and caravan sites, self-catering flats and cottages, youth hostels, family holiday parks, bed and breakfast establishments to luxury hotels, is available in Cornwall.

    Extensive and up-to-date lists of serviced accommodation such as hotels, family holiday parks and bed and breakfast establishments can be obtained from any Tourist Information Centre listed in this FactFile.

Information on self-catering holidays
Cornish Traditional Cottages
Blisland,
Bodmin, PL30 4HS
☎ (01208) 821666, Fax (01208) 821766
www.corncott.com

Cornish Cottage Holidays
The Old Turnpike Dairy
Godolphin Road, Helston, TR13 8GS
☎ (01326) 573808, Fax (01326) 564992
www.cornishcottageholidays.co.uk
Details of camping and caravan sites may be obtained from Tourist Information Centres listed in this Fact File. Ask for the *Cornwall, caravan, camping and holiday parks* brochure.

Youth Hostels

There are 10 youth hostels in Cornwall at Boscastle, Boswinger, Coverack, Golant, St Just, Lizard, Penzance, Perranporth, Tintagel and Treyarnon Bay. For further details contact the YHA Trevelyan House, Dimple Road, Matlock, Derbyshire DE4 3YH
☎ (01629) 592600, Fax (01629) 592702 www.yha.org.uk

BIRD WATCHING

Cornwall is one of Britain's best sites for watching seabirds. There is also a good variety of inland birds and the possibility of rare species that have been blown off course during storms. Recommended viewing points are:

Sea birds
Godrevy Point; The Island, St Ives; Pendeen Lighthouse; Gwennap Head; the Promenade from Newlyn to Penzance.

Inland
West Penwith Moors especially inland from the B3306 between Gurnards Head and Morvah.

Wading birds
Hayle estuary; Marazion marsh.

Water fowl
Drift reservoir west of Newlyn. Stithians Reservoir, south of Redruth.

BOAT TRIPS

Boat trips are on offer from almost every harbour around the Cornish coast. Some of the most popular are listed here. NB All are subject to tide and weather conditions.

Enterprise Boats
Prince of Wales Pier, Falmouth and Town Quay, Truro.
Run trips from Falmouth to Truro and return
☎ (01326) 374241/313234
Operate: Daily May to September

Pendennis Cruises
National Maritime Museum Cornwall

Trips around Falmouth Harbour
☎ (01872) 861910

St Mawes Tours
Roseland Visitor Centre, The Square, St Mawes
☎ (07940) 875309

Plymouth Boat Cruises
Phoenix Wharfe, Plymouth or Ashtorre Rock Community Centre, Saltash
Dockyards and Warships or

Tamar Valley cruises.
☎ (01752) 822797/671166
Operates: April to September

St Mary's Boatman's Association
The Quay, St Mary's,
Isles of Scilly
Variety of trips to other islands
and to view wildlife.

COASTGUARD

To report an emergency incident at sea dial 999.

CYCLING

There are few designated off-road cycle routes in Cornwall, though their number is increasing, but the following suggestions may be helpful:

Near St Agnes the **Tehidy Country Park Trail** has over 3 miles (5km) of cycle paths, ☎ (01209) 714494 for details.

The **Great Flat Lode Trail** between Redruth and Camborne explores one of the greatest concentrations of historic mine buildings anywhere in the world. $7\frac{1}{2}$ mile (12km), circular trail. Leaflet available from local TICs or information boards on route.

A trail linking the historic mining harbours of Portreath on the north coast to Devoran in the south is the **Coast to Coast trail**. It runs for 11 miles (18km) closely following the line of two early horse-drawn tramways. Leaflet available from TICs.

The **Camel Trail** is an 17 mile (27km) flat trail on a disused railway track which runs from Padstow via Wadebridge to Bodmin and on to Poley's Bridge. Most of it is suitable for disabled access. Parking is available in Padstow, Wadebridge, Bodmin and Poley's Bridge. ☎ (01872) 222000 for further information.

The **Cornish Way** is a much longer route, 180 miles (290km), running from near Bude all the way to Land's End and forming part of Route 3 of the National Cycle Route. Uses mainly minor roads and traffic-free off road routes. A special map is on sale at TICs, from Sustrans ☎ (01179) 290888 or Cornwall County Council ☎ (01872) 222000.

Cycle Hire

Bike Chain
Redruth
☎ (01209 215270

Bissoe Tramways Cycle Hire
Off A39 just north of Devoran.
☎ (01872) 870341
Open: 9.30am–5.30pm daily,
Easter to October; 9.30am–
4.30pm Saturday to Tuesday,
November to Easter.

Bridge Bike Hire
Wadebridge
☎ (01208) 813050
Open: 9am–5pm daily, all year.

Bridge Cycle Hire
Eddystone Road, Wadebridge
☎ (01208) 814545
Open: 7 days a week, all year.

Bugle Cycle Hire
A391 at Bugle
Cycle to the Eden Project and
gain reduced price admission.
☎ (01726) 852285   www.bugle-
cycle-hire.co.uk
Open: Easter to end of September plus October half-term.

Camel Trail Cycle Hire
Eddystone Road, Wadebridge
☎ (01208) 814104
Open: 8.30am–5.30pm daily.

Padstow Cycle Hire
South Quay, Padstow
☎ (01841) 533533
Open: 9am–5pm daily.

DIALECT

abroad(scat abroad) broken in pieces
bal — a mine
beal — beak of a bird
belong — (he belongs to go) he is accustomed to go
brave — well, in good health
bulhorn — a snail
bussa — large earthenware pot
cloam — crockery
croust — elevenses
direckly — later
fairmaids — cured pilchards
figgy-duff — plum pudding
flasket — two handled basket for washing
fogou — cave
hoggan — a heavy cake
kievea — large tub
klidgy — sticky
launder — gutter
logan-rock — a stone that can be moved
lurgy — illness of unknown type
muryans — ants
oggie — pasty
passage — ferry
praze — small common
pen — head
proper — good
quilkin — frog or toad
scat — break
shute — a stream of water
smeech — a disagreeable kitchen smell
soused — marinated
tre- — settlement, homestead, farmhouse

DOGS

Dogs are banned from many beaches in Cornwall because of the risk to health from fouling. Visitors should check before allowing a dog on to a beach. TICs have details in an excellent leaflet.

EATING OUT

Cornwall offers vast opportunities for eating out from the simple pasty bought at the local baker's shop to top-class restaurants. No attempt has been made to list any particular establishments here but Tourist Information Centres will be very pleased to make recommendations.

FACILITIES FOR THE DISABLED

Most visitor attractions offer facilities for the disabled wherever possible. Please telephone the attraction concerned for up-to-the-minute information. Tourist Information Centres will also be able to advise on accommodation and attractions that offer suitable facilities.

FISHING

There are excellent opportunities for all types of fishing in Cornwall: deep sea fishing, boat angling, fly fishing, coarse fishing, rock fishing, beach fishing. Digging for bait is now banned from a number of harbours and estuaries. Consult local tackle shops for information about this and where to fish and obtain licences or permits if necessary. Always take local advice when fishing at the coast, either on shore or from a boat, as the area can be affected by heavy Atlantic swells even in the height of summer.

Deep Sea Fishing

Boat trips are available from Bude, Newquay, Hayle, St Ives, Penzance, Falmouth, Mevagissey, Fowey and Looe for full day, half day or evening deep sea fishing. Details are available at the harbour side or from local tackle shops.

Boat Angling

There are boat launching facilities at most harbours but permission should always be sought from the harbourmaster, as should local advice on weather and sea conditions.

Fly Fishing

Argal Reservoir
West of Falmouth. Fly fishing, picnic area. 1 April to 31 October.
☎ (01579) 342366

Stithians Reservoir
About four miles west of Penryn. Open season April to October.
☎ (01209) 860301

Drift Reservoir
Three miles west of Penzance on A30. Season: 1 April to 12 October.
☎ (01736) 363869

Siblyback Water Park and Colliford Lake
Bodmin Moor.
Season: 15 March to 31 October.☎ (01579) 342366

Coarse Fishing

Boscathnoe
Nr Penzance.
All year, ☎ (01837) 871565

Bussow
Nr St Ives.
All year. ☎ (01209) 860301

Porth
Newquay
All year. ☎ (01837) 871565

Argal
Near Penryn
All year. ☎ (01209) 860301

GOLF

Full details of golf courses may be obtained from local tourist offices. A free guide entitled *Golf in Cornwall* is available from Tourist Information Centres. See also www.golfincornwall.co.uk.

HORSE RIDING

Efford Down Riding Stables
Bude
Beginners and experienced riders welcome.
☎ (01288) 354244

Lower Tokenbury Equestrian Centre
Caradon Town, Upton Cross, Liskeard
Beginners or experienced riders welcome. Booking essential.
☎/Fax (01579) 362747

Newton Livery and Riding Stables
Polhorman Lane, Mullion
Beginners or experienced riders welcome.

☎ (01326) 240388
Open all year.

St Veep Riding Stables
South of Lostwithiel
Beginners or experienced riders welcome. Livery available.
☎ (01208) 873521)

Timberdown Riding School
Stoke Climsland
Beginners or experienced riders welcome. Riding holidays.
☎ (01579) 370577

KARTING

Indoor

Camborne Powerhouse,
Pendarves Street, Camborne.
☎ (01209) 711993

Outdoor

Menheniot Supertrack,
near Liskeard
☎ (01579) 347229

LEISURE CENTRES/INDOOR POOLS

Bude Haven Leisure Centre
☎ (01288) 353714

Carn Brea Leisure Centre,
Pool nr Redruth, ☎ (01209) 714766

Dragon Leisure Centre,
Bodmin ☎ (01208) 75715

Lux Park Leisure Centre,
Liskeard ☎ (01579) 342544

Polkyth Recreation Centre,
St Austell, ☎ (01726) 223344

Saltash Leisure Centre
☎ (01752) 840940

Ships and Castles Leisure Pool,
Falmouth, ☎ (01326) 212129

St Ives Leisure Centre
☎ (01736) 797006

Fact File

The Splash Leisure Pool,
Bude, ☎ (01288) 356191

Waterworld
Newquay, ☎ (01637) 853828

MAPS

The best maps to use are Ordnance Survey Landranger Series 2cm to 1 km 1:50,000 numbers 190, 200, 201, 203, 204; Ordnance Survey Explorer Series 4cm to 1km 1:25,000 numbers 101, 102, 103, 104, 105, 106, 107, 108, 109, 111 and 126.

PUBLIC TRANSPORT IN THE AREA

Travel Southwest Public Transport Information Line
☎ (0870) 608 2608   www.traveline.org.uk

The *Cornwall Public Transport Timetable* covering bus, ferry, plane and train is available free from TICs.

Buses

Locally, an extensive network of bus services is run by a number of operators. Timetable information is available from **Western National,** ☎ (01209) 719988 for West Cornwall and ☎ (01208) 79898 for North and Mid Cornwall. **Truronian Travel** ☎ (01872) 273453, www.truronian.co.uk for services in the Truro, Helston and Lizard area.

Trains

Wessex Trains operate main line services throughout Cornwall. Rail enquiry line (08457) 484950   www.wessextrains.co.uk   They also operate the Looe Valley Line from Liskeard to Looe and the St Erth to St Ives branch line.

Park and ride schemes operate in season at Liskeard (for Looe) and Lelant Saltings (for St Ives). Parking is not easy at either resort and the park and ride schemes are well recommended.

Ferries

Ferries operate across a number of estuaries in Cornwall, regularly in summer, often less so in winter, subject to tide and weather conditions.

Torpoint to Plymouth*
Mount Edgecumbe to Plymouth
Cotehele Quay to Calstock
Fowey to Polruan
Fowey to Bodinnick*
Padstow to Rock
Falmouth to St Mawes
Falmouth to Flushing
Feock to Philleagh*
St Mawes to Place
Helford to Helford Passage
Smugglers Cottage, Tolverne to Falmouth

* Vehicles carried.

Falmouth has a unique Park and Ride scheme. During the summer cars can be parked between Penryn and Falmouth and the journey completed by classic wooden launch. Passengers alight outside the National Maritime Museum.

Isles of Scilly

There are helicopter flights (20 minute flight) to the Isles of Scilly daily except Sunday, with **British International** from Penzance Heliport. ☎ (01736) 363871 Fax (01736) 332253 www.helicopter-scilly.co.uk

A fixed-wing air service (15 minute flight) is operated all year by **Isles of Scilly Steamship**, Monday to Saturday to the Isles of Scilly from Land's End. A similar service operates from Newquay but with a reduced service in the winter months. Isles of Scilly Travel Centre ☎ (0845) 710 5555 www.ios-travel.co.uk

The sea crossing to the Isles of Scilly on Scillonian III leaves from Penzance and takes two and a half hours. Isles of Scilly Travel Centre as for fixed wing above.

ROCK CLIMBING

West Cornwall is the foremost sea cliff climbing area in Britain with the most popular cliffs being found at Bosigran, Sennen and Chair Ladder. There are granite, greenstone and killas cliffs offering climbs from Difficult to E8 grade for the experienced climber. **It is essential that climbers remember that these cliffs are affected by tidal movements and that Atlantic swells can hit the cliffs with explosive force, even in summer. Great care should be taken at all times.**

It is also important to bear in mind environmental considerations concerning flora and fauna, especially at bird nesting sites. A free booklet *The Green Guide* is available from the British Mountaineering Council. The used of fixed gear such as bolts or drilled pegs is not acceptable here.

British Mountaineering Council:
☎ (0161) 4454747
www.thebmc.co.uk.

National Trust Cornwall Office
☎ (01208) 74281.
The National Trust owns many of the climbing cliffs.

Climbing courses/guiding:

Compass West, operates June to September
☎ or fax (01736) 871447
www.compasswest.co.uk

Great Escapes
☎ (01637) 880951 evening booking line
☎ (0775) 952553 information and daytime mobile

SAILING

All types of sailing are available from reservoir sailing and small dinghies to sea cruising, creek hopping to voyages to France and Ireland, and excellent facilities abound in Cornwall. Many yacht clubs offer temporary membership to visitors. Amongst the many available are:

Helford River Sailing Club	☎ (01326) 231460
Newquay Sailing Club	☎ (01637) 878574
Pentewan Sands Sailing Club	☎ (01726) 817704
Royal Cornwall Yacht Club	☎ (01326) 312126
St Mawes Sailing Club	☎ (01326) 270686
Looe Sailing Club,	☎ (01503) 262559

Amongst companies which offer sailing tuition are:

Classic sailing, St Mawes
☎ (01326) 270027
www.classic-sailing.co.uk

Cornish Cruising, Falmouth
☎ (01326) 211800
www.cornishcruising.co.uk

Windsport International
☎ (01326) 376363

Peninsula Watersports, Stithians
Reservoir
☎ (01209) 860301
www.swlakestrust.org.uk
Or contact the **Royal Yachting Association** ☎ (0845) 3450400
or www.rya.org.uk
Visitors' moorings are available at most harbours, contact the appropriate harbourmaster.

TOURIST INFORMATION CENTRES

Further information on any specific activity or event may be obtained from the appropriate Tourist Information Office. * means open in summer only.

Bodmin
Bodmin Shire House
Mount Folly Square
☎/fax (01208) 76616
bodmintic@visit.org.uk

Boscastle
Visitor Centre, Cobweb Car Park
☎/fax (01840) 250010
budetic@visit.org.uk

Bude
The Crescent Car Park
☎ (01288) 354240
Fax (01288) 355769
budetic@visit.org.uk

Camelford*
North Cornwall Museum, The Clease
☎/fax (01840) 212954
camelfordtic@eurobell.co.uk

Falmouth
28 Killigrew Street
☎ (01326) 312300
Fax: (01326) 313457
falmouthtic@yahoo.co.uk

Fowey
The Post Office,
4 Custom House Hill
☎ (01726) 833616
Fax: (01726) 834939
foweytic@visitor.org.uk
Hayle*
☎ (01736) 754399

Helston (Lizard Peninsula and Tin Mining Country)
79 Meneage Street, Helston
☎ (01326) 565431
Fax: (01326) 572803
info@helstontic.demon.co.uk

Isles of Scilly
Garrison Lane, St Mary's
☎ (01720) 422536
Fax: (01720) 422049
tic@scilly.gov.uk

Launceston
Market House Arcade,
Market Street
☎ (01566) 772321
Fax: (01566) 772322

launcestontic@ukonline.co.uk

Liskeard
Foresters Hall, Pike Street
☎ (01579) 349148
tourism@Liskeard.gov.uk

Looe*
The Guildhall, Fore Street,
East Looe
☎ (01503) 262072
Fax: (01503) 265426
looetic@looetourism.freeserve.co.uk

Lostwithiel
Lostwithiel Community Centre,
Liddicoat Road
☎/fax (01208) 872207
tourism@lostwithiel.org.uk

Mevagissey
The Fish Quay
☎/Fax (01726) 844857
mevatic@aol.com

Newquay
Municipal Buildings, Marcus
Hill
☎ (01637) 854020
Fax: (01637) 854030
info@newquay.co.uk

Padstow
Red Brick Building, North Quay
☎ (01841) 533449
Fax: (01841) 532356
padstowtic@visit.org.uk

Penzance
Station Road
☎ (01736) 362207
Fax (01736) 363600
pztic@penwith.gov.uk

Perranporth
☎ (01872) 573368
Fax (01872) 573138
thevoice@perraninfo.co.uk

St Agnes
20 Churchtown
☎/Fax (01872) 554150
stagnes.tic@stagnes.com

St Austell
Bypass Service Station,
Southbourne Road
☎ (01726) 879500
Fax (01726) 874168
tic@cornishriviera.co.uk

St Ives
The Guildhall, Street an Pol
☎ (01736) 796297
Fax: (01736) 798309
ivtic@penwith.gov.uk

St Just
The Library, Market Street
☎ (01736) 788669
Fax (01736) 788586
stjust.library@cornwall.gov.uk

St Mawes
The Roseland Visitor Centre, The
Square
☎/Fax (01326) 270440
manager@roselandinfo.com

**South East Cornwall
Discovery Centre**
Millpool, West Looe
☎(01503) 262777
Fax (01503) 263266
discovery@caradon.gov.uk

Tintagel
Bossiney Road,
☎/Fax (01840) 779084
tintagelvc@ukonline.co.uk

Truro
Municipal Buildings,
Boscawen Street
☎ (01872) 274555
Fax: (01872) 263031
truro@touristinfo.demon.co.uk

Wadebridge
Rotunda Building, Eddystone Rd,
Wadebridge
☎ (01208) 813725
Fax: (01208) 813781
wadebridge.tic@virgin.net

WALKING

Coastal walking is excellent in Cornwall but there are opportunities
to explore inland as well. Here you will find heritage trails, pilgrim

routes and riverside walks as well as wild moors with ancient sites to visit.

The South West Coast Path long distance footpath, which celebrated 25 years in 2003, runs for some 630 miles (1014km), 268 of those miles (431km) around the coast of Cornwall. Many sections can be walked as day walks, using public transport to return to base in the evening. The South West Way Association produce a guide to the route with details of accommodation, transport, ferries and tide tables.

South West Coast Path Association ☎ (01752) 896237 www.swcp.org.uk

Passenger Transport Unit, Cornwall County Council ☎ (01872) 322000

In addition there are the Coast to Coast Trail, the Saints Way, St Michaels Way, The Tinners Way and the Mineral Trackways. The National Trust publish 22 leaflets detailing walks on all the coastal properties belonging to the Trust in Cornwall. Leaflets for all of these and many other walks in Cornwall may be obtained from all local tourist offices.

WATERSPORTS

Facilities for Bodyboarding, Surfing, Windsurfing, Canoeing and Diving are excellent in Cornwall. The Cornwall Tourist Board, ☎ (01872) 322900, can supply very good information on all aspects of watersports. It is essential that those who are new to these activities and to the area, seek local advice in order to undertake the sports safely.

Surfing:

British Surfing Association ☎ (01736) 360250 www.alsurf.com

Surf Line (for sea conditions and forecast) ☎ (09068) 360360

Harlyn Surf School, Padstow ☎ (01841) 533076 www.harlynsurfschool.co.uk

Sennen Surfing School, Sennen Cove. ☎ (01736) 871458 www.sennenbeach.com

Canoeing:

Falmouth Canoe Club, ☎ (01326) 317353 www.falmouthcc.org.uk

Inland: **Adventure Sports,** Carnkie, Redruth, ☎ (01209) 218962 www.adventuresportsuk.com

Diving:

British Sub-Aqua Club ☎ (0151) 3506200 www.bsac.co.uk

Specific information for Cornwall: www.cornwall-online.co.uk/waterside.

Falmouth Diving Club, ☎ (01326) 376928/(07967) 809734 www.falmouthdivingclub.co.uk

Porthkerris Divers, St Keverne, ☎ (01326) 280620/280877
www.porthkerris.com

Seaways Diving and Marine, Penryn, ☎ (01326) 375544
www.seawaysdiving.com

Inland waters offering a variety of watersports – tuition available

Roadford Lake, nr Launceston ☎ (01409) 211507

Siblyback Watersports Centre, nr Liskeard ☎ (01579) 346522

Stithians nr Helston ☎ (01209) 860301

Upper Tamar Lake, nr Bude ☎ (01288) 321712

WEATHER

Cornwall is a very narrow peninsula and the weather is much
influenced by the sea. In winter, temperatures rarely fall below
32°F (0°C) and thanks to the Gulf Stream the area is usually warmer
than the rest of mainland Britain. The driest months are likely to be
in early summer and May tends to be the sunniest. The weather
here can change very quickly and sunshine is never very far away.

Weatherline ☎ (09068) 500404

WEB SITES

Cornwall Tourist Board	www.cornwalltouristboard.co.uk
Cornish Riviera	www.cornish-riviera.org.uk
North Cornwall	www.northcornwall-live.com
All Areas	www.cornwall-online.co.uk
Scilly Isles	www.scillyonline.co.u

Published in the UK by
Landmark Publishing Ltd,
Ashbourne Hall, Cokayne Ave, Ashbourne, Derbyshire DE6 1EJ England
Tel: (01335) 347349 Fax: (01335) 347303 e-mail: sales@landmarkpublishing.co.uk
website: www.landmarkpublishing.co.uk

7th Edition 2004
ISBN: 1-84306-123-6

Print: Gutenberg Press Ltd, Malta
Design: James Allsopp
This edition was updated and edited by: Kay Coulson

Front cover: Polperro
Back cover, top: Mevagissey
Back cover, bottom: St Mawes Castle

Picture credits:
All photographs are supplied by Lindsey Porter
except the following:

The late G Irving: p11 bottom left.
Newquay & the Cornish Riviera Tourist Dept: p134, p151, p166.
Ron Scholes: p223.
West Country Tourist Board: p214, 218.
YHA: 203 top.

DISCLAIMER

While every care has been taken to ensure that the information in this book
is as accurate as possible at the time of publication, the publishers
and authors accept no responsibility for any loss, injury or
inconvenience sustained by anyone using this book.
